ECONOMIC DEPENDENCE AND REGIONAL COOPERATION IN SOUTHERN AFRICA

SADCC and South Africa in Confrontation

Olayiwola Abegunrin

Studies in African Economic and Social Development
Volume 2

The Edwin Mellen Press
Lewiston/Queenston/Lampeter

Library of Congress Cataloging-in-Publication Data

Abegunrin, Olayiwola.
Economic dependence and regional cooperation in Southern Africa :
SADCC and South Africa in confrontation / by Olayiwola Abegunrin.
p. cm. -- (Studies in African economic and social development
; v. 2)
Bibliography: p.
Includes index.
ISBN 0-88946-515-0
1. Africa, Southern--Economic integration. 2. Southern African
Development Coordination Conference. 3. South Africa--Foreign
economic relations--Africa, Southern. 4. Africa, Southern--Foreign
economic relations--South Africa. I. Title. II. Series.
HC900.A524 1989
330.968--dc20   89-12585
                                                     CIP

This is volume 2 in the continuing series
Studies in African Economic & Social Development
Volume 2 ISBN 0-88946-515-0
SAESD Series ISBN 0-88946-514-2

A CIP catalog record for this book
is available from the British Library.

The Edwin Mellen Press   The Edwin Mellen Press
        Box 450   Box 67
Lewiston, New York   Queenston, Ontario
     USA 14092   CANADA L0S 1L0

The Edwin Mellen Press, Ltd.
Lampeter, Dyfed, Wales
UNITED KINGDOM SA48 7DY

Printed in the United States of America

SEVEN DAY LOAN

This book is to be returned on
or before the date stamped below

1 4 JAN 2003

2 4 JAN 2003

1 8 DEC 2003

TO: Yetunde, Olayiwola Jr., Oladimeji, and Olayinka.

They know why.

CONTENTS

LIST OF TABLES

LIST OF MAPS

LIST OF FIGURES

PREFACE

I have written this book to fill a void in scholarly work that has existed on these new regional institutions of economic cooperation. This book came out of my five years' (1981-1986) research on the economic cooperation of Southern African States. During the course of the research for this book I travelled in three continents, in Africa, Europe and North America, and I visited eight countries. The research for this book took me to five countries in Southern Africa - Botswana, the seat of the headquarters of SADCC, Mozambique, Tanzania, Zambia and Zimbabwe. In Europe I visited the headquarters of the EEC in Brussels, Belgium and London and I visited Washington, D.C. twice for the purpose of collecting materials and talking to people for this book.

The basis of this book was the first article I wrote on SADCC in 1981 titled "The Southern Nine", and Published in the Current Bibliography on African Affairs, Volume 14, No. 4, 1981-1982 issue. It was a very short article in which I strongly emphasized the view that SADCC is a vitally needed new regional economic grouping in Africa. My view is that SADCC is the only alternative weapon, besides the armed struggles, to fight the white apartheid regime in South Africa against its hegemonic domination of its African majority-ruled neighbors in Southern Africa. And that "SADCC must fight to keep the faith that their economic and political liberation rests in their cooperation and unity".

This book examines the historical roots of SADCC, beginning from the Pan-African Movement for East and Central Africa established in Mwanza, Tanzania in 1958. Briefly it examines and analyzes the various Economic groupings that have existed in Africa since 1959. Throughout this iv

book emphasis has been laid on the importance of the 1980 Lagos Plan of Action as the corner stone, to lay a durable foundation for internally generated, self-sustained processes of development and economic growth based on the twin principles of national and collective self-reliance. One of the objectives of the Plan of Action which has also been adopted by SADCC is to bring about self-sufficiency in food production, and a diminishing dependence on exports and on expatriates technical assistance. SADCC as a new regional economic cooperation in Southern Africa is going to be a significant institutional factor in the Liberation process of Namibia and South Africa. With its initial success of one of its projects - SATCC, it is hoped that its other projects will succeed, but it must be realized that the members of the organization must be willing to promote liberation and self-reliance within their own national economies before extending it to the regional level. SADCC has a future, but a better promising future will not be secured without serious struggles - politically, economically, militarily and intellectually. A luta continual.

OLAYIWOLA ABEGUNRIN
OBAFEMI AWOLOWO UNIVERSITY
ILE-IFE, NIGERIA
JANUARY, 1987

ACKNOWLEDGEMENT

In writing this book, I owe a lot of gratitude to those who preceded me in the study of the economic cooperation in Africa, and I have benefited greatly from their works, most especially from the work and advice of my colleague and good friend Professor Ralph I. Onwuka of the Department of International Relations, Obafemi Awolowo University, Ile-Ife. I thank him for his constructive criticism and useful suggestions and for spending his valuable time to proof-read the entire manuscript. I am also indebted to Julius O. Ihonvbere for his useful advice and reviewing of Chapter Two on the theories of dependency and integration, and to John Nana, Alade Fawole and Biodun Alao.

I am grateful to Professor Douglas G. Anglin of Carleton University Ottawa, Canada, for permission to use the table from his article entitled "Economic Liberation and Regional Cooperation in Southern Africa: SADCC and PTA", which appeared in International Organization, Volume 37, No. 4. I am also grateful to the following people for their advice and useful suggestions, Professors Adeoye Akinsanya of University of Ilorin, Nigeria, S. S. Nyang of Howard University, Washington, D.C. and Fola Soremekun formerly of University of Ife. My gratitude to the SADCC Executive Secretary and his staff for their cooperation in giving me access to all SADCC documents during my research period at the Organization's Headquarters in Gaborone, Botswana.

I am indebted to the following people for their immense assistance in providing me with materials and otherwise in the process of the research for this book, Dr. Doris Hull of the Moorland-Spingarm Research Center, Howard University, Washington, D.C., Mrs. Laverne Page, Ms. Angel

Batiste, Ms. Beverly Gray all of the African Section of the Library of Congress, Washington, D.C., Mr. Abifarin, research assistant, for Department of International Relations, Obafemi Awolowo University, Ile-Ife, and Eric Johnson, Waheed Olaniyi and Sandy Wall who did the typing of the entire manuscript and to all my Southern African friends. I acknowledge the generous financial assistance from the Obafemi Awolowo University, Ile-Ife and the University of North Carolina at Charlotte which enabled me to conduct the research works for this book. Above all my sincere gratitude to my wife, Funmilola Atoke and to my children, Yetunde, Olayiwola Junior, Oladimeji and Olayinka, for their endurance and patience during my long absence from home in the course of my research trips for this project. My thanks to those that I have either by omission or oversight not mentioned their names but have contributed in one way or the other to the success of this book. Finally, any errors or omissions found in this work are my sole responsibility.

ABBREVIATIONS

ACDA	- Arms Control and Disarmament Agency
ACP	- African, Caribbean and Pacific Group (Lome Convention)
ADB	- African Development Bank
ACR	- Africa Contemporary Records
AED	- Africa Economic Digest
AID	- Aid for International Development
ARB	- Africa Research Bulletin
ANC(SA)	- African National Congress of South Africa
ANCZ	- African National Council of Zimbabwe
BLS	- Botswana, Lesotho and Swaziland
CAF	- Central Africa Federation
CARICOM	- Caribbean Economic Community
CCM	- Chama Cha Mapinduzi
CEAO	- Communaute Economique de l'Afrique de l'ouest (French West African Economic Community)
CEPGL	- Economic Community of Great Lakes Countries
COMIRA	- Military Committee for Angolan Resistance
CONSAS	- Constellation of the Southern African States
EAC	- East African Community
ECA	- Economic Commission for Africa
EEC	- European Economic Community
ECOWAS	- Economic Community of West African States
FAPLA	- Armed Forces for the Liberation of Angolan Peoples
FNLA	- National Front for the Liberation of Angola
FPLM	- Peoples' Forces for the Liberation of Mozambique
FRELIMO	- Frente de Libertacao de Mocambique
GDP	- Gross Domestic Product
GNI	- Gross National Income

GNP	- Gross National Product
GRAE	- Revolutionary Government of Angola in Exile
IMF	- International Monetary Fund
JMC	- Joint Monitoring Commission
LLA	- Lesotho Liberation Army
MANU	- Mozambique African National Union
MNR(RENAMO)	- Mozambique National Resistance
MPLA	- Popular Movement for the Liberation of Angola
MULPOC	- Multilateral Programming and Operational Centre
NIEO	- New International Economic Order
OAU	- Organization of the African Unity
OECD	- Organization for Economic Cooperation and Development
OPEC	- Organization of Petroleum Exporting Countries
OPIC	- Overseas Private Investment Corporation
PAC(S.A.)	- Pan African Congress of South Africa
PAFMESCA	- Pan African Movement for East and Central Africa
PF	- Patriotic Front
PTA	- Preferential Trade Area
RP-Z	- Republican Party of Zimbabwe
SACU	- Southern African Custom Union
SADCC	- Southern African Development Coordination Conference
SADF	- South Africa Defense Forces
SATCC	- Southern African Transport and Communication Commission
SWAPO	- South West African Peoples' Organization
UANCZ	- United African National Council of Zimbabwe

UDEAC	- Union Douaniere et Economique de l'Afrique Centrale (Central African Customs and Economic Union)
UDE NAMO	- Uniao National Democratic de Mozambique
UDI	- Unilateral Declaration of Independence
UN	- United Nations
UNAMI	- Uniao Nacional Africana de Mozambique Independents
UNIDO	- United Nations Investments Development Organization
UNITA	- National Union for the Total Independence of Angola
UPA	- United Party of Angola
ZANLA	- Zimbabwean African National Liberation Army
ZANU	- Zimbabwean African National Union
ZAPU	- Zimbabwean African People's Union
ZIMCORD	- Zimbabwe Conference on Reconstruction and Development (held in March 1981)
ZIPRA	- Zimbabwean Independence Peoples' Revolutionary Army

MAP 1
SOUTHERN AFRICA

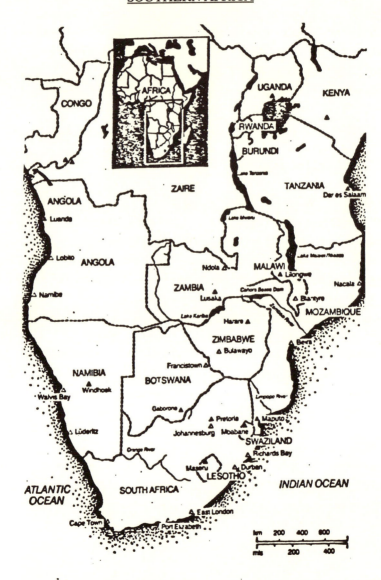

Southern Africa

INTRODUCTION

With the policy of the Apartheid regime to destabilize governments of the Southern African Sub-Continent, its continued occupation of Namibia in defiance to and in disregard of world opinion and its continued opposition to majority rule in South Africa, regional economic cooperation among South Africa's neighbors cannot be said to be over-emphasized. Specifically, emphasis should be on functional economic cooperation, because functionalists hold strongly that administration and construction for the common good is in itself part of the therapy for a disharmonious society. This therapy is all the more urgently needed in Southern African sub-continent, because economic, industrial and technological progress will make the attainment of the regional cooperation and economic self-sustenance of the black-ruled Southern African states an eventual realizable goal.

Southern Africa has become a battle ground between two ideologically and fundamentally opposed constellations of states. These are the Pretoria and the Lusaka Constellations. The conflict between the two groups concerns basically the racial policies and the future of South Africa [1]

The Pretoria constellation was launched on 22 July, 1980, and is led by P. W. Botha, South African President. The Botha's axis is a designed strategy which, essentially, is aimed at using South Africa's economic power and wealth to manipulate its nine neighboring black-ruled Southern African states; and to exert subtle pressure to ensure that they (its neighbors) "behave" themselves as far as the apartheid regime in South Africa is concerned. [2]

This ambition of the Pretoria constellation is a vital part of the total strategy of survival of the Botha government. This particularly involves the use of the economy as an instrument of maintaining ultimate political power and control based on the maintenance of the basic structures of apartheid. This has in turn motivated South Africa's opposition to the policies of economic and political liberation of the Southern African Development Coordination Conference (SADCC) states.

The second, the Lusaka constellation and also known as the "Southern Nine"[3] was launched on 1 April, 1980. It consists of nine Southern African states of Angola, Botswana, Lesotho, Malawi, Mozambique, Swaziland, Tanzania, Zambia and Zimbabwe. The declared aim of the "Southern Nine" is to form an alliance which would pursue an economic strategy that would reduce or eliminate their economic dependence on South Africa. To this end, the Southern Nine and SWAPO of Namibia unanimously adopted a Programme of Action, aimed at stimulating inter-state trade with the ultimate objective of eliminating economic dependence on South Africa.[4]

The objective of this study is to trace the evolution of this new regional institution of inter-state economic cooperation known as SADCC. The study will also examine the political and economic situation of the SADCC states particularly the role of South Africa in the economies of Southern Africa states and how the dependence of SADCC states on South Africa can best be explained within the context of centre-periphery. It will conclude with a discussion of the importance of SADCC in the liberation process of Namibia and South Africa, and speculate on its institutional prospect in the period ahead.

What is unique about SADCC is its institutional structure (see Appendix 1) and its most distinctive innovation. Building on the experience of the Frontline states, the Non-aligned Movement and the defunct East African Community, SADCC is pioneering a radically different and superior institutional framework. The rationale for this is that:

> "SADCC has viewed institutions as facilitating and consequential rather than causative forces or ends in themselves. Therefore, it has consistently sought to develop concrete areas of activity and to identify their actual servicing requirements first and only then to create institutional structure".[5]

With this emphasis on action not institutions, it is somewhat surprising that the formal structures and action orientation of SADCC is innovative in four important major ways: first, the emphasis placed on the sensitivities of members to infringements on their national sovereignties; second, the degree to which responsibility for operational programmes has been devolved to national governments; third, the balance of power between the political and bureaucratic organs; and fourth, the institutionalization of external dependency.

The insistence on the sanctity of national sovereignty is fundamental to SADCC's modus operandi. With painful memories of the defunct Central African Federation and the East African Community fresh in their minds, the Frontline states' leaders were determined that SADCC should not be in a position to dictate economic policy to its constituent members. SADCC members are determined to avoid creating a "Community"

or even a "Common Market"; hence the voluntarist basis
of cooperation implied by the term "Coordination
Conference", SADCC's unique character is that it is
essentially a project for cooperation, and the main aim
is to identify projects of national interest; but the
organization is heavily dependent on aid from the
capitalist countries particularly the European Economic
Community Countries. Therefore, for this reason I see
SADCC as another strategy for entrenching neo-
colonialism and it might extend apartheid policy of
South Africa to some Southern Africa States.

The study will fill a void in scholarly work that
has existed on this new regional institution of economic
cooperation. More significant, SADCC as a new regional
institution of economic integration in Southern Africa,
is going to be a significant institutional factor in the
liberation process of Namibia and South Africa, as well
as being a unifying factor for its nine independent
majority black-ruled states in Southern Africa. The
modicum of unity afforded within the institutional
framework will further encourage member-states to work
together for the ultimate liberation of the remaining
territories still under white minority rule in the
Southern African sub-region.

NOTES

[1]"Pretoria's Constellation" known as the Constellation of Southern African States (CONSAS), was originally supposed to include all of Southern Africa states. South Africa's initiative in 1979 regarding the formation of CONSAS was to counter and oppose the establishment of SADCC. At present CONSAS is apartheid regime's domestic constellation of P. W. Botha, launched on 22 July 1980, while Lusaka Constellation of the "Southern Nine" was launched on 1 April, 1980. CONSAS includes South Africa, and its so-called independent homelands (the Bantustans) of Bophuthatswana, Ciskei, Transkei and Venda. For details see "The Collapse of Botha's Constellation Strategy" Africa (London), III (November 1980), pp. 47-50.

[2] See Olayiwola Abegunrin, "The Southern Nine", Current Bibliography on African Affairs, Vol. 14, No. 4, (1981-82), p. 331.

[3] In this book SADCC and the Southern Nine will be used interchangeably.

[4]Olayiwola Abegunrin, "The Southern Nine", op. cit.

[5]"SADCC: From Dependence and Poverty Toward Economic Liberation" Blantyre (SADCC 3), Annual SADCC Conference held in Blantyre, Malawi, 19-20 November 1981.

CHAPTER 1

AFRICAN EXPERIENCE
WITH REGIONAL COOPERATION

"Our salvation is economic cooperation. With this free trade idea African unity now is here".[1]

Various affective slogans were employed by Africans in their bid to gain freedom after independence and to secure unity between diverse groups. In the 1960s "Uhuru na Umoja" was the East African "freedom and unity" watchword while the Southern African quest for liberation was in 1970s expressed in one word "chimurenga" - "war for liberation".[2]

Economic cooperation among developing countries has been generally advocated as a vital element in the international strategy for development. Thus the aspirations towards unity and cooperation in Africa began with the emergence of the African Countries' independence in the 1960s. These aspirations found institutional expression in a variety of ways. The succeeding inter-governmental political organizations of African states had objectives which included the promotion of measures for economic cooperation. Of all these organizations, the Organization of African Unity (OAU) founded in May 1963, is the most inclusive. Its formation represents the first comprehensive attempt to organize continent-wide African cooperation on a

permanent basis. Established to replace all existing
sub-regional political groupings, its formation was in
fact accompanied by the liquidation of the Casablance
and Monrovia groupings,[3] the Pan-African Movement for
East and Central Africa (PAFMESCA),[4] and the Ghana-
Guinea-Mali Union. The purpose of this chapter is to
examine African experience with regional cooperation
since the 1960s, and to examine and analyse the Southern
African Development Coordination Conference (SADCC)
attempt of a regional economic cooperation for Southern
Africa.

The enthusiasm that marked the early history of
European economic integration, and the eventual
establishment of the European Economic Community (EEC)
that came out of the Treaty of Rome of 1957 signed by
six European Countries - Belgium, France, Italy,
Luxembourg, Netherlands and West Germany, proved highly
ineffective in the developing countries; nowhere more so
than in Africa. The progressive integration of
adjoining national economies is generally believed to be
a powerful means of promoting economic development as
well as political unity. Experience has shown the
following factors to be the principal motivations
leading the under-developed countries (the so-called
developing countries) to integrate their economies:
first, industrial development and technical progress;
second, expansion of trade and better use of existing
productive capacity; third, increase in the capacity to
negotiate with third parties; and fourth, improvement of
political relations between states.[5]

Ever since the early 1960s, closer economic union
between the African countries has been forcefully
proclaimed as a pre-condition for the continent's
economic progress. The United Nations Economic

Commission for Africa (ECA) has been particularly active in this respect, since its inception in 1958.[6] It is assumed that most African countries are too small individually, in terms of population, national income and resources generally, to provide a viable basis for dynamic economic change. According to World Bank figures for 1981, only 31 of the 53 African countries had populations of more than 10 million, whereas 12 had less than one million inhabitants.[7] Because of the prevailing poverty, the purchasing power of the vast majority of African peoples is very low.

The African efforts towards closer economic cooperation have not been diminished by the failure or at best, indifferent performance of such groupings as the defunct East African Community (EAC), the Economic Community of West African States (ECOWAS), the Economic Community of the Countries of the Great Lakes (CEPGL), the Mano River Union, the Communate Economique de l'Afrique de l'ouest (CEAO) and many others.

The Scope of Economic Cooperation in Africa

There is a vast literature on the almost innumerable regional economic groupings that have subsequently come and gone in Africa. Table 1.1 (page 11) shows the past and present economic groupings in Africa since 1959. It is fashionable now to postulate that the OAU had neglected economic progress since it was founded. There is a degree of truth in this contention. However, without seeking to provide an apology for this benign neglect of economic issues I feel there is a need to sympathize with and understand the dreams of its founding members and their desire to consolidate their formal, political independence. They had sought to ensure good governance of member countries

and the systematic functioning of their colonially-
inherited institutions by seeking only such political
ties as their conceptions of, or apprehensions about
their new sovereign status would permit. While
continental cohesion was promoted by the OAU, the
continent's recognized diversities and the subsequence
of conflicting ideological positions have combined to
create centrifugal forces that constrained and hampered
economic integration.

Nevertheless, with the task of national
consolidation and regional emancipation now nearly
complete, Africa can now plan for its future. From
peripheral neglect, economic issues have therefore moved
to centre stage. Visions of a glorious dawn free of the
shackle of poverty by which African countries are
chained had dictated the necessity of immediate
attention to economic survival and protection in
attempts at regional integration.

The OAU's quest to consolidate Africa's political
independence and to assure Africa's economic future
found support and encouragement in an organization with
similar objectives - the ECA. The Economic Commission
for Africa created by the United Nation's General
Assembly Resolution 1155 (XII) of 26th November, 1957
and the United Nation's Economic and Social Council's
Resolution 671A (XXV) of 29th April, 1958[8] provided the
first opportunity for the articulation of African
social-economic aspiration on a continental scale. The
ECA in its multifaceted operations on this continent has
operated as an African economic think tank. It has
played a catalytic role in reinforcing the OAU and has
also organized various conference and seminars to its
advantage.

TABLE 1.1
SCHEMES FOR ECONOMIC COOPERATION IN AFRICA*

Schemes and Year of Establishment	Members
1. Council of the Entente, 1959	Benin, Burkina Faso, Niger, Togo
2. Permanent Consultative Committee of the Maghreb, 1964	Algeria, Morocco, Tunisia
3. Central African Customs and Economic Union, 1966	Central African Empire, Congo, Gabon, United Republic of Cameroon
4. East African Community, 1967	Kenya, Uganda, United Republic of Tanzania
5. Union of Central African States, 1968	Chad, Zaire
6. West African Economic Community, 1973	Burkina Faso, Ivory Coast, Mauritania, Mali, Nigeria, Senegal
7. Mano River Union, 1973	Liberia, Sierra-Leone
8. Economic Community of West African States, 1975	Benin, Burkina Faso, Cape Verde, Gambia, Ghana, Guinea, Guinea Bissau, Ivory Coast, Liberia, Mali, Mauritania, Nigeria, Niger, Senegal, Sierra-Leone, Togo

9.	Economic Community of Great Lake Countries, 1976	Burundi, Rwanda, Zaire
10.	Southern African Development Coordination Conference, 1979	Angola, Botswana, Lesotho, Malawi, Mozambique, Swaziland, Tanzania, Zambia, Zimbabwe
11.	Preferential Trade Area for East and Southern African States, 1981	Angola, Botswana, Djibouti, Ethiopia, Kenya, Lesotho, Malagasy, Malawi, Mauritius, Mozambique, Seychelles, Somalia, Swaziland, Tanzania, Uganda, Zambia, Zimbabwe
12.	Economic Community of Central African States, 1983	Angola, Burundi, Cameroon, Central African Republic, Chad, Congo, Equatorial Guinea, Gabon, Rwanda and Zaire

---

*Source: Compiled from various Sources, especially United Nations Records.

The Lagos Plan of Action of 1980

The OAU-ECA cooperation reached a climax in their joint organization of the Lagos Special OAU Economic Summit in April 1980, and the adoption at the Conference of the Lagos Plan of Action - an economic blueprint for the rapid socio-economic transformation of the African continent.[9] The Lagos Plan of Action basically had two objectives: the achievement of economic cooperation through integration, and self-reliance.[10] The first objective is manifest in the Plan's call for the creation of an African Common Market which is to be the forerunner of an African Economic Community expected to come into existence by the year 2000. Implicit in the creation of the Economic Community is the Plan's other goal of promoting collective, accelerated, self-reliance and self-sustaining development of the African continent. The Plan's provision of a two-staged programme of implementation for the two decades leading to the year 2000 was indeed commendable.[11] In the 1980s, African states would concentrate on dividing the continent into functional economic units, and coordinating and harmonizing these groupings. This decade would also witness the strengthening of sectoral integration of the region in the fields of agriculture, communications, industry and energy.

In the 1990s, Africans are expected to witness further integration through harmonization of strategies, policies, development plans and promotion of joint projects. These efforts are expected to lead to abundant agricultural yields, human resource development, the development of African multinational industrial complexes, establishment of institutions for the identification and exploitation of shared natural resources and the setting up of financial institutions to promote financial flows and regional technological acquisition.

As a sequel to the Lagos Conference of April 1980, the ECA, acting as the monitoring agency, has set up the machinery to evaluate the Plan's progress. It has had several follow-up conferences and makes a yearly assessment of the Plan's progress. A preliminary perspective study for Africa's socio-economic development to cover a twenty-five year period, from 1983-2008, contains certain recommendations about Africa's demographic situation, social condition, food crisis, energy problems, the industrialization dilemma, the transportation and communication bottleneck, unexploited natural resources, imbalances in external trade and financial arrangements, institutional inadequacies and the overall macro-economic set-up.[12]

While examining these preliminary recommendations, we are realistic enough to allow for a difficult passage ahead. Africa's inherited political economy had condemned it to the role of raw materials producer. The continent can therefore not make progress without combating the pervasive regional dominance by multinational corporations, who as the new flag bearers of their various states, have effectively integrated Africa into their capitalist economies. The socio-economic distortions created by the parasitic relationship between Africa and these giant international corporations continue to have destructive manifestations. These manifestations, among others, include a monopoly of extractive resources at Africa's expense as the real owner of these resources, exploitation of Africa's cheap and abundant labour without reciprocal benefits, encouragement of the drain of the continent's best brains and the refusal to transfer the needed technology for Africa's industrial take-off. These multinationals add insult to Africa's injured pride by their operation with such high-handedness to the point of seriously jeopardizing the continent's sovereignty.

In the meantime, the vagaries of the international economic systems, aggravating drought that undermines the continent's feed production capacity causing an annual decline of about 4 percent, political upheavals, and an exploding annual population rate of 3 percent have all combined to obstruct Africa's efforts. Fiscal problems particularly the headaches of raising finance from exports, management of inflation, the containment of runaway deficits, debt amortization and payment of high energy bills continue to hinder development. Management and national planning problems are equally formidable obstacles. These problems notwithstanding, it is gratifying to note strides are being made towards the Plan's fulfillment. Many African countries have increased their budgetary allocation to agriculture. Marketing methods are being improved and public sector reforms are being instituted.

The most significant contribution to the Plan's progress however has been made in the field of regional economic integration. The Preferential Trade Area (PTA) for Eastern and Southern African countries to advance steadily with the introduction of a common list of commodities to be traded among members and the establishment in February 1984 of a P.T.A. - Clearing and Payments House.[13] On 18th October 1983 two rival customs unions namely the Union Douaniere et Economique des Etat de L'Afrique Centrale, better known by its acronym of UDEAC, and the Communate Economique de Pays de Grand Lacs - the CEPGL, merged together to form the

Economic Community of Central African States. The ten-member organization also includes the Lusophone states as shown in Table 1.1 (page 11). The formation and development of the two economic groupings side by side with the ECOWAS gives some room for optimism about the possible realization of the dreams for an African Economic Community by the turn of the century.

Africa's future, however, lies in self-reliance. Indeed, only a self-reliant strategy would advance African development on the national level, enhance autonomy and unity on the continental level and advance the continent's interests at the global level. Self-reliance here should serve to minimize the dangers of external institutions and forces replacing indigenous ones and should serve as links between the nation or region and the international community. While Africans are expected to be masters of their own destiny, self-reliance in this context should not connote an inward looking approach for indigenous solutions that must be developed from first principles. Rather, it is Africa's ability to tap her domestic resources to develop locally what we are potentially capable of, while simultaneously keeping abreast of external technological advancements whose adoptable capability and subsequent transplantation should be a matter of continuous examination. The picture I wish to paint here precludes dependences on external aid flows, goods and services. It requires a determined structural domestic political and administrative adjustment. This in effect means that individually as nations, Africa's self-reliance will be measured by her people's ability to initiate economic policies that will transform societies, and represent a definite shift away from the peripheral orbit in which we find ourselves lobbying around the developed and industrialized (Northern capitals) western powers.

The United Nations Conference on "Regionalism and the New International Economic Order (NIEO)" of May 8-9, 1980 recommended that developing countries should urgently and seriously study the feasibility of implementing the "Regional and Inter-Regional Strategy for Collective Self-Reliance" not as a substitute for, but as a positive necessary complement to the global negotiations on the New International Economic Order.[14] It was also agreed that regionalism was necessary with "its roots in the soil of real economic, social and financial cooperation" and proposed such cooperation among developing countries "on the sub-regional, regional and inter-regional levels in a number of areas".[15]

The major and most conspicuous attempts at regional cooperation in Africa are ECOWAS, Mano River Union and CEAO. The Economic Community of West African States, with a total population of 149 million in 1980 and a Gross National Product (GNP) of $85 billion, was formally established in 1975 on the initiative of Nigeria and Togo. The draft establishing ECOWAS was formally signed in Lagos on 28 May, 1975 by eleven Heads of State and four plenipotentiaries representing fifteen West African countries.[16] It aims at a common market with free movement of goods, capital, and labour for a period of 15 years.

The Communaute Economique de l'Afrique de l'ouest (CEAO) comprises six Francophone West African countries of Burkina Faso, Ivory Coast, Mali, Niger, Mauritania and Senegal with a total population of 32 million by 1980. It was established in Abidjan in 1973, reportedly upon a French initiative designed purposely to kill the

West African Community founded in 1968.[17] Like ECOWAS,
CEAO   seeks   to   restructure   fundamentally   the
participating economies of its member states. It aims
at being able to institute a common external tariff
after a period of 12 years. All its members also belong
to ECOWAS, and it remains to be seen whether the two
economic communities will ultimately merge.

Southern African Objectives for Cooperation

Southern Africa shares the belief in the benefits
that may be reaped from closer economic cooperation in
the region. Except for the Southern African Customs
Union (SACU) which was concluded between South Africa
and former High Commission territories in 1910, (and re-
negotiated in 1969) Botswana, Lesotho and Swaziland (the
BLS states), and the Rand Monetary Area which was
established in 1974. No other tangible attempts have
since been made at promoting inter-state economic
cooperation in the Southern African sub-region.
However, the prospect for the independence of Zimbabwe
which the 1970s war of national liberation in Southern
Africa engendered, ostensibly encouraged the
establishment of the Southern African Development
Coordination Conference (SADCC), and to a lesser extent
the initiation of the proposed preferential trade area
(PTA) for East and Southern African states.[18] Later
development in Southern Africa was characterized by the
coming together of all the nine majority-ruled
independent states of the sub-region to form an economic
cooperation now known as Southern African Development
Coordination Conference (SADCC).[19]

The main objective of the SADCC members is to
integrate their economic development in the areas of
agriculture, industrial energy conservation and

security, transport and communications and manpower
development. The SADCC states' strategies of
integration are based on the need for devising a
collective economic strategy that would lessen their
economic dependence on Pretoria.[20] SADCC's intention is
to commit its member states to end white political
domination and economic hegemony. Towards this end the
SADCC would wish to minimize potential conflict among
its members. Each of the participant states has been
asked, but not forced, to select a sector such as
communications, transport, food security or manpower
development for which it will assume initiative and
responsibility. All members may contribute ideas and
join discussion in the area not assigned to them even if
primary responsibility has been assigned to another
member state. "SADCC members are encouraged to consider
what they do best and how deeply they can afford to be
involved at any given time in any of their
programmes".[21] See SADCC Action Programme in Appendix 2
(page 297). There is a division of labour to prevent
duplication and over-loading of responsibilities yet
sufficient inclusiveness to discourage any role from
being monopolized. Each state will have some tangible
SADCC activity which will draw it into closer
relationships with at least some of the others.[22]

At the end of the first SADCC Summit, in Arusha,
Tanzania, member states adopted a draft declaration
expressing four main development objectives to be
pursued within the framework of SADCC; "reduction of
economic dependence particularly, but not only, on the
Republic of South Africa; the forging of links to create
a genuine and equitable regional integration; the
mobilization of resources to promote the implementation
of national interstate and regional policies; and

concerted action to secure international cooperation within the framework of their strategy for economic liberation".[23] In addition, one of the main objectives for SADCC's creation was to enable its members to free themselves from the economic, political and military stranglehold of the racist regime in Pretoria. SADCC, then must be seen as a continuation of the "ever-evolving African strategy of achieving the total liberation of Southern Africa". In doing this, however, there are numerous problems involved. First, there are the countermeasures taken by the apartheid regime in South Africa to frustrate the efforts of the SADCC states, which are striving to end their dependence on Pretoria. For instance Botha's Constellation of States should be seen in that light, as being used by the white regime in South Africa to manipulate its black-ruled neighbours[24] and to exert subtle pressure so that they (the SADCC states) "behave" themselves as far as the apartheid regime in South Africa is concerned.

The significant features of SADCC include its size, geographical spread, and the political commitment and solidarity of its memberships. The core States of SADCC comprise the Frontline states which since 1974, were closely involved in assisting and, to some extent, directing the Southern African Liberation Struggles particularly in Namibia, Zimbabwe, and in South Africa. In November 1979 in Dar-es-Salaam the five Frontline member states resolved to broaden their membership to include "all genuinely independent Southern African states".[25] However, the motives of the Frontline states' Presidents in extending the hand of friendship to their less resolute comrades in Southern African struggles was, no doubt, founded on the hope that they (Lesotho, Malawi and Swaziland) might thereby be weaned

from their errant ways.[26] For example, since the Lusaka
Economic Summit of April, 1980, which formally brought
SADCC into existence, Namibia has been given an observer
seat in the Organization pending its independence.
Without any doubt, once Namibia achieves its
independence, its admission will be automatic.

The insistence on confining SADCC membership to
countries clearly within the Southern African sub-
continent is one explanation for the continuous refusal
to approve Zaires' application for admission into this
new economic cooperation (See Table 1.1 (page 11) and
Map 2 (page 22) for member states of SADCC). However,
this was not the major reason. Mobutu's persistence in
pressing his claim is particularly embarrassing to the
Frontline states. On the ground of geographical and
economic dependence on South Africa, Zaire's records
clearly cannot be compared with that of Tanzania, the
only member of SADCC that is not from the Southern
African sub-continent. Another reason is that since the
inception of the Organization of African Unity (OAU) and
its Liberation Committee with its headquarters based in
Dar-es-Salaam, Tanzania has been in the forefront of the
Southern African Liberation Struggles. Based on the
Code of Conduct adopted by the SADCC members, inter
alia, membership required, first an "avoidance of
territorial expansionism and occupation of each other's
territory", and second, a "refusal by each member
country to serve as a base for subversion and
destabilization of another member country".[27] The above
condition was a clear reference to Zaire's annexation of
two villages in Kaputa district in Northern Zambia in
1980, and the 1984 arrest and imprisonment of Zambian
nationals in the same district,[28] regarded at least by
Zambia as provocative. Another condition reflected

22

MAP 2
SADCC MEMBER STATES

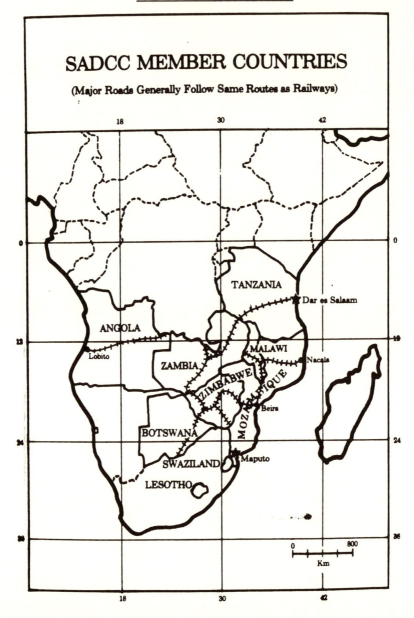

SADCC MEMBER COUNTRIES

(Major Roads Generally Follow Same Routes as Railways)

Angola's complaint that Zaire was harbouring alleged
Angolan subversives.[29] The worst of all is that
President Mobutu is a collaborator of the enemies of
Southern Africa, with its diplomatic, economic and
military ties with the state of Israel and the U.S.
Central Intelligence Agency (CIA).[30]

The roots of SADCC are a little bit remote, though
President Mugabe of Zimbabwe has traced its roots to
both Pan-African Freedom Movement of Eastern, Central
and Southern Africa of 1958 to 1964 and the Conference
of East and Central African States of 1966 to 1974.[31]
However, the immediate impetus for its emergence, can be
traced to the prospects for early independence of
Zimbabwe in particular and the war of national
liberation in Southern Africa of 1970s in general. As
rightly stated by Professor Anglin, "Zimbabwe is the hub
of the transportation network north of the Limpopo, and
the key to the success of any serious endeavour to
promote economic liberation from South Africa and
collective self-reliance".[32]

The idea of regional economic cooperation that is
coming together and pooling together of economic
resources on a regional basis in Southern Africa dated
to 3 July, 1974, when President Kaunda of Zambia,
proposed the "establishment of a trans-continental belt
of independent and economically powerful nations from
Dar-es-Salaam and Maputo on the Indian Ocean to Luanda
on the Atlantic".[33] However, the Southern African
Development Coordination Conference emerged out of
efforts on the part of Sir Seretse Khama of Botswana to
maintain and expand the trend toward regional
cooperation in Southern Africa, which started by the
establishment of the Frontline states.[34] President
Khama intended to avoid the "sterile confrontation"

between the majority ruled nations of Angola, Botswana, Mozambique, Tanzania, Zambia and the newly-independent Zimbabwe, and the racist minority-ruled South Africa. Rather, he foresaw the development of an organization comprising all independent majority-ruled states in Southern Africa committed to the development of the area. According to Richard Weisfelder the reasons behind the acceptance of the other Frontline states of President Khama's idea were both political and economic:

> By early 1977 there were signs that the consultative body of Frontline states' Presidents could evolve toward a more comprehensive organization promoting regional conflict resolution had already begun to anticipate the consequences of impending Zimbabwean independence. The next logical step was consideration of appropriate means to consolidate political gains, rebuild shattered economies, take advantage of new options and anticipate the inevitable new challenges.[35]

The series of high-level meetings took place in rapid succession with the Foreign Ministers of the Frontline states conferring in Gaborone, Botswana in May 1979, economic Ministers meeting in Arusha, Tanzania in July 1979 and Heads of State in Dar-es-Salaam, Tanzania in November 1979.[36] Finally on 1 April 1980, the five Frontline states now joined by Lesotho, Malawi and Swaziland as well as the newly independent Zimbabwe, solemnly signed the Lusaka Declaration on Economic Liberation which formally brought SADCC into existence. Thus, SADCC is a logical outcome of the longstanding economic liberation struggles and the building and strengthening of political solidarity of the nine independent black-ruled Southern African states. The

late President Seretse Khama of Botswana, the first
Chairman of SADCC, characterized it as an economic
cooperation of the Southern African states that will
lead to their economic liberation and reduce "our
economic dependence on the Republic of South Africa".[37]

SADCC Versus Consas

The launching of the Lusaka constellation on 1
April 1980 before the Pretoria constellation was
launched on 22 July, 1980 was a major political and
psychological setback for the South African white
minority regime. It was so because in terms of the
original grandiose plans, South Africa was convinced
that its constellation would include (at least) some of
its neighbouring states (that formed the Southern Nine)
in Southern Africa[38]. The Lusaka meeting took place
between the representatives of a group of nine Black-
ruled Southern Africa countries now known as the
"Southern Nine" which evolved from the Southern African
Development Coordination Conference (SADCC). This
economic cooperation has proved to be of an historic
significance in the struggle to overthrow the apartheid
regime of the Republic of South Africa. This was a
month after Zimbabwe's elections in which the ZANU-PF
was victorious and its leader Robert Mugabe was elected
the Prime Minister (now President) of the first black
led genuine majority government in Zimbabwe. This event
finally crushed all hopes of any African ruled
government in Southern Africa joining the white minority
regime of South Africa, which had confidently predicted
that at least Malawi, Lesotho and Swaziland would join
the Pretoria constellation.[39] As it was reported
elsewhere, "the six Frontline states - Angola, Botswana,
Mozambique, Tanzania, Zambia and Zimbabwe were joined by

Lesotho and Swaziland which relied heavily on the South
African economy, and Malawi, the only African country
having diplomatic relations with Pretoria".[40]   It was
also significant that Sam Nujoma, President of the South
West African People's Organization (SWAPO) was present
at the Lusaka Conference as an observer representing
Namibia.   On the other hand when the Pretoria
constellation was launched in July 1980 (four months
after the launching of the Lusaka constellation) it was
something of a non-event in the sense that the launching
of the Pretoria Constellation took place between
President Botha and the Presidents of the four South
African so-called "independent", areas of the Bantustans
of Transkei, Bophuthatswana, Ciskei, and Venda.   These
four homelands are islands within the apartheid regime
in South Africa, and these so-called "independent
nations" created by South African Boers have been
refused recognition by the World Community.

Pretoria's (Botha's) proposed constellation known
as "The Constellation of Southern African States
(CONSAS)", was originally supposed to have included all
of the Southern African states.[41]   South Africa's
initiative in 1979 regarding the formation of CONSAS was
to counter and oppose the establishment of the SADCC.
At present CONSAS is apartheid South Africa's domestic
constellation of Southern African States includes South
Africa and its so-called independent homelands (the
Bantustans) of Bophuthatswana, Ciskei, Transkei and
Venda.

SADCC's regional economic cooperation is being
complemented by a Preferential Trade Area (PTA) for East
and Southern African states.   Unlike CONSAS, which was
accepted only by South Africa and its so-called homeland
states, most of the SADCC member states are signatories

to a draft treaty establishing the PTA.[42] The CONSAS's objective is essentially a strategy to use South Africa's economic power and wealth to manipulate the Southern African states, to exert subtle pressure to ensure that the SADCC states "behave" and accept the white minority regime in South Africa. Most important, CONSAS's goal is the total strategy of survival of the white minority rule, "which especially involves the economy as an instrument of maintaining ultimate political power and control based on the maintenance of the basic structures of apartheid, hence its opposition to the SADCC's policies".[43]

On the other hand, the PTA was established at a Summit Meeting of 20 Heads of State of Central, Eastern and Southern Africa in Lusaka, Zambia in December 1981. The remote origins of PTA can be traced to the determination of successive executive secretaries of the UN Economic Commission for Africa (ECA) to force the pace of cooperation among African states, in trade, transport and industry through the mechanism of sub-regional coordinating bodies.[44] The aims of PTA are to coordinate sub-regional development, particularly by relaxing and eventually eliminating trade barriers; and to break its member-states' economic dependence on the developed world. The treaty establishing the PTA came into effect on 30 September 1982, upon ratification by seven members.[45] The negotiations leading to the establishment of the PTA predated the Lagos Plan of Action and the Final Act of Lagos, that the OAU adopted in Lagos, Nigeria in April 1980.[46] Nonetheless, the results were consistent with the decisions of the Lagos session, which included a proposal for an African Common Market by the year 2000. So also the SADCC aims and programmes fit neatly within the OAU Policy of encouraging regional economic groupings as the basis for an eventual all-African economic Community and Continental Unity which is also the objective of the Lagos Plan.

One major friction between the PTA and SADCC is that, while the emphasis in SADCC on reducing dependency is focused especially but not exclusively, on Pretoria, PTA with its broader membership makes no direct attempt to address the issue of South Africa. Instead, it advocates a positive approach to the problem, contending that, to the extent it succeeds in promoting intra-regional trade and development, the present dangerous dependence on South Africa will decrease.[47] However, most SADCC members, cannot afford the luxury of such a detached stance. The pervasive presence of Pretoria - economically, politically, and militarily is an inescapable daily preoccupation and loosening its grip on virtually every aspect of national life is inevitably a foremost concern. The belief is that economic liberation should enable SADCC states to strengthen their economies, minimize their vulnerability to South African pressure, and join more actively in the liberation struggles in Namibia and in South Africa.

Equally important is whether SADCC and PTA can learn to coexist, if necessary in creative tension. "If they fail to complement and reinforce each other but instead dissipate their energies in wasteful competition, they are both certain to suffer, and possibly fatally".[48] There will be inevitable disputes about overlapping jurisdictions (See Table 1.2 (page 30) on PTA and SADCC Action programmes). For instance SADCC and PTA will be appealing to the same roster of aid agencies and (governments) foreign powers, for the financing of often similar projects. Furthermore, there is danger that ideological differences between Kenya and Tanzania or Malawi and Mozambique, economic rivalry between Nairobi and Harare, or political misunderstandings between the EEC and ECA might spill over to complicate the delicate relations between the two organizations (PTA and SADCC).

Africa must actively strive to reduce its dependence on external nations and replace this dependence with self-sustaining development strategy based on the maximum internal use of the continent's resources. This I referred to as a "self-reliant" strategy of development and it must become the overarching theme for Africa in general and Southern Africa in particular, for the remaining parts of this twentieth century. Therefore, the only realistic hope for the continent's development lies in greater economic cooperation and self-reliance, a fact which the African leaders have recognized as their long-term development needs as defined in the Lagos Plan of Action of 1980.[49] Collectively, self-reliance would assure continental integration by increased exercise of political will and determination to associate and integrate Africa's efforts for the common good. Such an all embracing commitment would facilitate active financial support for the common purpose and engender various cooperative gestures among African states. It could also help contain some of the continent's increased ideological posturing and consequent polarization of views.

TABLE 1.2
PTA AND SADCC ACTION PROGRAMMES

PTA (Committee Agenda*)	SADCC (Functional Areas)
TRANSPORT AND COMMUNICATIONS COMMITTEE	TRANSPORT AND COMMUNICATIONS (SATCC)
Road transport	Road transport
Air transport	Air transport
Railway transport	Railway transport
Inland waterway transport	
Shipping, ports and freight booking centres	Shipping
Telecommunications	Telecommunications
AGRICULTURAL COOPERATION COMMITTEE	AGRICULTURAL DEVELOPMENT
Food security	Food security
Agronomic research: crop production, livestock fisheries, forestry	Crop research in the semi- arid tropics
Livestock production and disease control	Fisheries, forestry, wildlife
Regional agricultural trade	Animal disease control
	Soil conservation and land utilization
INDUSTRIAL COOPERATION COMMITTEE	INDUSTRIAL DEVELOPMENT
Industrial development	
Multinational industrial enterprises	INDUSTRY AND TRADE COORDINATION
Industrial manpower training	
Investment laws	
Marketing	Security printing

TABLE 1.2
PTA AND SADCC ACTION PROGRAMMES

PTA (Committee Agenda*)	SADCC (Functional Areas)
CUSTOMS AND TRADE COMMITTEE	
Trade liberalization	
Customs cooperation	
Rules of origin	
Transit trade and facilities	
CLEARING AND PAYMENTS COMMITTEE	
Clearing House Trade and Development Bank	Development Fund ENERGY CONSERVATION AND SECURITY MANPOWER DEVELOPMENT

*Report of the First Meeting of the Councils of Ministers of the PTA for Eastern and Southern Africa, 22-25 June 1982, ECA/MULPOC/Lusaka/PTA/CM/1/2. Annex VI.

32

[1]West African Calypso quoted from Peter Robson, Economic Integration in Africa (Evanston: Northwestern University Press, 1968), p. 25.

[2]David Martin and Phyllis Johnson, The Struggle for Zimbabwe: The Chimurenga War (New York: Monthly Review Press, 1981), p. 10.

[3]The Casablanca group was the radical group meeting in Casablanca in January 1961 between the Heads of States of Egypt, Ghana, Guinea, Mali and Morocco together with representatives from other African countries including the leaders of Front for the National Liberation (FNL) of Algeria. In July 1961 the Casablanca group agreed on political and economic cooperation, including the creation of a common market over a period of five years, beginning in January 1962, and the setting up of an Africana payments union, an economic development bank and joint air and shipping lines. These measures were never implemented. Within the Casablanca group, closer relations had already been established between Ghana, Guinea and Mali since December 1960. The Ghana-Guinea-Mali Union proposed "to establish the union of our three states; and to promote a common economic and monetary policy".

The Monrovia group regarded as the Conservative Group met in May 1961 at a Conference of Heads of Independent African States that was held in Monrovia. The Monrovia group consisted of the members of the Brazzaville group together with Ethiopia, Liberia, Libya, Nigeria, Sierra-Leone, Somalia, Togo and Tunisia. At their second meeting in July 1961 the group produced an economic programme similar to that of the Casablanca group, including the creation of a common market and an economic development bank. The reconciliation of their differences and merging of two groups led to the formation of the Organization of the African Unity in May 1963. For details on these two groups see Adekunle Ajala, PAN-AFRICANISM: Evolution, Progress and Prospects (London: Andre Deutsch, 1973), pp. 23-40.

[4]Pan-African Freedom Movement of East and Central Africa (PAFMESCA) came into existence at the end of a meeting of twenty-one representatives of political parties from East and Central Africa, held at Nwanza,

Tanzania 16 to 18 September 1958. See Joseph S. Nye, Jr., Pan-Africanism and East African Integration (Cambridge, Mass: Harvard University, Press, 1967), p. 122.

[5]Lynn K. Mytelk, Regional Development in a Global Economy: Multinational Corporation, Technology and Andean Integration (New Haven: Yale University Press, 1979).

[6]The United Nations' General Assembly Resolution 1155 (XII) of 26th November, 1957 and the Economic and Social Council of the United Nations Resolution 671 (XXV) of 29 April 1958, established the Economic Commission for Africa. For details see Economic Commission for Africa: A Venture in Self-Reliance (Ten years of ECA 1958-1968) (New York: United Nations, 1972), p. 2.

[7]See the World Bank, Accelerated Development in Sub-Saharan Africa: An Agenda for Action (Washington, D.C.: The World Bank, 1981), p. 143.

[8]Economic Commission for Africa: A Venture in Self-Reliance, op. cit.

[9]For details see Lagos Plan of Action for the Economic Development of Africa 1980-2000 (Geneva: International Institute for Labour Studies, 1981).

[10]Ibid.

[11]Ibid.

[12]J. K. Thisen, "ECA and Africa's Economic Development 1983-2000: A Preliminary Perspective Study" in Onwuka, Abegunrin and Ghista (eds.), African Development: The OAU/ECA Lagos Plan of Action and Beyond (Lawrenceville, VA: Brunswick Publishing Company, 1985), p. 87.

[13]"Regional Developments: PTA Clearing House Inaugurated", Africa Economic Digest, Vol. 5, No. 6 (February 10-16, 1984), p. 6.

[14]"UNITAR Conference holds that Regionalism is an integral part of New Economic Order" UN Monthly Chronicle (New York), Vol. 17, No. 6, July 1980, P. 49.

[15]Ibid.

[16]The Eleven Heads of State who signed the ECOWAS treaty on May 28, 1975 were, Mathieu Kerekou (Republic of Benin), Dauda Jawara (Gambia), Luiz Cabral (Guinea Bissau), Felix Houghouet-Boigny (Ivory Coast), William Tolbert (Liberia), Moktar Daddah (Mauritania), Seyni Kounkche (Niger), Yakubu Gowon (Nigeria), Siaka Stevens (Sierra-Leone), Gnassingbe Eyadema (Togo), Sanguoule Lamizana (Upper Volta), four countries not represented by Heads of State were: Ghana, Guinea, Mali and Senegal. See Ralph I. Onwuka, Development and Integration in West Africa: The Case of the Economic Community of West African States (ECOWAS), (Ile-Ife: Obafemi Awolowo University Press, 1982).

[17]Ibid.

[18]See the Draft Principles for the establishment of a Preferential Trade Area for Eastern and Southern African States as the first step towards the creation of sub-regional common market (Addis Ababa, Ethiopia: Economic Commission for Africa, 27-30 June, 1978). ECA/MULPOC/Lusaka/116 (May 1978), pp. 1-3. A treaty for the establishment of the PTA was signed in Lusaka, Zambia on 21 December 1981, by the following East and Southern African Countries: Angola, Botswana, Comoros, Djibouti, Ethiopia, Kenya, Lesotho, Malagasy, Malawi, Mauritius, Mozambique, Seychelles, Somalia, Swaziland, Tanzania, Uganda, Zambia, Zimbabwe. See "Lusaka Summit to approve PTA Plan", Africa, 124 (December 1981), pp. 92-93.

[19]See "SADCC: Toward Economic Liberation: Declaration by the Frontline States made at Arusha, Tanzania 3-4 July 1979", African Contemporary Record: Annual Survey and Documents 1979-1980, pp. C. 117-120.

[20]Christopher R. Hill, "Regional Cooperation in Southern Africa", African Affairs, Vol. 82, No. 327 (April 1983), pp. 215-239.

[21]Richard F. Weisfelder, "SADCC: A New Factor in the Liberation Process", in Thomas C. Callaghy (ed.), South Africa in Southern Africa (New York: Praeger Publishers, 1984).

[22]Ibid.

[23]African Contemporary Record (ACR), Annual Survey and Documents 1979-1980 (1981), p. A. 38.

[24]O. Abegunrin, "The Southern Nine", A Current Bibliography on African Affairs, Vol. 14, No. 4, (1981-82), p. 331.

[25]Douglas G. Anglin, op. cit., p. 686.

[26]Ibid.

[27]For details see Record of SADCC Summit Meeting held in Harare, Zimbabwe on 20 July, 1981 in SADEX Vol. 3, No. 5, September/October 1981, pp. 1-10.

[28]John Mukela, "Border Watch", Africa Now (London), 14 (June 1982), p. 38. See also Mkwapatira Mhango, "Zambia-Zaire: Border Flare-up", New Africa (London), August 1984, p. 25.

[29]See The Guardian (London) 17 August, 1982, p. 3.

[30]See "The Star of David and Mobutu's Torch" Africa, 131 (July 1982), pp. 44-46.

[31] SADCC Blantyre 1981: The Proceedings of the Southern African Development Coordination Conference held in Blantyre, Republic of Malawi on 19-20 November 1981 (Zomba, Malawi: Government Printer 1982).

[32]Douglas G. Anglin, "Economic Liberation and Regional Cooperation in Southern Africa: SADCC and PTA" International Organization Vol. 37, No. 4, 1983, p. 685.

[33]An Address by President Kaunda of Zambia to the Lusaka Economic Summit of Southern African Development Coordination Conference held in Lusaka, Zambia on 1 April 1980 (Lusaka, Zambia: Government Printer, 1980), pp. 3-4.

[34]For a historical background of the Frontline States, see Carol B. Thompson, Challenge to Imperialism: The Frontline States in the Liberation of Zimbabwe (Harare: Zimbabwe Publishing House, 1984).

[35]Richard R. Weisfelder, "The Southern African Development Coordination Conference (SADCC)", South African International, Vol. 13, No. 2 (1982), p. 76.

[36]Amon J. Nsekela (ed.) Southern Africa: Toward Economic Liberation (London: Rex Collings, 1981).

[37]See "In Memoriam: Opening Statement of the 1 April 1980, Southern African Development Coordination

Summit" by the Chairman, His Excellency Sir Seretse Khama, President of the Republic of Botswana, SADEX, Vol. 2., No. 3, May/June 1980, p. 20.

[38]"Southern Africa: Union of the Southern Nine" Africa (London): 105 (May, 1980), p. 45.

[39]"The Collapse of Botha's Constellation Strategy", Africa (London), No. III (November 1980), p. 48.

[40]Ibid., p. 49.

[41]Ibid., pp. 47-50.

[42]See The PTA Treaty: Articles 30, 31 and 37.

[43]O. Abegunrin, "SADCC: Politics of Dependence" in Onwuka and Sesay (eds.), The Future of Regionalism in Africa (London: Macmillan Press, 1985), pp. 190-191.

[44]For details see Adebayo Adedeji "Foreward" Second Revised Proposed Treaty for the Establishment of a Preferential, Trade Area for Eastern and Southern African States, UN document ECA/MULPOC/Lusaka/PTA/X. pp. 1-22.

[45]C. M. B. Utete, "PTA: Toward an African Common Market", Africa Report, (January-February, 1985), p. 73.

[46]For details on the long-term development needs for Africa, see Organization of African Unity, Lagos Plan of Action for the Economic Development of Africa 1980-2000 (Geneva: International Institute for Labour Studies, 1981), p. 7.

[47]PTA has established a Technical Committee of Experts to advise on "ensuring economic restructuring of the BLS States and reduction of their dependence on South Africa" (See PTA Treaty, Annex XII).

[48]The London Liaison Committee prepared a factual paper on the overlapping SADCC-PTA jurisdictions. This was revised by Zimbabwe and submitted to the Gaborone summit of July 1982.

[49]Lagos Plan of Action for the Economic Development of Africa 1980-2000, op. cit., p. 7.

CHAPTER 2

THEORETICAL PERSPECTIVES
ON SOUTHERN AFRICA COOPERATION

The Southern African Development Coordination Conference is a form of liberation movement through regional cooperation based on economic interdependence. SADCC has no single ideology, its members are pursuing different ideologies. Four of its members: Lesotho, Malawi, Swaziland and Zambia, pursue capitalist ideology; two of its members: Botswana and Zimbabwe[1], are adopting mixed economy with long term commitment to transition to socialism, while Angola, Mozambique and Tanzania[2] are leaning towards socialist strategies. The fundamental differences between these political economic ideologies are in varying degrees of state intervention and participation in the first two groups while the states take full control of activities in socialist states. The pattern of production and exchange also differs, while capitalism emphasizes private ownership of means of production, socialism emphasizes state ownership. Despite these ideological differences SADCC is firmly bound together on common issues, concerns, and interests, especially on issues of economic development and a possible military threat from the apartheid regime in South Africa.[3]

Concept of Integration

Integration means the bringing together of parts into a whole. The concept of "economic integration" does not have a clear-cut meaning. In the economic literature, many economists have argued that "the mere existence of trade relations between independent national economies is a sign of integration".[4]

To Peter Robson integration is:

"a situation that is normally attained as a result of a process, extending over time, during which progressive adjustments are made with the object of bringing about a state of affairs in which, within the group, specialization and exchange are expanded."[5]

Joseph S. Nye defines integration as "the process by which two or more actors in the global system form a new set or cooperate to unite for the common benefit".[6]

Nevertheless, integration can be said to exist when units join hands in order to satisfy common objectives which they cannot meet individually. In such a case, integration can be a process with the certain objectives in the interest of a larger body. Such a process would involve the shifting of loyalties, expectations and political activities toward a new and larger centre whose institutions and processes demand jurisdiction over those of the individual national states. The extent of such a transfer of loyalties and jurisdiction enjoyed by the new centre, would depend mainly on the level, and goals of the integrating scheme as well as the socio-economic and political environment under which such integration policies are to be implemented. The economies within the international division of labour influence integrative or cooperative efforts among developing countries. If we consider SADCC based on the criteria presented by integration theorists, one would lose hope for the organization's future. Yet, it is the unconventional nature of SADCC that has made it to succeed so far, where other regional integration schemes have failed. Regional integration theorists have identified a number of obstacles to effective integration in the Third World. Recognition of these problems emerged due to the resounding failure of regional integration schemes in the Third World, and SADCC is no exception. Here are some of the problems.

Problems of Integration

The disappointing result of the attempts by African and other developing countries at regional economic integration can be explained in the first instance by the failure to understand adequately the nature of the development problems facing them (the developing countries), and hence, the subsequent choice of unsuitable development strategies for these countries. The model or analogy of the developed countries with its emphasis on trade liberalization and economies of scale with respect to industrialization invites failure by ignoring structural stumbling-blocks such as agricultural backwardness, lack of physical and service infrastructures, mismanagement of their economies, and many other features. Furthermore, what is often overlooked is that regional integration is not an end in itself but a means to promote some objectives, usually development.

Experience has shown that the prospects for regional integration in the developing world are improved only if the levels of development of the participating countries are not too disparate and their economies are competitive rather than complementary.

Thus, ECOWAS faces the problem that the GNP of Nigeria (the most populous member) is several hundred times larger than that of Gambia (the least populous member) and several times larger than that of the second largest member, the Ivory Coast. The 1978 per capita income of the Ivory Coast was 7.3 times as high as that of Gambia while Nigeria's population accounts for about 58 per cent of the ECOWAS total.[8] Whatever the reasons for the pre-eminence of some constituent areas at the time when integration begins, the fact of the matter is that their advantage tends to increase rather than decrease as has been proved by Kenya in the EAC, Zimbabwe in the former Central African Federation and the Ivory Coast in CEAO.[9]

Unequal development naturally involves geographically unevenly distributed infrastructures. The basic pattern of African transport and telecommunications routes was established before independence, in accordance with the colonial powers' commercial and administrative interests - rather than promoting intra-African traffic needs. It mirrors the relative resource endowment and general development of particular areas. Unless this pattern is changed, efforts to integrate trade and production cannot possibly be successful;

> "the low degree to which African production structures are complementary is reflected in the small volume of intra-African trade. Of the continent's total trade in 1977, only about 4 percent was intra-African as against 19 percent in the case of Asia and 20 percent for Latin America. The trade over time has certainly not been encouraging; from 1955 to 1977, intra-African trade fell from 7 percent to 4.3 percent while the increase in the

actual volume of trade was very small. The share of manufactured goods in intra-African trade declined from 26 percent in 1955 to 18.3 percent in 1976. Intra-trade in agricultural raw materials rose from 2.1 percent in 1955 to 4 percent in 1977 but at the same time total African trade with Western countries rose ten fold".[10]

Indeed, it is a paradox when one considers the immense human and natural resources of the continent. In addition to its reservoir of human resources, African continent has 97 percent of world reserves of chrome, 85 percent of world reserves of platinum, 64 percent of world reserves of manganese, 25 percent of world reserves of uranium and 13 percent of world reserves of copper, without mentioning bauxite, nickel and lead; 20 percent of world hydro-electrical potential, 20 percent of traded oil in the world (excluding the U.S.A. and USSR); 70 percent of world cocoa production; one-third of world coffee production, 50 percent of palm produce just to mention a few. However, Africa, despite all efforts made by her peoples, remains the least developed continent. It has 20 of the 31 least developed countries of the world.[11] Africa is susceptible to all kinds of disastrous efforts of natural endemic diseases of the cruelest type and is victim of settler exploitation arising from colonialism, imperialism, racism and apartheid. Indeed, Africa was directly exploited during the colonial period and since the end of the Second World War this exploitation has been carried out through neo-colonialist external forces which seek to continue to influence the economic policies and direction of African states.[12]

It is very distressing that in spite of all its human and natural resources the African continent still remains the least developed of all the continents. For example the total Gross Domestic Production (GDP) of Africa is only 2.7 percent of the world's per capita income and averaging $166.00. Thus, in the 20 years from 1960 to 1980 the average annual rate of growth continent-wide has been just 4.8 percent a figure which hides divergent realities ranging from 7 percent growth rate for the oil exporting countries down to 2.9 percent for the least developed countries. Yet, the Lagos Plan of Action Report predicted that "if the world economic forecast for the next decade is to be believed, the over-all performance of the African economy over the past 20 years may even be a golden age compared with future growth rate".[13]

African experience, as exemplified by the demise of the (EAC), shows that no other problem has a more disruptive effect on integration schemes than the distribution of gains and losses. In the African context, benefits and costs are measured above all by the extent to which member countries gain from new industries, generate new employment opportunities, and the ability of nationals from the member states to fill senior and other posts in these organizations. The extent to which the growth of aggregate income appears to be affected by integration will presumably become more significant over time, but is impossible to measure at any one moment in time.

In respect of highly industrialized economies, the size of production structures and the degree of complimentarity are such that the distribution issue is secondary, relative to the question of overall growth generated by integration. However, the distribution issue is critically important in those economies that have barely emerged from subsistence production and are at the same time expected to meet proliferating expectations while trying to cope with explosive population growth. The dynamics of integration have no inherent tendency to even cut intra-regional inequalities in respect of income and industrial activity. On the contrary, the play of market forces tends to increase the income differentials in an integration area and to strengthen "polarization" around existing growth centres.

The most extensive literature on empirical computation and analysis of the distributional impact of a regional grouping has perhaps been that on the East African experience. All the main instruments introduced to correct distributional imbalances (transfer taxes, industrial licensing system, the disbursements of the General Fund Services, the disbursements of the East African Development Bank) were largely inadequate. Countries generally seek development and not just revenues and the former depends greatly on the location of activities.

Thus no plausible general solution is yet in sight for the problems of the distribution of benefits and costs of integration among SADCC member countries. Integration schemes should, from the start, pay more attention to the distributive aspects when dealing with the problems of integration and not postpone till later the solution of distribution problems. If this is not done the programme in question is unlikely to progress very far.

The significance of political and ideological factors in promoting or impeding economic integration can be dealt with briefly in the present context. We

will deal more fully on the ideologies of the SADCC
states in the next chapter. Generally, economic and
political factors interact very closely in integration
schemes. If economic conditions militate against
integration, political determination alone will not make
it work e.g. the EAC. Even favourable economic
conditions cannot ensure success in an adverse political
climate like Southern Africa. For example the apartheid
regime's invitation to Botswana, Lesotho and Swaziland
(the BLS states) to join the so-called "The
Constellation of Southern African States" proposed by
the apartheid South Africa,[14] in 1979, was rejected by
the BLS states.

Economic integration of sovereign independent
states demands that they voluntarily surrender part of
their sovereignty to either a supra-national
institution, or the anonymous forces of the market or
both. This is a major problem. SADCC is trying to
overcome these kinds of problems by de-emphasizing the
idea of recreating a "community" or even "Common
market", but instead emphasizing the voluntarist basis
of cooperation implied by the term "coordination
conference". In those states where national
independence is recent and the central government's
authority uncertain, the issue is particularly
difficult. Changes of government are frequent, thus
there is no political stability, and new rulers readily
ignore commitments made by their predecessors. As a
consequence, most developing countries are not prepared
to remain participants in integration schemes that would
require the surrender of important instruments of
economic policy, or substantial limitations on their
use.

Too much criticism has perhaps been made of the disruptive effect of diverging ideologies in the East African Community with Tanzania committed to African Socialism or Ujamaa, Kenya to a capitalist economy while Uganda had always had an unstable economy (under erratic Idi Amin). However, the existence of different economic systems probably caused fewer problems than the emergence of a growing tendency for them to give priority to local interests rather than to the common East Africa cause. Dissatisfaction over the distribution issue, coupled with the difficulties resulting from disastrous mismanagement of some of the common services, clearly played a significant role.

The significance of administration and management, as distinct from economic and political factors, in the implementation of African integration efforts deserves far more attention than it has received. The poor management of African economies generally, and of intra-African trade as well as integration schemes in particular, account for many problems and failures that are erroneously attributed to political ill-will. Blue-prints for the future of intra-African trade are inevitably likely to outstrip Africa's capacity to manage and implement them. This applies equally to integration schemes. The optimistic assumption that the pooling of resources guarantees economic progress, overlooks the fact that if a country lacks managerial and administrative know-how, national incapacities are simply transferred into the regional realm. Cultural and linguistic differences, such as those between SADCC states in which there are both Anglophone and Lusophone countries, add to the practical problems of interstate relations in Africa. In any case the only hope for the continent's development lies in greater cooperation and self-reliance, a fact which the African leaders have already recognized in their adoption of the Lagos Plan of Action in 1980.[15]

Theoretical Frameworks

As already stated in the introduction to this study, its theoretical frameworks are functional integration and the dependency approach. These are the two relevant approaches to the study of SADCC as an example of regional economic cooperation for the liberation of Southern Africa. The relevance of these two theories to SADCC states' attempts towards regional economic cooperation in Southern Africa will be examined and analyzed in this chapter.

First, the theory of functionalism is applied in this study because functionalism stresses the question of what contributions are essential to the creative work of solving common problems (in this case South African economic domination of its neighbours - SADCC states'), rather than what sacrifices are needed for the task of reconciling conflicting interests. According to Ernst B. Haas, "the essence of functionalism was that economic decisions were superior to crucial political choices".[16] Therefore, a shared interest in SADCC states economic welfare would ultimately bring about their liberation from the South African economic hegemony, and the final liberation of the remaining of the Southern African territories still under the apartheid rule. Secondly, dependency theory is also used in this study because of the colonial experience of the SADCC states. These were the states colonized, suppressed and ruled for many centuries by the imperialist European powers. "Dependency is the process of incorporation of the underdeveloped or less developed countries into the global capitalist system, and structural distortions resulting therefrom".[17] In other words dependency is the domination of weaker economies by the stronger ones. In this case the economies of the SADCC states are dominated by South Africa and its Western industrialized capitalist allies.

The Functionalist Approach

We are using functional integration in this study, because functionalists hold strongly that administration, and construction for the common good is in itself part of the therapy for a disharmonious society. This therapy is all the more urgent in the Southern African sub-continent, because economic, industrial and technological progress will make the attainment of the regional cooperation, and economic liberation of the SADCC states an eventual realizable goal.

Functionalism, and the functional approach to human relations is very old indeed, its roots can be traced as far back as Hugo Grotius (1583-1645).[18] In the twentieth century, Paul Reinsch has written on and reviewed the theory of functionalism. But in contemporary times, it first reappeared in the writings of David Mitrany of Oxford University. In his book entitled, A Working Peace System, [19] Mitrany argued for a new international system to replace the one whose breakdown had led to two World Wars.

The theory of functionalism, as an essentially asserted defense of the proposition that the development of international economic and social cooperation is a major prerequisite for the ultimate solution of political conflicts and the elimination of war, has been most elaborately developed and persuasively stated by

Mitrany.[20]   "...the   functional   approach   or
cooperation...may be the means of persuading the powers
(governments) ultimately to make wide sacrifices in the
interest of their national sovereignty which is needed
for the preservation of peace."[21]

According to Mitrany, "the problem of our times is
not how to keep the nations peacefully apart, but how to
bring them actively together".[22]   Mitrany did not
approach the problem directly by organizing around the
points of national conflict, but indirectly by seeking
out the areas of mutuality and "binding together those
interests which are common, where they are common, and
to the extent to which they are common".[23]   Mitrany
abjures the effort to devise a comprehensive blueprint
for   the   organization   of   international   relations,
preferring   instead   to   rely   upon   blueprint   for   the
pragmatic development of special purpose organizations
e.g. regional economic cooperation which he thinks will
tend   to   evolve   their   own   distinctive   structural
patterns, procedural system, and areas of competence in
accordance   with   the   inherent   requirements   of   their
functions or missions.

This method is recommended as one which seeks to
link authority and a specific activity, to break away
from   the   traditional   link   between   authority   and   a
definite area.   It is a horizontal approach, shifting
attention   away   from   theoretical   divisions   of   human
society which are symbolized by the sovereignty of
states toward the various strata of social needs which
cut across national boundaries.   Functionalism stresses
the question of what contributions are essential to the
creative work of solving common problems more than what
sacrifices   are   needed   for   the   task   of   reconciling
conflicting,   interests: Mitrany   in   his   theory   of

functionalism sees the ideal peace in terms of international cooperation instead of international coexistence. He puts his faith not in protected peace but in what he called, A Working Peace System. He believes that a peaceful world society is more likely to grow through doing things together in workshops and market places through international agencies rather than through signing pacts, treaties in embassies and chancelleries.

Mitrany's model of functionalism is Gesellschaft, but not Gemeinschaft; in other words, society instead of community. His image is nearer to that of the pluralists, with its implications of individuation and discretion. He commented, "...the functional way...leaves the individual free to enter into a variety of relationships...religious, political, professional, social and cultural, and so on...each of which may take him into different directions... Man's choice is assured by multiple access to the association of the modern world."[25] And Mitrany's main thesis is as follows:

> Sovereignty cannot in fact be transferred
> effectively through a formula, only through a
> function. By entrusting an authority with a
> certain task, carrying with it command over
> the requisite powers and means, a slice of
> sovereignty is transferred from the old
> authority to the new; and the accumulation of
> such partial transfers, in time, brings about
> the translation of the true seal of authority.
> Functionalism is a method which
> would....overlay political divisions with a
> spreading web of international activities and
> agencies, in which and through which the

interests and life of all the nations would be gradually integrated.[26]

The advocates of functionalism maintain that there is a basic difference between political aspects of international relations and activities related to the satisfaction of human welfare needs. The political aspects of International Relations are divisive, stressing power as the main objective of state action; while activities (economic activities) related to the satisfaction of human welfare needs represent common and mutual interests of mankind, stretching across national boundaries and therefore generating cooperative behavior. The functionalists believe that international action organized to meet "functional", i.e. welfare needs will make it possible to build, gradually, solid foundations for cooperation. As people and governments work together and produce common benefits, incentives to conflicts will be counter-balanced and hopefully, outweighed, as national loyalties give way to international attachments and cooperation.

Functionalism in this sense has thus stressed the importance of international organizations and activities devoted to the promotion of economic and social development, and technical cooperation in such fields as communications, health, education and scientific exploration. The functionalists believe that the human condition will improve only when the government of men is replaced by the administration of things; but whereas the liberals assume merely a quantitative distinction between politics and administration and recognize their mutual dependencies, the functionalists insist on a rigorous qualitative difference. For them, politics is identified with the pursuit of power and with residual infantile behaviour or traits.

The functional theory focuses on the global system as a set of self-regulating mechanisms. The <u>self</u> which is regulated is the system as a whole; the mechanism describes the way in which a functional or dysfunctional movement of one variable reacts on another. Some components are acted upon in such a way that they tend to vary only within certain specified ranges. These mechanisms constrain and secure a chain of mutual adjustment among the variables so that the system moves towards a given state of equilibrium which is identified as the system's goal. The system theorists treat the set of relationships as a whole system. Thus, the term <u>needs</u> refers to the needs of the system - for example, a sub-regional organization as SADCC - but not the individuals, whose relationship might compose this sub-regional organization.

<u>Functional Integration</u>, then, means the alignment and adaptation of the parts with the goals of the system. The mutual adjustment of the variables toward the maintenance of some desired state are characteristic properties of functional systems. As equilibrating systems which are integrated, adaptive, goal-achieving, and environment-determining, although all these qualities may be present in various degrees and may be achieved in different ways.[27]

<u>Functionalist Doctrine in International Relations</u>

Mitrany hypothesizes the development of successive layers of functional collaboration, creating "increasingly deep and wide strata of peace - not in the stand-offish peace of an alliance, but one that would suffuse the world with a fertile mingling of common endeavor and achievement. This gradual evolution constitutes what Mitrany calls "progress by installments", and Frederick Schuman characterizes as "peace by pieces".[28]

There seems to be a doctrine of "ramification" in Mitrany's thesis whereby the development of collaboration in one technical field contributes to collaboration in other technical fields. Functional collaboration in one sector, resulting from a felt need, generates the necessity for functional collaboration in another sector. Mitrany assumes that functional activity could re-orient international activity and contribute to world peace. And eventually such collaboration would encroach upon, or even absorb the political sector. In other words, regional and economic cooperation and integration would build the foundation for political agreements and consequently perhaps make politics superfluous. Mitrany's basic strategy was to shift the focus of attention from divisive political issues to non-controversial technical problems.[29]

Neo-Functionalism

Ernst B. Haas developed a modified version of Mitrany's functionalism by studying the operations of the European Coal and Steel Corporation. The modified version of functionalism is called neo-functionalism. To Ernst Haas the essence of functionalism was that step-by-step economic decisions were superior to crucial political choices. He claimed that the operation of ever more controversial politics, starting from a shared interest in economic welfare, would ultimately bring about the establishment of a new super-national authority regardless of the wishes of the individual actors. Haas's neo-functionalism assumed that economic self interest was more important than political commitment and that unintended consequences and incremental decision-making were more effective in bringing about integration than purposeful behaviour and the construction of elaborate grand designs.[30]

The central theme of Haas's studies of the classical functionalist like Mitrany was the concept of Spillover or what Mitrany called the doctrine of ramification. In his study of the European Coal and Steel Corporation, Haas found that among Europeans directly concerned with coal and steel, relatively few of them were initially strong supporters of the European Coal and Steel Corporation (ECSC). It was only after the ECSC had been operationally successful for many years that so many or several trade union leaders and political leaders in Europe became proponents of the Corporation. Such groups, as a result of gains which they experienced from ECSC, placed themselves in the vanguard of other efforts for European integration, including the creation of European Common Market (ECM) or (EEC) in 1957. Thus there was a marked tendency for persons who have experienced gains from supra-national institutions in one sector to favour integration in other sectors. Haas then concluded that decisions made in organizations at the international level may be integrative. "Earlier decisions spill over into new functional contexts, involve more and more people, call for more and more inter-bureaucratic contact and consultations, meeting with new problems which grow out of the earlier compromises".[31]

According to the functionalists, functional activity prevents and eliminates sources or causes of conflict. A preventive orientation does not emphasize the static aspects of cooperation and integration, but rather the task of reconstruction and continued collaboration for the solution of economic and social problems, and this is one of the SADCC objectives. One of the causes of the unrest and disharmony on the international scene is the existing disparity between economic and social advantages among world population.

Pragmatism seems to be the dominant factor in functionalism. Probably this is the reason why the constitutional approach is avoided, and step-by-step schemes in the direction of an international system of cooperation are advanced. In functionalism, man will seek the rational advantage in maximizing his physical welfare through cooperation with other men. The most desirable route to international community is to proceed gradually from initial cooperation.

Functionalists advocated building on existing foundations, extending the network of international agencies and increasing their powers. This is a practical approach which is one of the chief attractions of functionalism. Functional international organizations have been in existence for well over a century, and their number has steadily increased since the Second World War. In one of Mitrany's studies, he stated that:

> "Apart from the work of the UN with its specialized functional agencies, the international network of functional agencies now includes over one hundred inter-state agencies and more than one thousand and five hundred non-governmental unions and association, and both groups are growing steadily in response to new problems and needs".[32]

The growing interdependence of the nations of the world as a result of the enormous rate of technological change has been the subject of many comments on the international level. However, this interdependence of the nations has by no means led to internationalism or a sense of world community. Because of the UN Charter and more particularly because of the difficulties obstructing the performance of its organs, the search for cooperation or additional strength through regional arrangements has increased in the past few decades, and in view of the fact that the interest or attraction is in regionalism or sub-regionalism it is essential to distinguish between regional division and regional devolution. "A fully integrated regional union would inescapably acquire the nature of a nation-state and would be bound to act as such in playing its part at the United Nations."[33]

One way to clear the atmosphere of ideological obstruction would be for international organizations to assume authority for specific issues and activities through functional linkage projects. According to Joseph S. Nye, functional linkage projects are schemes which are formally owned and maintained by states and form a link between them as an integrative variable.[34] In essence, the scope of the functional line of action are: (a) to take as many issues as possible out of the field of competition and friction, and at the same time; (b) to develop a web of common activities which will be serving all peoples impartially according to their needs and which would gradually build a living regional community.[35]

Functional integration proceeds through progressive delegation of the decision-making power. The decisions may begin in individual countries on the basis of recommendations from an intergovernmental group; then they are made jointly by representatives of countries in an international conference, and finally, they are made by the international agency itself, in this case the appropriate agency for the function to be carried out, thus contributing to interstate and regional integration.

Another consequence of functional integration is the emergence of a new type of international actor, The Functional Specialist. The functional specialist may be an international civil servant or a national specialist, e.g. a career diplomat, but in either case, preliminary studies had indicated that he develops a special interest in maintaining the system. His increasing decision-making power, or course, reinforces this interest and allows him to initiate creative personal action to further the cooperative or integrative process.

Mitrany, Haas, Balassa, Robson, Nye and others used systems theory in developing functional integration models. In the work of each of these theorists there is emphasis upon the effect of integration in one sector upon the ability of participating units to achieve integration in other sectors. In general, functional integration theorists hold strongly that people adopt integrative behavior because of expectations of joint rewards or penalties. Thus, we shall, therefore, regard in this study SADCC as an attempt towards economic integration of the nine-African majority-ruled independent Southern African states. Therefore, the common benefit for their efforts towards economic cooperation will be to end their political domination and economic hegemony by the white apartheid regime in South Africa. To that end, member states are encouraged to contribute effectively to the SADCC programmes.

From our analysis of functional theory, we see that functionalism in its actual formation, specified a course of development which will eventually end the supremacy of the nation state. In its conceptualization of the processes which would lead to the replacement of national interest oriented politics, the functionalist theory essentially ignored considerations of power politics, and political influence of the nation-state. Therefore, functional developments are not supposed to be the result of political processes. Therefore, in our opinion economic cooperation of (Southern Africa) SADCC states would offer avenues for altering the traditional political system of the Southern African sub-region in which the white minority regime in South Africa dominates the whole sub-region economically and militarily. The economic cooperation of the SADCC states would move beyond just mere contacts to stress what essentially amounts to role-playing in a regional structure. Professional and technical skills, bureaucratic norms and tasks would be emphasized; national certitudes and commitments would be shifted to the (new organization) SADCC complete with functional interdependence and shared expectations.

By seeking a pragmatic and regional-wide solution, peaceful change will come to Southern Africa, not through a shift of national boundaries but by a means of actions taken across national boundaries. A peaceful change in apartheid South Africa, and settlement of the Namibian independence issue will augur well for the survival of SADCC as a regional economic cooperation for Southern Africa. The SADCC's future plans of a functional and viable economic integration of Southern Africa will be achieved. Economic hegemony of SADCC will gradually be broken once there is a peaceful change to a representative democratic majority rule in Namibia and South Africa. It will also help to promote the regional security cooperation of the region, which the Frontline states have been working towards achieving since the independence of Zimbabwe to become a reality. Furthermore, the achievement of the objectives of the Lagos Plan of Action - i.e. restructuring the economy of Africa, based on the twin principles of national, and collective self-reliance, and self-reliant and self-sustaining development; and the continental integration of Africa by the year 2000, which SADCC also subscribed to will be strengthened.

The first and the most successful action programme of SADCC is the Southern African Transport and Communications Commission (SATCC), located in Maputo, Mozambique. The success of SATCC is very encouraging, and with the current action moods among the SADCC members, the achievements of SATCC will spill over into another sector of its programmes, possibly its food security programmes which is gaining very rapid momentum.[36]

It is difficult to find regional integrative or cooperative efforts in the developing world falling within a single theoretical perspective, and SADCC is no exception. The functionalist theory focuses strictly on the working technical institutions of an integrative or cooperative region as shown by its proponents. However, it is not wide enough to cover the political, security, (military), self-reliance and psychological implication of SADCC.[37] In view of the limitations of functionalist theory to integration in developing countries, it becomes necessary to transcend them and emphasize an alternative approach which puts into consideration the specific, and peculiar problems, and contradictions which inhibit successful cooperation in the Third World and especially in Africa.

Dependency Theory

One fact is clear from the existing literature, the African countries have not had many problems with establishing economic groupings, setting up elaborate institutions and drafting beautiful and well-worded treaties. The question then follows as to what factors and forces have continued to encourage dormancy, increase costs, conflicts and disintegration instead of benefits, cooperation and self-reliant development.[38]

In this section we shall examine and analyze dependency theory only as it relates to regional cooperation in the Third World, and we are not going to deal with all the aspects of the "dependency" approach as a "theory" per se. It must be pointed out also that the dependency perspective on regional cooperation in under-developed regions goes beyond Pan-Africanist and neo-classical explanations, prescriptions and projections. This is because its approach is "political economy" and its methodology critical. It notes the impact of the historical contact between imperialism and the periphery as well as the internal factors and forces which reproduce and influence the connections between the centre and the periphery. The focus of dependency perspectives on cooperation in the Third World relates class interests, the nature of the state and the structure of production and accumulation to the specificities of the social formations in order to comprehend how external forces affect cooperation efforts. Thus, the condition of dependence is taken as a starting point for evaluating and analyzing nationalistic economic policies, internal social relations, the new international economic order, terms of trade and international relations of exchange.

Patrick J. McGowan defines dependency as an "asymmetrical structure of control relations wherein a controller, such as a state, multinational enterprise, or parent, regularly and hence predictably, changes or maintains the behaviour of a controllee, such as another state, an economic sector, or a child".[39] McGowan's definition of dependency falls within the structuralist framework. However, in this study, we hope to emphasize the specificity of the Southern Africa sub-region. Classical dependency theory, which draws an unmatched link between the periphery and the metropole obviously explains little, particularly in the effort to understand internal socio-economic and political dynamics which shape the attitudes and commitment of participating states to integration efforts. In fact, Southern Africa is unique in the context of African geo-politics.

Considering McGowan's definition, an asymmetrical control relationship represents dominance (the capitalist powers) whereas for the controlled (the Third World countries) their underdevelopment represents dependency and often exploitation. As shown in Figure 1, (page 62) the contemporary structures of economic dominance and dependency are encouraged and promoted by the industrialized world powers through international trade, world-wide division of labour, product specialization, and multi-national enterprise operations. The economic and political control of the Third World, especially the African states by the capitalist industrialized powers was achieved during the 19th and early parts of the 20th centuries through imperialism and colonialism. Today, this strategy still continued by the colonial policies of the capitalist powers featuring various forms of penetration.[40]

The dependency approach to regional integration at the levels of theory and practice, which will serve as the alternative theoretical framework for this study, emphasizes the consideration of four major aspects.[41] First the colonial experiences of the integrating economies. This will enable us to comprehend the origins, nature and dynamics of institutions, policies, relations between internal forces and problems affecting political stability and so forth. The second aspect is the nature and pattern of internal structures of production and exchange. This would involve an understanding of the nature of the peripheral state, how it legitimizes and rationalizes production and exchange, and how these are most likely to impact upon its ability to support collective self-reliance. The third aspect is the location and role of the integrating states in the international division of labour, and how this location, and role informs relations with transnational actors particularly Multinational Corporations (MNCs).[42]

The dependency theory identifies MNCs as one of the principal obstacles to successful cooperation among dependent and underdeveloped countries, this is because MNCs fail to transfer technology, discourage local initiative, kill infant industries, do not make use of local resources, corrupt politicians, transfer wrong tastes, transfer profits and inhibit national economic independence.[43] Thus, as far as collective self-reliance is concerned, the dependency theory contends that any integration scheme which does not have a viable and comprehensive institution dedicated to the vigorous regulation and control of these powerful vertically integrated institutions - the MNCs in the primary interest of the integrating economies is bound to lead to more costs than benefits. Such control measures must

FIGURE 1
A SYSTEMATIC VIEW OF ECONOMIC DEPENDENCY RELATIONS

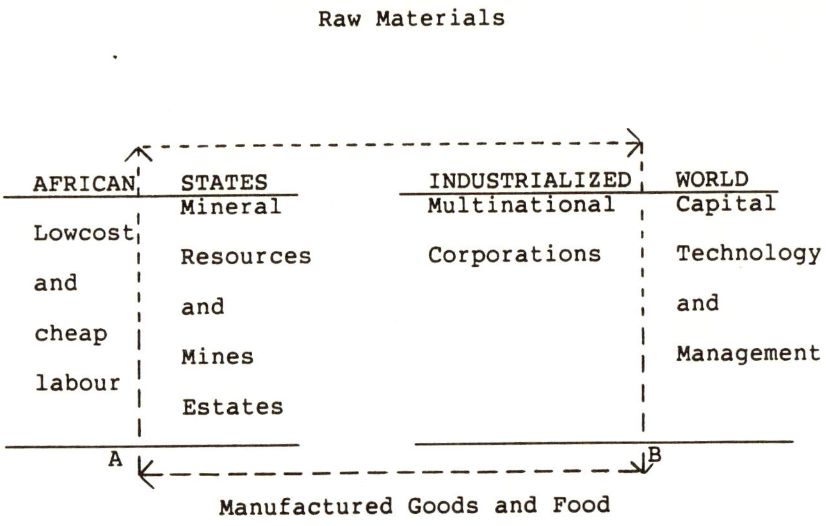

Raw Materials

AFRICAN STATES	INDUSTRIALIZED WORLD
Lowcost and cheap labour	Mineral Resources and Mines Estates	Multinational Corporations	Capital Technology and Management

A   B

Manufactured Goods and Food

---------->   Exported Raw Materials to Developed World

<- - - - -   Imported Finished Products to Underdeveloped World

include the delineation of certain sectors where MNCs are completely excluded, policies aimed at encouraging the use of local resources, technology and skill transfer, formation of sectoral linkages and the use of MNC locational patterns to balance inherited spatial distortions. These are certainly crucial areas which regional cooperation schemes cannot pretend to ignore because they influence and determine on a daily basis the dynamics of accumulation, development and crisis in the integrating economies.

Finally, the fourth aspect is that the dependency theory demands that integration schemes in underdeveloped regions must pay special attention to the particular regional problems of uneven development and availability of resources, natural problems such as drought or access to the sea and problems arising from historical legacies.[44] In the case of SADCC for instance, the problem of South Africa as an economic and military power in Southern Africa must be addressed. Similarly, problems arising from the system of apartheid, dependence on the South African economy, transport and communication net-works, the landlocked nature of some SADCC member-states, the uneven level of development (both economic and political); the geo-strategic use of South Africa by the Western powers,[45] and the role of the MNCs in the perpetuation of South Africa's system of apartheid, and aggression against SADCC states and Western economic domination are issues, and problems that would definitely affect economic cooperation in the sub-region. In addition, the question of Namibia's independence and the ideological postures of some of the Frontline states will affect the perception of other states, foreign actors and the

benefits or usefulness of regional integration of SADCC
itself.

The Dependency Model and Underdevelopment of Africa

Having (outlined) examined the main features of
dependence theory as it relates to regional cooperation
in the Third World, how do we relate them to the
economic underdevelopment of Africa (Southern Africa)?

As suggested by Stratchey:

> The backward regions assumed a dependency
> status (the last stage before outright
> control) in relation to the metropolitan
> powers chiefly because the former were in debt
> to the latter. What was significant about the
> shift from consumer goods to capital goods in
> the world trade was that the colony-to-be
> needed long-term credits or loans to pay for
> the capital goods and that finally, the
> relationship between the backward country and
> the metropolitan country was one of debtor and
> creditor. And from this it was but a small
> step to dependence and domination.[46]

From this, therefore, dependency is the situation
that the history of colonial imperialism has left and
that modern imperialism creates in underdeveloped
countries. As Dale Johnson puts it, "Dependency is
imperialism seen from the perspective of
underdevelopment".[47] Dependency is a "Conditioning
situation" in which the specific histories of
development and underdevelopment transpire in various
societies. Specifically, as defined by Theotonio dos
Santos, dependency is:

> a situation in which a certain group of
> countries have their economy conditioned by

the development and expansion of another
economy, to which the former is subject. The
relation of interdependence between two or
more economies, and between these and world
trade, assumes the form of dependence when
some countries (the dominant) can expand and
give impulse to their own development, while
other countries (the dependent) can only
develop as a reflection of this expansion.
This can have positive and/or negative effects
on their immediate development. In all cases
the basic situation of dependence leads to a
global situation in dependent countries that
situates them in backwardness and under the
exploitation of the dominant countries. The
dominant countries have a technological,
commercial, capital resource, and social-
political pre-dominance over the dependent
countries (with pre-dominance of some of these
aspects in various historical moments). This
permits them to impose conditions of
exploitation and extract part of the
domestically produced surplus.[48]

Historical situation of dependency have conditioned
contemporary underdevelopment in Africa and other
underdeveloped countries. Thus underdevelopment is not
an original state as modernization theorists want us to
believe. The beginnings of African underdevelopment can
be traced to the trans-Atlantic slave trade, the
abandoning of that trade in favour of "legitimate trade"
and the eventual partition of Africa in 1884/85.[49] In
other words, the basis of African underdevelopment
(dependency) can be found in slave trade and colonial
imperialism. Colonial imperialism in Southern Africa

will be treated in the next chapter. During the period of slave trade the African supplied the white man with human cargo (often, at least at the initial state, Europeans raided African coasts for captives whom they enslaved) who were taken to the North and Central American plantations to work on the lands stolen from the owners - the American Indians. In return the African received guns, gunpowder and silky items that began his process of dependency on the Europeans.

In the second stage, the colonial imperialism stage, the African became oriented to the export of primary products (principally agricultural products), under the control of metropolitan capital, and constituted as markets for imported manufactures from the same metropolitan countries. Foreign capital came in to construct social overheads - transportation facilities and utilities that would enhance the exploitation of the African people, and their natural resources, and for the maintenance of law and order. With their economic and military power the metropolis successfully kept African countries as de facto colonies. Governments of the underdeveloped countries and their businessmen have no control over international markets for primary products, the prices of which fluctuate and quite often are manipulated by the rich and powerful (developed) nations. Such fluctuations almost always result in unfavourable terms of trade in relation to imports.

Dependency relations have also shaped the social structure of underdevelopment. Africa has played and is still playing a definite role in the international economy, but the internal development of Africa has been severely curtailed or "conditioned" by the needs of the dominant (developed) economies within the international (economy) market. No nation has ever developed completely outside of the world market nor has any nation operated without constraints upon policy chores. But, the difference between dependent and interdependent development is that growth in the dependent nations occurs as a reflex of the expansion of the dominant nations, and is geared toward the needs of the dominant economies i.e. foreign rather than national needs.[50] This is exactly what is happening in Southern African states in which their growth occurs as a reflex of the expansion of the (West) industrialized nations, and is geared toward the foreign economies rather than the Southern African needs. The economy of the SADCC states is a service economy to that of the Western industrialized economy and South Africa.

In the dependent countries, foreign factors of production, such as capital and technology have become the main determinants of economic progress and socio-political life. And while this same world market promoted the expansion of development in Europe and North America, it has a tendency to limit development in the (dependent countries) African countries.[51] This historical tendency has been the root problem of African underdevelopment.

> Dependency then, means, that the development alternatives open to the dependent nation are defined and limited by its integration into and functions within the world market. · This limitation of alternatives differs from limitations in the dominant nations in so far as the functioning of the basic decisions in the world market...are determined by the dominant nations. Thus, the Southern African states (dependent nations) must make choices

in a situation in which they do not set the terms or parameters of choice.[52]

The international system upon which Southern Africa depends implies a "structure" that is, a structure of institutions, classes, and power arrangements. The dynamic·process that takes place within that structure is called "imperialism". "Imperialism" therefore, is an institutionalized system of control which systematically shapes the institutions and structures of dependent, dominated countries (SADCC states) and limits their freedom of action, if they are to avoid the system's sanctions, to system-defined alternatives".[53] The international system is not merely economic; it is a stratified system of power relations, as Irving Louis Horowitz has emphasized by the title of his book Three Worlds of Development: The Theory and Practice of International Stratification.[54]

Central to this power relations within the international system are the multinational corporations. There are four main features of these global giants: (1) horizontal integration, the tendency to take advantage of a profitable opportunity to buy out their opponents who produce similar commodities, and vertical integration, the tendency to own the plant, produce their own raw materials, and also become their own wholesaler. Thus, monopolizing the three stages rather than one "stage of production"; (2) the tendency toward conglomeration or diversification; (3) mounting "internationalization" or "multinationalization" of the operation of capital; and (4) the growing cooperation among the capitalist world as opposed to the rivalry of about from 1870 to 1914, and the growing disunity of "the secondary capitalist powers thus far to offer a serious challenge to Western hegemony".[55]

These characteristics of modern capitalism have prompted a need for cooperation among the multinational corporations with respect to their overseas operations. There has arisen a need to control the production process, from the sources of supply and processing of raw materials to markets or outlets for commodities. Their emphasis has turned to "long range-planning, maximum security and avoidance of risk and preservation of a favourable climate (ideological, and social, as well as economic) for the perpetuation of corporate operations and for long-range profits".[56] Furthermore, increase in the scale, monopolistic concentration, conglomeration and internationalization of private capital, leads to the reduced dependence upon immediate profit return from overseas investment.[57]

Third, a limited measure of "development" takes place and the resulting moderate redistribution of income provides a wider market for metropolitan exports, and may even lead to relative stability. A relatively "developed" African economy is quite healthy for foreign investment and trade. In this respect contemporary capitalism has an ingredient of "welfare imperialism". The problem is that under these conditions African development is controlled fundamentally by the needs of foreign corporation, rather than response to African needs.

Fourth stage, there are efforts at regional integration of markets, such as the French Economic Community, the Commonwealth of Nations which tie African countries to their former colonial masters, the European Economic Community which former colonies can join only as associate members, and lastly, the Organization of American States (OAS) in which the U.S. dominates.

Since the nature of private corporate operations abroad is such that they need protection by the imperialist power, therefore, the multinational corporations have employed their power and influence to shape the foreign policies of their governments. In no other country is this more evident than in the United States. Here the U.S. interests quite often are synonymous with the corporate interests of its companies abroad. This is demonstrated by this statement:

During the 25 years in which the United States was the most powerful nation on earth, the tighter and more notorious were the links between Washington, Wall Street, and Detroit, the better it was for the U.S. Companies. When the CIA removed Mohammed Mossadeq an obstreperous Iranian premier who "irrationally" tried to interfere with Gulf's and Standard Oil's prospects for taking over his country's oil, or when the same agency rescued Guatemalan banana land for United Fruit from a popularly elected "subversive" nationalist, these were U.S. patriotic initiatives applauded by businessmen. Capital and ideological purity were preserved together. The readier the Pentagon and CIA were to bring down or raise up governments in underdeveloped countries, the better the investment climate for U.S. Corporations. United States military power was used to establish the ground rules within which American business could operate. The U.S. Government acted as consultant for rightist coups in Bolivia, Brazil, Chile, Greece, Indonesia and Zaire, and their generals opened their countries to U.S. investment on the most favourable terms. Wherever the flag was been planted around the world, in some 500 major military interventions, U.S. Corporations have moved in. The construction of a world wide military empire has been good business.[58]

The relationship between the U.S. government and its multinationals became even stronger during the Nixon Administration. Richard Nixon was a candidate put forward and also supported by the American conglomerates. Having been put in office by the business giants of America, Nixon had every reason to reward his supporters. Thus, he went out of his way to demonstrate that his was a "Business Administration" and that he was all out to "protect American business".[59] Of course, President Nixon could not have the courage to tell the American people that he was using the American resources to promote the interest of a few economic elites. The CIA was the instrument for implementing Nixon's economic policies. National interests became synonymous with the economic interests of the global giants. Of vital importance is the fact that the presence of U.S. business in a dependent country "entitles" her to become very actively involved in the domestic politics of the people, buying and selling local politicians and nationalists. This is exactly what the Reagan administration is doing in Southern Africa, especially, Reagan's support to the UNITA in Angola. Similarly, the white minority in South Africa is financing and training the MNR rebels against the legitimate FRELIMO Government in Mozambique.

Before ending this review of dependency, it is significant to recognize a very important work in this area. Walter Rodney in his popular book, How Europe

Underdeveloped Africa,[60] has given in much more detail the information about how Western European Governments and trading companies deliberately and systematically worked hard to bring about the underdevelopment of the African continent. Walter Rodney emphasizes that bringing Africa into the world economy may have had a few advantages but it did create the conditions for the present economic problems encountered by Africa. Integrating Africa into the international economic system at the time was premature and it was the beginning of increasing disequilibrium between the poor and the rich economies. This was so because Africa was forced into the international market system at a competitive disadvantage. Since Africa did not, nor does it possess the kind of advanced technology known in the west, it was virtually impossible for Africans to compete with the Europeans and the result was a one-way trade. Not only was the trade a one-way affair but the Europeans had made African (Southern African) countries their de facto colonies.

In their vantage position as the conqueror, the (Western) dominant powers, both militarily, economically and politically were able to exploit Africa's natural resources, (this is diagrammatically shown in Figure 1) (page 62) which they sent home without paying just prices. In addition, Africa served as a dumping ground for their cheap and surplus products. The end product of all these events was that Africa became a dependent economy, serving European interests and thus externally controlled and regulated by the developed countries.

What I have examined and analyzed in this section is that development and underdevelopment are both comparable terms as well as having a dialectical relationship. By this is meant that the interaction of both produces each other. In the interaction between Europe and Africa the former was the master while the latter was the servant, and the result was the transfer of wealth from Africa to Europe. This relationship has resulted in a great imbalance or disequilibrium which has remained the fundamental problem of African underdevelopment. It goes without saying that Africa must find a way to liberate herself from economic dependence. And this is what the struggle is all about in Southern Africa.

Dependency theory advocates that regional integration must be directed at winning control over the domestic and regional economies, political independence and stability, self-reliance and the redefinition of the peripheral location and rule of underdeveloped regions in the international division of labour.[61] SADCC claims to have all these goals either explicitly or implicitly.

We cannot examine all the questions raised by dependency theory in this study, as it has been stated in the earlier section of this chapter, when and where it illuminates our explanations and conceptualisations we shall endeavor to apply the dependency framework. However, in subsequent chapters we shall examine the extent to which SADCC institutions, policies and environment are capable of ensuring the attainment of "a durable foundation for internally generated, self-sustained processes of development and economic growth based on the twin principles of national and collective self-reliance".[62]

74

NOTES

[1]President Robert Mugabe, The Construction of Socialism in Zimbabwe: Policy Statement No. 14 (Harare: Zimbabwe, Department of Information, 9 July, 1984), pp. 1-11.

[2]See John Dimsdale, "Tanzania-Mozambique: Two Roads to Socialism", Africa Report, September-October 1982, pp. 14-17. Also R. H. Green, "Southern African Development Coordination: The Struggle Continues", Africa Contemporary Records (ACR) 1980-1981, (1981), pp. A24-25.

[3]The most serious threat to the survival of SADCC is the apartheid South Africa. There are many sources of information on the South African threat to its black neighbouring states. See The Report of Committee of Foreign Relations, House of Representatives, Subcommittee of Africa, Hearings before the Subcommittee on Africa of the Committee of Foreign Affairs, U.S. House of Representatives, 97th Congress, 2nd Session, December 8, 1982, Regional Destabilization in Southern Africa (Washington, D.C.: U.S. Government Printing Office, 1983). See also Joseph Hanlon, "Hostage to apartheid: Frontline Angola:, South (London), June 1983, pp. 12-13.

[4]Bela Balassa, The Theory of Economic Integration (London: George Allen and Unwin, 1973), p. 1.

[5]Peter Robson, Economic Integration in Africa (Evanston: Northwestern University Press, 1968), p. 26.

[6]Joseph S. Nye, Pan-Africanism and East African Integration (Cambridge: Harvard University Press, 1967).

[7]Bela Balassa, op. cit., p. 2.

[8]Ralph I. Onwuka, Development and Integration in West Africa: The Case of ECOWAS (Ile-Ife: Obafemi Awolowo University Press, 1981), p. 3.

[9]See Arthur Hazlewood, Economic Integration: The East African Experience (London: Heineman Books, 1975). See also Ralph I. Onwuka, op. cit., pp. 39-48.

[10]Statistical Year Book 1979/80 (New York: United Nations, 1981), pp. 48-51.

[11]For details see The World Bank, Accelerated Development in Sub-Saharan Africa: An Agenda for Action, op. cit., p. 121.

[12]Kwame Nkrumah, Neo-colonialism: The Highest State of Imperialism (New York: International Publishers, 1966).

[13]See the Documents, Organization of African Unity Lagos Plan of Action for the Economic Development of Africa 1980-2000 (Geneva: International Institute for Labour Studies, 1981), pp. 7-8.

[14]Botha's proposed "Constellation" known as "The Constellation of Southern African States (CONSAS)", was originally supposed to have included all of Southern African States. South Africa's initiative in 1979 regarding the formation of CONSAS was to counter and oppose the establishment of the SADCC. At present CONSAS is apartheid regimes' domestic constellation of Mr. P. W. Botha, launched on 22 July 1980. CONSAS includes South Africa, and its so-called independent homeland (the Bantustans) of Bophuthatswana, Ciskie, Transkei and Venda. See "The Collapse of Botha's Constellation Strategy", Africa, III (November 1980), pp. 47-50.

[15]See Organization of African Unity, op. cit.

[16]Ernst B. Haas, The Unity of Europe: Political, Social and Economic Forces 1950-1957 ˙ (Stanford University Press, 1968), p. 16.

[17]James A. Caporaso, "Introduction to special issue of International Organization on Dependence and Dependency in the Global System" International Organization, Vol. 32, No. 1 (1978), p. 1.

76

[18]James P. Sewell, <u>Functionalism and World Politics</u>, (Princeton, NJ: Princeton University Press, 1966), pp. 4-5.

[19]For details on the Theory of Functionalism see David Mitrany, <u>A Working Peace System</u> (Chicago: Quadrangle Books, 1966).

[20]_____, <u>Functionalism</u> (New Haven: Yale University Press, 1950), pp. 196-199.

[21]_____, <u>A Working Peace System</u>, <u>op. cit.</u>, p. 40.

[22]<u>Ibid</u>.

[23]<u>Ibid</u>. p. 43.

[24]<u>Ibid</u>., p. 28.

[25]See James Sewell, <u>op. cit.</u>, p. 49.

[26]Mitrany, <u>op. cit.</u>, pp. 9-14.

[27]<u>Ibid</u>., pp. 51-62.

[28]Inis L. Claude, Jr. <u>Swords Into Plowshares</u> (New York: Random House, 1971), pp. 378-407.

[29]Mitrany, <u>op. cit.</u>, p. 97.

[30]Ernst B. Haas, <u>The Unity of Europe: Political, Social and Economic Forces 1950-1957</u> (Stanford: Stanford University Press, 1968), p. 16-19.

[31]_____, "International Integration: The European and the Universal Process", <u>International Organization</u>, XV (1961), pp. 366-392.

[32]David Mitrany, "The United Nations After 25 Years, Regional and Functional Devolution", <u>International Relations</u>, III, 10 (November, 1970), pp. 816-834.

[33]Joseph S. Nye, _International Regionalism_ (Boston: Little Brown and Company, 1968), pp. 337-428.

[34]_Ibid._

[35]There are six integrative variables, as given by Joseph Nye, _Ibid._, pp. 337-428.

[36]Sue Turner, "SADCC: Lusaka, Food Security emerges as the key issue", _Africa Economic Digest_ (London), Vol. 5, No. 4, (27 January-2 February, 1984). pp. 2-4.

[37]R. H. Green, "Constellation, Association, Liberation: Economic Coordination and the Struggle for South Africa", _ACR 1979-1980_ (1981), p. A32.

[38]Unlike in the developed regions of the world where integration serves other purposes, in the case of the underdeveloped countries the theory and practice of economic integration cannot be separated. See John P. Renninger, _Multinational Corporation for Development in West Africa_ (Toronto), Pergamon Press, 1979.

[39]Patrick J. McGowan and Dale L. Smith, "Economic Dependency in Black Africa: An Analysis of Competing Theories" _International Organization_, Vol. 32, No. 1 (1978), p. 180.

[40]For details in the case of U.S. Penetration of Africa and Latin America see Anthony Sampson, _The Sovereign State of ITT_ (New York: Stein and Day Publishers, 1973); Walter Rodney _How Europe Underdeveloped Africa_ (Washington, D.C.: Howard University Press, 1974) John Stockwell, _In Search of Enemies: A CIA Story_ (New York: Norton, 1978); Olayiwola Abegunrin and H. E. Newsum, _United States Foreign Policy Towards Southern Africa; Andrew Young and Beyond_ (London: Macmillan Press, 1987), in this book see especially Chapters 1 and 2; and Kwame Nkrumah, _Neo-Colonialism: The Last State of Imperialism_ (New York: International Publishers, 1966).

[41]Lynn K. Mytelka, _Regional Development in a Global Economy: The Multinational Corporation Technology and Andean Integration_ (New Haven: Yale University Press, 1979).

[42]For full details on the role of Multinational Corporations in Southern Africa see Ann Seidman and Neva Seidman Makgetta, Outposts of Monopoly Capitalism: Southern Africa in the Changing Global Economy (London: Zed Press, 1980).

[43]Ibid.

[44]See Walter Rodney op. cit., on the European powers in the underdevelopment of Africa.

[45]For details on the Geo-strategic importance of Southern Africa see, O. Abegunrin, "South Africa and West" Renaissance Universal Journal Vol. 4, No. 2 (1984). Also see Western Massachusetts Association of Concerned African Scholars, U.S. Military Involvement in Southern Africa (Boston: West End Press, 1978); and Ann Seidman and Neva Seidman Makgettla, op. cit.

[46]James O'Connor, "The Meaning of Economic Imperialism", in K. T. Fann and Donald C. Hodges (eds.) Reading in the U.S. Imperialism (Boston: F. Porter Sargent, 1971), p. 33.

[47]Dale Johnson, "Dependence and the International System", in Cockcroft et al. Dependence and Underdevelopment: Latin America's Political Economy (New York: Anchor Books, 1972), p. 71.

[48]Ibid., pp. 71-77.

[49]R. J. Gewin and J. A. Betley, The Scramble for Africa (Ibadan: University Press, 1973).

[50]Ira Katznelson et al. (eds.) The Politics and Society Reader (New York: David McKay Co. 1974), pp. 175-176.

[51]Ibid.

[52]Ibid.

[53]Cockcroft et al. Dependence and Underdevelopment, p. 9.

[54]Irving Louis Horowitz, Three Worlds of Development: The Theory and Practice of International Stratification (New York: Oxford University Press, 1972).

[55]Katznelson et al., The Politics and Society Reader, pp. 192-193.

[56]Ibid., p. 194.

[57]Ibid.

[58]Richard Barnet and Ronald Muller, Global Reach (New York: Simon and Schuster, 194), pp. 78-79.

[59]Ibid., p. 83.

[60]See Walter Rodney, How Europe Underdeveloped Africa (Washington, D.C.: Howard University Press, 1974).

[61]Lynn K. Mytelka, op. cit., see also Julius O. Ihonvbere "Social Aspects of Integration: The Case of ECOWAS" Korean Journal of International Studies 14 (1) (1982/83) Julius O. Ihonvbere, "Integration in a Dependent Regional Economy: Goals and Problems of ECOWAS" unpublished M.A. Research Essay, The Norman Paterson School of International Affairs, Carleton University, Ottawa, May 1981.

[62]For details see Organization of African Unity, Lagos Plan of Action for the Economic Development of Africa 1980-2000 op. cit.

CHAPTER 3

IMPERIALISM AND LIBERATION STRUGGLES IN SOUTHERN AFRICA

Arnold Toynbee had predicted that future historians would say that:

> the great event of the twentieth century was the impact of the western civilization upon all other living societies of the world of that day. They will say of this impact that it was so powerful and so pervasive that it turned the lives of all victims upside down and inside out - affecting the behavior, outlook, feelings and beliefs of individual men, women, and children in an intimate way, touching chords in human souls that are not touched by external material forces - however ponderous and terrifying.[1]

Despite the exaggeration, there is some element of truth in this statement. The impact of Western civilization is found everywhere in Africa and will be felt by generations yet unborn. Although there may have been individuals and institutions that worked hard and sincerely for the good of Africans, their saving labours were palliative and peripheral. Let us take a look at how the European incursion affected Southern Africa in the area of economics.

Since the main focus of this chapter has to do with the colonial imperialism in Southern Africa, our concern here is primarily with economic imperialism. Thus from our discussion, we can define economic imperialism and the economic subordination or domination of one country or a group of countries by another for the main purpose of formal or informal control of domestic economic resources for the benefit of the subordinating or dominating power, and at the expense of the local people and their economy. The imperialist powers control foreign exchange and public and private savings; and agricultural, mineral, transportation, communication, manufacturing and commercial facilities and other assets of the Southern African states. In other words, western imperialist power controls both the liquid and real economic resources of the Southern Africa (countries) sub-continent especially, and the African continent as a whole.

The colonial experience of SADCC States differs in many respects. The route to political independence from colonial domination as well as contemporary socio-economic and political strategies to extricate themselves from the neo-colonial yoke also differ tremendously. While states like Botswana, Lesotho, Malawi, Swaziland, Tanzania and Zambia had a "peaceful" route to political autonomy, the case was different for other states like Angola, Mozambique and Zimbabwe, which won political independence through armed struggle for Liberation.[2] This chapter will examine and analyze the following; colonial-settler imperialism in Southern Africa; ideology and communist Countries in the liberation struggle in Southern Africa; and western economic imperialism, in Southern Africa.

Their colonial experiences of liberation struggles have served to determine as well as influence political efforts toward collective self-reliance in the area. There is no doubt that the political and economic liberation goal of SADCC which has dedicated itself to redefining regionalism as self-reliance, requires strong institutional support and political commitments. Seretse Khama former President of Botswana rightly pointed out in the case of SADCC that:

> ...political and economic liberation are phases in the same struggle...achieving economic liberation must be a regional as well as a national struggle. In the political realm, the struggle for the liberation of Angola, Mozambique and Zimbabwe and the continuing struggle for the liberation of Namibia have taught all of us in Southern Africa that lesson.[3]

The above statement gives credence to the view that "negotiated" political independence is and has always been incapable of redressing problems which contribute to national and regional disintegration. In the case of Angola, Mozambique and Zimbabwe the struggle for political freedom was by itself an ideological struggle. The salience of the political experience to successful cooperation and economic liberation in Southern Africa was made quite clear in President Khama's keynote address to the SADCC Conference in 1979:

> We are gathered here today to try to chart a new course for the future of Southern Africa, or to launch a new type of struggle for liberation... Our colonial past has ensured that we will continue to depend on others for our economic survival... Some of the countries

on which we depend for our economic survival
do not share the ideals on which our own
societies are found... Unfortunately we find
ourselves at their mercy... We can wage a
successful struggle for economic liberation
provided we can begin now, in the free states
of Southern Africa, to plan together for our
economic future.[4]

No doubt, the attainment of such ideals requires
extensive and solid "political will" among the
participating countries. The fact that the attainment
of economic liberation is in itself a political issue,
is not lost to Southern Africans.

Colonial-Settler Imperialism in Southern Africa

SADCC's aim of economic liberation is at variance
with a South African plan for the Southern Africa
subregion. The Apartheid regime would like to see a
constellation of states emerging from Southern Africa.
This is P. W. Botha's idea which he exposed in March
1979. Critically examined, one observes that the
constellation ideal is nothing other than a grand design
to entrench the dependence of Southern African states on
the white settler controlled South Africa. By coming up
with the constellation idea, South Africa seeks to
increase its neighbour's economic dependence on it and
to exert control over their policies and development.[5]

The constellation dream is at variance with
economic emancipation which is the aim of the SADCC.
Botha's idea of constellation of states means perpetual
colonial-settler imperialism in Southern Africa. In
fact constellation and economic liberation of Southern
Africa (which SADCC stands for) are diametric. Both
cannot coexist. Through constellation, South Africa

wishes to bring the SADCC states under its sphere of influence. However, it is the wish of the Southern African states to lessen their dependence on the apartheid regime. In Botha's design, the constellation of states can even be extended not only to Southern African countries but even also to the so-called Bantustans.[6] The argument for a constellation of state is that: "... It is only if a group of African states can be coerced, convinced or otherwise induced to enter a stable relationship with South Africa are either global or regional threats to domestic stability likely to be reduced."[7]

Having realized that the SADCC economic independence programme is becoming a reality, the apartheid regime in South Africa thinks the best way to bring about its demise is to infiltrate their rank and file. South Africa wishes to force Southern African states to cooperate with it. President Nyerere of Tanzania has however, laid bare the collective aim of the SADCC countries. For him there is no basis for cooperation between apartheid South Africa and SADCC states.[8] However, it is unfortunate that South Africa has been able to intimidate two of the SADCC states to sign accords with it. These are the Nkomati accord between Mozambique and South Africa and a secret accord between South Africa and Swaziland. The Nkomati accord has a lot of implications vis-a-vis the aims and aspirations of the SADCC (these implications are dealt with in Chapter 6).

The security implication of cooperation with the South African white regime is played down by Botha in his constellation scheme. South Africa calculates that being friendly with its neighbours they will not allow their territories to be used by liberation movements fighting a war of national liberation against South Africa. This implies that as soon as a constellation of states is formed, liberation movements activities in the region will be stemmed. If South Africa could have its way it will force members of the constellation to expel liberation movements from the region. South Africa has been doing this on its own before and still continues. But if a constellation of states dominated by it materialized, it will be a total war on Liberation Movements in the region. For example, in 1981 the racist regime in South Africa, carried out a raid on Matola, a town in Mozambique.[9] In this raid many innocent people were killed by racist troops, under the pretext that they were flushing out the African National Congress freedom fighters. South African forces have done the same in Angola. Killing thousands of the Angolan citizens and Namibian refugees inside Angola, under the pretext that they were flushing out the SWAPO Nationalist fighters.[10] South African Defense forces have carried out many raids and still continue raiding Botswana, Lesotho, Swaziland, Zambia and Zimbabwe, killing thousands of innocent citizens in those countries in order to force them to submit to South African wishes and join its so-called constellation of states.[11]

The existence of the white-settler minority regime in South Africa is hampering the socio-economic development of the Southern Africa sub-region. For instance, a country like Angola which is endowed with many natural resources, but has not seen peace for one week since its independence in 1975, by bombing of its territory[12] nearly everyday by South African troops. Given a chance and peace to stabilize itself, Angola has all the potential to achieve rapid economic development in Southern Africa. All strategic minerals are available in Angola, and it is the only Southern African country with a large petroleum production.[13] Continual raids on its neighbours, destroying bridges, railway lines, and other infrastructures including towns, villages,and rendering thousands of the Southern African citizens homeless.[14] As a result of this the Southern African refugee problem is increasing at an alarming rate.[15] The Ian Smith led white minority settler regime did the same thing in the former Rhodesia before it became independent under the African majority rule, Mugabe led government in April 1980.[16]

Botha conceives of the constellation along a separate development basis. According to him the constellation has to take care of the Bantustans - the so-called homelands. Having achieved the aim of apartheid, that is separate development which forced millions of Africans in South Africa into barren and unproductive areas of the country, in the so-called tribal homelands (see Table 3.1 (page 88) on population of SouthAfrica), a kind of cooperation with those the apartheid system has treated unjustly is sought. After banishing the blacks to the so-called homelands (the barren areas) the white minority took the prime and fertile areas.

The SADCC strategy is a way of putting an end to separate development, not entrenching it. It is based on the premise that regional coordination must be among formally equal states, which are objectively equal enough for none to be the dominant.[17] In the South African calculations, the constellation will widen the way for the export of goods and capital to other African states with the attending profit. This has been one of the aims of the apartheid regime in South Africa which

TABLE 3.1
POPULATION OF SOUTH AFRICA, 1985

Races ·	Numbers	Percentage of Total	Growth Rate
Blacks	22,800,000*	72.8%	2.9
Whites	4,820,000	15.5%	0.9
Coloureds	2,800,000	8.9%	2.0
Asians	880,000	2.8%	2.3
TOTAL	31,300,000	100%	

*12,000,000 of Africans have been forced into the so-called tribal homelands, while 10,800,000 live outside the homelands, mostly in the urban areas. Distribution of urban blacks outside the homeland is as follows:

Transvaal Province	- 5,973,600
Cape Province	- 1,687,200
Orange Free State	- 1,680,000
Natal Province	- 1,459,200

Source: "Population Profile", Africa Research Bulletins (April 15, 1986), p. 7575.

is becoming increasingly isolated from the world community. Although one is not saying that trade relations do not exist between the South African minority regime and some African states, a constellation will widen and broaden these trade relations, and even formally legalize them. South African private firms will have a tremendous role to play in the constellation. The racist settler government in South Africa is floating the idea of a free trade area among the Southern African states. This is because it will be the dominant power and gain immensely from such an arrangement.

However, we must bear in mind that while SADCC is opposed to private firm exploitation in the region, they do not aim at a gradual move towards total state control of their economies. This is because the region is made up of countries with different economic and political ideologies. Their intention is that the public sector will play an important role in the regional coordination. However, SADCC reserves the right to determine how far private capital can go in their scheme of things. The SADCC also wants to prove that "...dependence on South Africa and the lack of linkages between members were artificially imposed by colonialism".[18]

Ideology and Communist Countries in the Liberation Struggle in Southern Africa

The SADCC is made up of countries with different ideological orientation and is already finding it difficult to define the extent of reliance on South Africa. While some members want to limit reliance to unavoidable areas, others are dependent to a very large extent on South Africa. Geographically one of the member states of the SADCC, Lesotho is engulfed by South

Africa. The implication of this is that South Africa will always bring pressure to bear on these countries and make them spokes in the wheel of progress of SADCC objectives. Already, while some countries are considering sanctions, Swaziland and Malawi have made it clear at least until 1985, that they would not support sanctions of any degree against South Africa. Swaziland Prime Minister, Prince Bhekimpi told the OAU Chairman, President Abdou Diouf of Senegal in September 1985 that:

> The international community is imposing sanctions against South Africa. We in Swaziland cannot support any action which will eventually threaten our own survival. Unless sanctions against South Africa are accompanied by a large inflow of aid and investment in Swaziland, our survival will be endangered.[19]

In fact Swaziland has signed a secret treaty with South Africa since 1982 in which it has agreed to flush out ANC members on its own territory fighting the racist regime in South Africa. The only University in Swaziland had to be closed down in 1984 because of what the authority described as an unhealthy students preoccupation with the philosophies, aims and objectives of the ANC.[20]

Botswana has accepted that sanctions against South Africa are a very real possibility with the recent situation inside South Africa. The effect of sanctions will be felt in Botswana. For this reason the Gaborone authority is "formulating contingency plans to keep operations running after the Southern Supply line either dries up or is cut off".[21]

Malawi was one of the Southern African countries which met in Lusaka on 1st April 1980 to declare their commitment to pursue policies aimed at economic

liberation from South Africa, and yet is the only
African country that maintains diplomatic relations with
the Pretoria regime. Malawian authority has always
argued that isolation and boycott of South Africa will
not change the situation in Southern Africa. Instead,
Malawi maintains that "only constant dialogue with the
South African government will have positive result. In
other words, Malawi supports SADCC but does not
subscribe to its views".[22] SADCC member states are
already suffering because of the apartheid policy which
is not their own making. One remembers that South
Africa has proposed a constellation of states in
Southern Africa which the SADCC has rejected.
Ideological differences among members leads to the
problem of perception. Differences in ideological
pursuit leads to differences in what constitutes
development and what ought to be done, among the SADCC
member states.[23] Obviously, projects that a socialist
centrally planned economy with state control of
production has as its priority for economic development
will be different from those of the "mixed" or
capitalist economy.

The Communist countries did not have any colonial
contact with the countries making up the SADCC. While
not branding them saints, one can make bold to say that
they represent the better of two evils. The Eastern
European Countries' non-investment with the (apartheid)
colonial imperialism in South Africa in terms of
diplomatic and economic relations makes them the natural
ally of the SADCC. Many western countries because of
their economic links with South Africa were not ready to
extend even moral support to the liberation movements in
Southern Africa. The Communist countries are comrades
in the struggles, and offered training facilities on

their own territories for nationalist soldiers from
Southern Africa.[24]

> Sometimes instructors went to Africa from the
> communist world to impact their skills of
> guerrilla warfare and jungle strategy. There
> were also occasions when Africans went to
> countries ranging from Russia to North Korea
> as part of the military preparations for the
> struggle in Southern Africa.[25]

The countries of the Communist bloc have been able to
establish themselves in many Southern African countries.
Even before the military coup in Lisbon in April 1974,
the Russians had been giving support to the nationalist
fighters against Portuguese rule in Angola.[26] When
independence was attained they stayed and joined forces
with the MPLA government in Angola. The Russians
identified themselves with the majority of African
States which recognized the MPLA government in Angola.
Angolan-Russian relations culminated in the signing of
the treaty of friendship and cooperation between them in
October 1976. The treaty regards an attack on Angolan
territory as on the USSR.[27] The Russians would then
come to Angola's aid.

In Zimbabwe, the Russians, Chinese, and the North
Koreans helped the nationalist fighters in their war of
liberation. The USSR supported Joshua Nkomo (ZAPU)
while the Chinese and North Koreans supported Robert
Mugabe (ZANUPF). These countries supplied arms and even
helped in the training of liberation fighters. North
Korea is a very close ally of Zimbabwe. North Korea
gave military equipment and military advisers to
Zimbabwe after its independence in 1980. The North
Koreans helped train the Zimbabwean army especially the
fifth brigade.[28] President Mugabe personally commended

the North Koreans in 1983, when he said that Zimbabwe's
real friends were those who came to her rescue in a time
of need.   However, relations with the USSR picked up
rather slowly.   This was because Moscow had backed ZAPU
against the rival ZANU before the formation of the
Patriotic Front and had maintained rather distant
relations with Robert Mugabe even after the front came
into being, the USSR found itself at least temporarily
shut out of Zimbabwe in the wake of Mugabe's election
victory in 1980.   It was not until 1981 that Mugabe's
government agreed to open formal relations with
Moscow.[29]

In the case of Tanzania, President Nyerere has
always been a fully fledged fighter against minority
rule and colonialism, and his role in African liberation
struggles has been exemplary.   At the height of the war
in Southern Africa Nyerere's name and that of Tanzania
became synonymous with anti-colonial guerrilla action.
Ian Smith once described him as "the evil genius behind
the war in former Rhodesia".[30]   Tanzania has been the
headquarters of the Liberation Committee of the OAU
since its inception in 1964.   In the sixties Tanzania
earned a reputation as a Mecca for freedom fighters from
many parts of Africa.   Tanzania support for African
Liberation struggles continues today by the practical
training and education facilities provided for Southern
Africa's liberation Movements - (the ANC and SWAPO), in
Tanzania in their continued struggles against the
apartheid regime in South Africa.

This constant commitment to the anti-colonial
struggles has been at great cost to Tanzania in both
economic terms and in relations to attitudes towards
Tanzania, especially in the West.   However, Nyerere has
never stopped thinking and acting for the freedom of

Africa as a whole and Southern Africa in particular. He initiated the formation of the Frontline States in order to expedite strategic decision-making without having to wait for the OAU. He travelled throughout the world to talk with the allies of colonialism and racism reiterating time and again that the war in Southern Africa would not stop until victory and freedom were achieved. Nyerere was very serious on the liberation struggles in Southern Africa, and therefore declared that:

> The Southern part of Africa is governed by powers which claim to be part of the western bloc and which are accepted by their allies as part of the free world. This is not denied. Africa is determined that Africa shall be governed by Africa. That is also undeniable.[31]

Making a farewell speech to Nyerere for his retirement on behalf of the SADCC member states in August 1985, the late Mozambican President, Samora Machel, spoke of him as a symbol of liberation.

> To speak of Nyerere is to speak of the liberation of Africa. It is a founding father of the OAU whom we see departing from our midst. It is the political monument who made his country a sanctuary for liberation movements, who made the Tanzanian people an example of solidarity, who understanding that the struggle of other people was also his struggle, offered Dar-es-Salaam, The Harbour of Peace, as the capital City against colonialism, racism and exploitation.[32]

Nyerere's tremendous influence in the Third World and the developed world does not hinge only on his practical refusal to be a pawn on the superpower political chessboard, but he is a thinker, and the creator of a national economic and political philosophy which is essentially African in character and known as Uhuru na Ujamaa - meaning freedom and socialism. "Ujamaa is Tanzanian socialism".[33] Ujamaa is based on building society along African lines, respecting the traditional ethics of cooperation, the extended family, mutual obligation and concern for one another, with all the elements necessary for the life in the society properly integrated.[34]

Ujamaa philosophy is based on state control of the major means of production and the country's wealth, so that the government will have the power and means to implement the development of rural areas where 90 percent of Africans live. It is based on collectivization, living in planned villages in which the state can supplement people's own efforts by making the country's wealth available to them through improved infrastructure, free clean water facilities, education and medical care. Ujamaa philosophy believes in narrowing the glaring gap between the rich and the poor; and the rich contributing more to the government coffers through progressive taxation. Ujamaa-African socialism which has its critics both inside and outside Tanzania, deals with the division between the urban elites and the peasantry and attacks kleptocracy. It is based on self-reliance, which means national resources being the basis of development plans, but at the same time leaving the doors open for aid from anywhere, so long as it is free from strings and is intended to further the government policies and the aspirations of the people.[35]

Nyerere's incorruptible character has made it possible for him to get genuine aid and loans from the

East, West and even from the developing countries. He has also established balanced mutual relations with other nations both big and small without having to suppress his conscience or his words. But in the true sense of it Tanzania is very close to the Eastern bloc, especially to China which has been very helpful to Tanzania in terms of aid and development assistance. The Tanzanian rural organizations and agricultural development under the Ujamaa philosophy were patterned after the Chinese communes.[36] Most significantly, China helped "build and finance the Tanzania-Zambia railway".[37]

Nyerere has been very vocal in the international issues and a selfless advocate of the New International Economic Order. He has been criticized by some Western Critics that his socialism has failed. But Nyerere believes that his socialism has not failed, and that his country's economic difficulties were not a result of the socialist policies, but that those policies actually gave Tanzania the strength to deal with its economic difficulties in unity and with understanding and hope. "At present the country's situation is bad and will remain so for a long time, but there are encouraging signs. Tanzanians have started to see light at the end of the economic tunnel."[38]

However, we should not fail to realize one important fact. This is that the West is a very powerful bloc as far as influence on the World economy is concerned. It is also true that the West has pumped more aid to developing countries, especially in Africa than the Eastern European countries and other socialist countries combined. The result of Western aid and investments as I have said earlier has been counter productive. Western aid has not helped Africa out of its economic predicament. Instead Africa is becoming increasingly dependent on the industrialized countries for support. The involvement of Eastern European and Communist countries in Southern Africa can be seen in this way: "In comparison with the West, Communist States may give little economic aid, but they are not smeared with the South African connection, and they provide arms and military training for the liberation movements".[39] As things are now, the SADCC has to choose between getting as much aid and grants from Western sources and still remain at their apron strings or scout for investments which will be of mutual benefit to all the parties involved in the transaction.

While on balance Russian aid to African economic development has been only a fraction of Western aid, Russia's support of African liberation movements has been more substantial than Western aid. Many Western countries, because of their special economic and political relations with the minority regime in South Africa, have all along been reluctant to extend even moral support to liberation movements. For as long as Lisbon was under fascist rule and was reluctant to liberate Africa, the U.S. was strongly loyal to Portugal. Even after all the countries in the world have recognized the MPLA Government in Angola, the U.S. still refused to give diplomatic recognition to Angola after twelve years of Angolan independence. The Soviet Union and its allies have remained strong champions of African liberation in Southern Africa, and have often extended considerable financial and material support to the movements engaged in that liberation.

Western Economic Imperialism in Southern Africa

The crimes committed by imperialism are endless. Within this century 60 million people have been killed in wars generated by imperialism. As many as 100 million·people have been crippled, tens of additional millions have died from disease and epidemics, all generated by wars of imperialism. About 10 million men, women and children have been slaughtered in gas chambers, shot or hanged. Not less than 2 million have been killed by air raids, by napalm bombs. Since 1870 the imperialists have conducted over 120 wars and military operations against the people of Africa, and the result has been the staggering casualties of 5.3 million Africans. Therefore, what then is this imperialism?

In their essay on the political economy of nineteenth century British imperialism, Jon Gallagher and Ronald Robinson defined imperialism thus:

> imperialism, perhaps, may be defined as a sufficient function of this process of integrating new regions into expanding economy; its character is largely decided by the various and changing relationships between the political and economic elements of expansion in any particular region and time. Two qualifications must be made. First, imperialism may be only indirectly connected with economic integration in that it sometimes extends beyond areas of economic development but acts for their strategic protection. Secondly, although imperialism is a function of economic expansion, it is not a necessary function. Whether imperialist phenomena show themselves or not is determined not only by

the factors of economic expansion, but equally by the political and social organization of the regions brought into the orbit of the expansive society, and also by the world situation in general.

It is only when the politics of these new regions fail to provide satisfactory conditions for commercial or strategic integration and when their relative weakness allows, that power is used imperialistically to adjust those conditions. Economic expansion, it is true, will tend to flow into the regions of maximum opportunity, but maximum opportunity depends as much upon political considerations of security as upon questions of profit. Consequently, in any particular region, if economic opportunity seems large but political security small, then full absorption into the extending economy tends to be frustrated until power is exerted upon the state in question. Conversely, in proportion as satisfactory political frameworks are brought into being in this way, the frequency of imperialist intervention lessens and imperialist control is correspondingly relaxed. It may be suggested that this willingness to limit the use of paramount power to establishing security for trade is the distinctive feature of the British imperialism of free trade in the nineteenth century, in contrast to the mercantilist use of power to obtain commercial supremacy and monopoly through political possession.[40]

In the 1950's African and Asian leaders began to denounce what they considered to be "economic control, intellectual control, and actual physical control by a small but alien community, within a nation". The Third All-African People's Conference held in Cairo in 1961 listed some of the basic manifestations of neo-colonialism:

This conference considers that Neo-Colonialism, which is the survival of the colonial system in spite of formal recognition of political independence in emerging countries, which became the victims of an indirect and subtle form of domination by political, economic, social, military or technical forces, is the greatest threat to African countries that have newly won their independence or those approaching this status...

This conference denounces the following manifestations of Neo-Colonialism in Africa:

(a) Puppet governments represented by stooges, and based on some chiefs, reactionary elements, anti-popular politicians, big bourgeois compradors or corrupted civil or military functionaries.

(b) Regrouping of states, before or after independence, by an imperial power in federation or communities linked to that imperial power.

(c) Balkanization as a deliberate political fragmentation of states by creation of artificial entities, such as, for example, the case of Katanga, Mauritania, Buganda, etc.

(d) The economic entrenchment of the colonial power before independence and the continuity of economic dependence after recognition of national sovereignty.

(e) Integration into colonial economic blocs which maintain the underdeveloped character of African economy.

(f) Economic infiltration by a foreign power after independence, through capital investments, loans and monetary aids or technical experts, of unequal concessions, particularly those extending for long periods.

(g) Direct monetary dependence as in those emergent independent states whose finances remain in the hands of and directly controlled by colonial powers.

(h) Military basis sometimes introduced as scientific research stations or training schools introduced either before independence or as a condition for independence.[41]

Taking the chief manifestations as spelt out by the third All-African People's Conference and the definition of imperialism by Gallagher and Robinson, we can say that contemporary imperialism cannot function well without the active involvement of the state in international economic relationship; that there has to be a state capitalism before neo-colonialist policies can be implemented. Furthermore, contemporary imperialism works hard to prevent the (newly independent) Southern African States from consolidating their political independence, and thus makes it possible to keep them economically dependent. In the particular case of neo-colonialism, "the allocation of economic resources, investment effort, legal and ideological structures, and other features of the old society remain unchanged",[42] except for the substitution of "internal colonialism" for formal colonialism; in other words, power is now transferred to the domestic ruling classes i.e. thòse "negotiators worth talking to". These are the local (marionettes) puppets who are sure not to rock the colonial boat. It is this kind of situation that Reginald Green and Ann Seidman refer to as arising out of "false decolonization".[43] This kind of independence has ignored the basic needs of the Southern African states, promotes disunity within Southern African countries, and in practice prevents them from attaining real sovereignty. It was these kinds of (experiences) conditions that prompted the late Kwame Nkrumah of Ghana to write his books Africa Must Unite, published in 1963[44] and Neo-Colonialism: The Last Stage of Imperialism, published in 1965.[45] In these books, he concluded that the underdeveloped countries and especially Africa would not make a forward march towards economic independence until neo-colonialism or neo-imperialism is defeated.

It appears that the SADCC has not come up with an entirely different strategy to achieve economic development. The traditional system in which the West brings in investments to third world countries in order to bring about economic development has been found to be inadequate. This is because it leads to a dependency cycle which the third world countries find difficult to break. Transnational companies investments in the third world seen in Western view as aid has been found to entrench the dependence of the third world countries on the metropolis. It is unfortunate that the SADCC did not take into consideration this fundamental point. It has been found that transnational investments in the third world countries lead to the extraction of huge profits from them rather than helping to bring about economic development.

The fact about the matter is that the West will only invest in SADCC projects when it seems likely there will be acceptable returns on capital.[46] With the invitation sent to foreign investors, especially from the West, one is being led to the conclusion that the organization (SADCC) is engaged in an activity which is likely to mortgage the entire economy of Southern Africa to the international capitalist system.[47]

Another important question concerns the sincerity of the foreign partners of the SADCC referred to by the organization as cooperators. It does not appear that the investors or cooperators in the SADCC projects have the same goals and aspirations as the SADCC. Most of the investors are private companies looking for profits. They do not feel they should be concerned with any goal which the SADCC might want to pursue, especially if it does not favour them. The only goal these foreign investors have is to make profit from their investments. For them investors in the SADCC projects should have no political concerns and should not be expected to subscribe to some kind of SADCC political goal.[48] This is a view held by Wilfred Turner, Director of the Southern Africa Association, which represents the main British firms involved in the region. Undoubtedly, the SADCC has a political goal and it is on this goal that the whole idea of forming the organization rests. As Tanzania's Minister of Industry, Basil Mramba said, "the SADCC is the child of the liberation movement in Southern Africa. It is the economic side of the liberation coin".[49]

Turner's assertion is very important because British investments are traditionally the most important in seven of the nine SADCC member states. If the investors do not feel themselves concerned with the goals of the SADCC, that means the probability of the scheme succeeding in the long run is very slim. The aim of forming the SADCC is to free the nine countries in the organization of dependence on racist South Africa and Western economic imperialism. As things are now, most of the cooperators in SADCC projects already have investments both capital and human in South Africa which they intend to make use of. Since the inauguration of SADCC in 1980, the West has been claiming that they are in support of the scheme. The European Economic Community (EEC), claims that the SADCC has its backing. However, the present dilemmas are a mirror of the community's own ambiguity faced with the weight of the trade and investment links between the EEC member states and racist South Africa.[50] The fact is that most of the Western countries who claim they want to see the SADCC succeed have huge investments in South Africa. Shown in Table 3.2 (page 105) are six EEC Countries including U.S. and Japan that are South Africa's top trading partners, (see also Table 3.3 (page 106) on Western investment in South Africa). Therefore, the important question is whether the west really wants to see SADCC succeed?

South African Boer authority intimidates the West to continue their investment in the apartheid enclave by saying that moving western investments from the country will increase unemployment and social unrest in all European countries. The Pretoria argument is that investment in South Africa creates job opportunities at home for the West. If the West does not continue its

TABLE 3.2
INTERNATIONAL TRADE WITH SOUTH AFRICA IN 1983 (In M)

Country	Export to South Africa	Imports from South Africa	Total	Rank
U.S.	2,467.0	1,753.8	4,220.8	1
Japan	1,903.8	1,546.7	3,455.0	2
U.K.	1,892.9	1,324.1	3,217.0	3
West Germany	2,236.0	753.4	2,989.4	4
France	622.7	378.7	1,001.4	5
Italy	516.4	398.9	915.3	6
Netherlands	224.0	351.5	595.5	7
Belgium	231.2	348.3	579.5	8
Total	11,094.0	6,855.4	16,973.9	

Source: An adapted version of a table on "The Sanctions Factors", Africa (June 1986), p. 40.

106

TABLE 3.3
BREAKDOWN OF WESTERN INVESTMENT IN SOUTH AFRICA

Country	Percentage of Investment
U.K.	34
U.S.	25
West Germany	25
Other Countries	16
Total	100

Total investment of $15.6 billions at 1981 Exchange rate.

Source: "Botha Peddles his Shopsoiled Line", South (London) July 1984, p. 67.

investments many jobs will be lost at home with its implications. This is an attempt to lure the West to continue its investment programmes in South Africa. While Britain, the U.S. and West Germany pay lip service to SADCC's aims, they continue in more tangible ways to support South Africa.[51]

It is doubtful if the West is really sincere in its goodwill for the SADCC. Scholars have asked whether it is realistic to suppose that the West will provide enough aid to enable the SADCC truly break South Africa's stronghold on the region.[52] One wonders if the statement of people like Edgard Pisani, former EEC Commissioner for the development policy is actually sincere. He said "the EEC considers it more important to try and build up the economic infrastructures and independence of members of the SADCC".[53] Is the EEC not just paying lip service to the cause of the organization? This question is especially important if one considers the fact that apart from the implications of the investment in South Africa, the amount the EEC has committed to the SADCC so far amounts to just peanuts compared to what they have invested in South Africa. One should not be carried away by the EEC argument that between 1980 and 1984 the community has committed 870 million ECU to SADCC projects. The contention that the EEC has also made contributions to national programmes of the SADCC in areas of agriculture and rural development is also meant to divert the world's attention from the continuing and growing investments of the Western countries in South Africa.

It has been argued by many Europeans that the EEC is sincere towards the SADCC. They pointed out the various projects that the EEC has carried out in the Southern African sub-region. They argued that the completion of the Botzam road linking Botswana and Zambia, the rehabilitation of the Tazara railway linking Tanzania and Zambia are projects undertaken by the EEC to show solidarity with the SADCC. They have also argued that annual community aid to the SADCC countries could total about $200 million by 1986. In fact EEC experts say that overall European aid (including bilateral aid from member states) could be running at an annual rate of some $1 billion a year by mid 1980s.[54] However, the truth is that all these are small compared with their investments in South Africa. One should therefore, not be deceived by the figures quoted by the EEC.

The fact that the West by and large welcomes the SADCC initiative and in particular the methods and institutions which the SADCC intends to use in implementing the policies confirms that the West does not perceive any immediate danger to their long-term interests in the area.[55] It also reinforces the argument that the master-servant relationship between the north represented by the West, and the South represented by the SADCC will be maintained in the SADCC scheme. Therefore, the role of the South as suppliers of raw materials to the industries of the north will not change. On the other hand the West's role as suppliers of finished products to the South will also remain. The West therefore, do not have to oppose a system that will eventually benefit it.

By aligning with the West, the SADCC will find it difficult to change the role of the South as hewers of wood and drawers of water for the north. The supply of cheap raw materials from the South will still continue to flow to the (West) north. The West on the other hand will continue to manipulate market forces to suit their own purpose, and continue to entrench imperialism in Southern Africa.

110

NOTES

[1]Arnold J. Toynbee, <u>Civilization on Trial</u> (New York: Oxford University Press, 1948), p. 214.

[2]For details on the armed struggles and war of liberation in Southern Africa see the following sources: Fola Soremekun, <u>ANGOLA: The Road to Independence</u> (Ile-Ife: Obafemi Awolowo University Press, 1983), John Marcum, <u>The Angolan Revolution: Exile Politics and Guerrilla Warfare 1962-1976 - Volume II</u> (Cambridge: MIT Press, 1978), Louis B. Serapiao and Mohamed A. El-Khawas, <u>Mozambique in the Twentieth Century: From Colonialism to Independence</u> (Washington, D.C.: University Press of America, 1979), Leonard T. Kapungu, <u>RHODESIA: The Struggle for Freedom</u> (Maryknoll, NY: Orbis Books, 1974), David Martin and Phyllis Johnson, <u>The Struggle for Zimbabwe: The Chimurenga War</u> (New York: Monthly Review Press, 1981), and Richard Gibson, <u>African Liberation Movements: Contemporary Struggles Against White Minority Rule</u> (London: Oxford University Press, 1972).

[3]Amon J. Nsekela (ed.) <u>Southern Africa: Toward Economic Liberation</u> (London: Rex Collings, 1981), p. vii.

[4]See Sir Seretse Khama, Keynote address to SADCC members, Arusha, Tanzania (3 July 1979).

[5]Guy Arnold, "SADCC's Fatal Flaw", <u>Africa Now</u> (October 1984), p. 92.

[6]"Building the Apartheid Empire", <u>op. cit.</u>, p. 28.

[7]See R. H. Green, "Constellation, Association and Liberation: Economic Coordination and Struggle for Southern Africa", <u>Africa Contemporary Record</u> 1979/80 (1980), p. A36.

[8]Guy Arnold, <u>op. cit</u>.

[9]Marcelino Komba "Mozambique's return to Arms" <u>Africa</u> June, 1981, pp. 52-62.

[10]See "South Africa: The Total Strategy Policy"
ACR 1979/80 (1981), pp. B766-767.

[11]On South Africa's raids into SADCC states see
Andrew Meldrum, "Zimbabwe under Threat of Invasion"
AfricAsia January 1986, pp. 14-15. "Pretoria's midnight
raids" Newsweek International, December 20, 1982, p. 16,
see also "Racists raid Botswana", Daily Sketch (Ibadan)
June 15, 1985, p. 6.

[12]Gerald J. Bender, "ANGOLA: Left, Right and
Wrong", Foreign Policy, 43 (Summer 1981), p. 55. See
also Layi Abegunrin, "South Africa's War Against its
Neighbours" The Punch (Lagos) September 28, 1985 and
"Racist forces Raid Angola", Daily Sketch (Ibadan),
January 7, 1986, p. 6.

[13]See J. T. C. Simoes (ed.) SADCC: Energy and
Development to the Year 2000, op. cit., pp. 85-96.

[14]"We will like to try out new areas of
cooperation", Africa Now (August 1984), p. 65.

[15]See Mark Doyle "ANGOLA: Sharks and Refugees"
West Africa, 26 September, 1983, p. 2220.

[16]David Martin and Phyllis Johnson, The Struggle
for Zimbabwe: The Chimurenga War, op. cit.

[17]R. H. Green, "Constellation, Association,
Liberation: Economic Coordination and Struggle for
Southern Africa" ACR 1979/80 (1980), p. A36.

[18]Joseph Hanlon, "The Business of Liberation, The
SADCC fights to keep the taint of apartheid out of its
trade", South (December 1984), p. 70.

[19]Norman Sowerby "SWAZILAND: Any sanctions pill
should have SADCC antidote" African Business (DEcember
1985),p. 21.

[20]Ibid.

112

[21]Linda Van Buren "When sanctions come, all the equations will change", African Business (October 1985), p. 26.

[22]"Malawi: Landlocked Southern Africa" African Business (December 1985), p. 17.

[23]E. J. Kisanga, "options for the SADCC" Africa (February, 1985), p. 37.

[24]Layi Abegunrin, "Soviet and Chinese Military Involvement in Southern Africa", A Current Bibliography on African Affairs Vol. 16, No. 3, 1983/84, pp. 195-206.

[25]Ali A. Mazrui, Africa's International Relations: The Diplomacy of Dependence and Change (London: Heinemann Press, 1977), p. 186.

[26]Ibid., p. 188.

[27]Fola Soremekun "Instant Socialism: Angola's Approach to Development since Independence" Lusophone Areas Studies Journal, No. 2 (July 1983), pp. 1-21.

[28]"Operation Turkey Revived" Africa Now (April 1983), p. 49.

[29]South Africa: Time Running Out, The Report of the Study Commission on U.S. Policy Toward Southern Africa (Berkeley: University of California Press, 1981). p. 325.

[30]Africa (November 1985), p. 10.

[31]Ibid., p. 11.

[32]Ibid.

[33]For details on Nyerere's economic and political philosophy read his works on Ujamaa, Julius K. Nyerere, Uhuru Na Ujamaa: Freedom and Socialism (Dar-es-Salaam: Oxford University Press, 1968).

[34]Ibid.

[35] Ibid.

[36] Ibid.

[37] Alan Lawrence, China's Foreign Relations since 1949 (Boston: Routledge and Kegan Paul 1975), p. 192.

[38] "Tanzania's economy: light at the end of the tunnel" Africa Now (December 1985), p. 49.

[39] James Barber et al., The West and South Africa (London: Routledge and Kegan Paul, 1982), p. 21.

[40] John Gallagher and Ronald Robinson, "The Imperialism of Free Trade", Economic History Review, 2nd Series (August 1953), pp. 5-6.

[41] "Neo-Colonialism", Voice of Africa 1/4 (April 1961), p. 4.

[42] See James O'Connor, "The Meaning of Economic Imperialism", op. cit., p. 40.

[43] Reginald H. Green and Ann Seidman, Unity or Poverty (Baltimore: Book, 1968).

[44] Kwame Nkrumah, Africa Must Unite (New York: International Publishers, 1963).

[45] _____, Neo-Colonialism: The Last Stage of Imperialism (New York: International Publisher, 1965).

[46] Guy Arnold, op. cit., p. 895.

[47] E. J. Kisanga, op. cit., p. 37.

[48] Joseph Hnalon, op. cit., p. 69.

[49] Ibid.

[50] "Ten Years of Lome Convention", West Africa (February 1985), p. 357.

[51]Guy Arnold, op. cit., p. 95.

[52]Ibid.

[53]Shade Islam: "Playing   the   SADCC   Card"   West Africa (February 1985), p. 365.

[54]Ibid.

[55]E. J. Kinsanga, op. cit.

CHAPTER 4

SADCC DEPENDENCE ON SOUTH AFRICA
AND EXTERNAL SOURCES

The Lusaka economic declaration was a remarkable
policy statement reflecting the ever-evolving African
strategy toward achieving the total liberation of
Southern Africa, based on the 1969 Lusaka Manifesto and
the Dar-es-Salaam Declaration of 1975. These
declarations were clear expressions of a desire to fight
against colonialism, and white minority rule. With this
background in mind the aim of this chapter is to examine
and analyze whether SADCC states have any real
capabilities to eliminate forces of dependence and
parameters of its dependence on South Africa, and
external sources. We will also examine whether effort
for self-reliant development is feasible or not and
problems of appropriate technology for Southern Africa.
The (1980) Lusaka declaration clearly reflected the
growing concern of black Southern Africa over their
continued dependence on white-ruled South Africa.[1] The
Lusaka declaration also realized the need for devising a
collective economic strategy to lessen the economic
dependence of the SADCC States on Pretoria. The
Organization has won formal endorsement from the U. N.
General Assembly in this regard. SADCC has become
effective in two ways: it has provided an umbrella

under which aid and investment can be sheltered for the member-states. SADCC is in effect offering a seal of respectability to the donor or financing countries who would otherwise be concerned about bilateral involvements or the existence or absence of formal links between individual states in Southern Africa and the European Economic Community.[2]

SADCC Objectives to Eliminate Forces of Dependence

The primacy given to regional economic cooperation and economic liberation supported by the whole of Africa reflects the shift toward pre-occupation with economic survival on a continental scale. As if to emphasize its importance the Lusaka economic summit was attended by both the former OAU Secretary-General, Edem Kodjo and the United Nations Economic Commission for Africa (ECA) Executive Secretary, Adebayo Adedeji. Furthermore, the Southern Africa Development Coordination Conference fits neatly with the OAU policy of encouraging regional economic groupings as the basis for an eventual all-African economic community and continental unity. President Kaunda of Zambia puts the SADCC in a proper historical continental perspective when he said:

> the journey to SADCC started many years ago. The founding fathers of the OAU expressed our aspiration when they adopted the Charter of the Organization... The SADCC is an expression of Africa's deliberate and planned effort in forging links which not only have political objectives but also economic and social meaning... African unity must be given economic substance out of which the social – cultural fabric will grow so strong that our continent will no longer be vulnerable.[3]

Reduction of dependence on South Africa is a necessary means to achieve development centered on the fulfillment of the basic human needs of the people of Southern Africa. South Africa's apartheid system denies its citizens their dignity, while the regime's military and economic power is increasingly being used to systematically destabilize its black neighbouring states. So long as SADCC member states lack an integrated transport, food security and communication system distinct from that of South Africa, it will be difficult for them to prevent such destabilization from crippling their national development efforts.

Another aspect of the SADCC programme is regionally coordinated industrialization and energy projects. Angola has been assigned the responsibility for regional energy conservation while Tanzania is responsible for harmonization of a regional industrialization programme.[4] Angola's oil reserves are sufficient to meet a substantial portion of the needs of the SADCC countries. For this reason, Angola will supervise the SADCC energy programme. The SADCC's aim is to reduce the region's economic dependence on South Africa and other external economic powers. Angola's oil fields are exploited mainly by an American Company - Gulf oil and the product exported to the West. The energy plan is to harness and harmonize collectively, the energy resources of the SADCC states. Under a joint energy programme, Mozambique will supply electricity from the Cabora Bassa Dam[5] to countries like Lesotho and Swaziland which will consequently be no longer dependent on electricity supply from the South African Electricity Supply Commission (ESCOM).

The programmes of SADCC also embraced regional agricultural development for self-sufficiency in food.

Food security which is highly rated by the OAU Lagos Plan of Action of April 1980 is clearly also at the top of SADCC priorities. The objective of the 1980 Lagos Plan of Action is to lay a durable foundation for internally generated, self-sustaining processes of development, and economic growth based on the twin principles of national and collective self-reliance; to bring about self-sufficiency in food and a diminishing dependence on exports and on expatriate technical assistance; and to create an African Economic Community with a common market by the year 2000.[6] Regional responsibility for food and agricultural development is devolved on Botswana, Zambia and Zimbabwe. Crash plans are being drawn up, that would make the SADCC countries much more self-sufficient as far as food production is concerned with Zimbabwe and Zambia having been assigned a special role in this regard.[7] Within the context of agricultural development, SADCC envisages the establishment of a regional agricultural research centre whose functions are yet to be spelt out.

The SADCC plan on regional agricultural development also includes the control of "foot and mouth" disease on cattle. Botswana has approached the "Commission of the European Communities to under-take a feasibility and design study for a system of coordinated control of foot and mouth disease in cattle on a region-wide basis".[8]

SADCC programmes include a "review of existing training facilities in the region". Swaziland is expected to make recommendations for the better usage of such facilities. The exploration by Zambia of the prospects for establishing a Southern African Development Fund is one of the last items on the programme of the SADCC countries as shown in Appendix 2 (page 297).

SATCC has 112 capital projects already identified for execution at the estimated cost of $2.3 billion. These capital projects are on the development of harbours, railways, roads, food and agriculture, aviation and telecommunications. Forty percent of the total development budget will go to Mozambique for the development of Nacala, Beira and Maputo harbours and the upgrading and improvement of the railway links between Mozambique and Zimbabwe. "This is vital for the success of the medium and long term strategy for rerouting the goods to and from the SADCC states at present, mostly going through South African harbours".[9]

All but three of the SADCC states - Angola, Mozambique and Tanzania are landlocked. These countries are natural exit and entry points for the region's trade but for various reasons their road, rail and port facilities have become quite inadequate to the task. Therefore, most of the SADCC goods have to pass through South Africa. Beira, Dar-es-Salaam, Lobito, Maputo and Nacala ports it is hoped, will then be modernized and be able to handle the export and import trade of the SADCC states. Pretoria will no longer then be able to generate artificial shortage of goods through the delay of the SADCC imports at its ports.

The fourth SADCC Summit held in Maputo in July 1984 approved a progress report that recorded finance pledges of more than $1,000 million for projects in the SADCC action programme (See Appendix 2, page 297). SADCC has been given priority to improving regional transport and communications. The schemes that were proposed and studies in this sector entail costs of $2,500 million. The progress report approved in July 1984 Summit shows that $647 million had already been allocated or committed. SADCC has proposed 119 projects in the transport and communications sector alone: 5 are completed, 39 are under implementation, 44 are submitted for finance, 7 are ready for submission and 24 are at the early preparatory state. An example of a project in the implementation phase is the railway between the Mozambique port of Nacala and Malawi, whose needs are served by the port. Rehabilitation of the entire line will cost a total of $190 million, but already work is beginning on a $95 million project for the section of nearly 200km. between Nacala and Nampula.[10] Typical is the sharing of the finance between several countries: France $45 million, Canada $12 million, Portugal $27 million and Mozambique $11 million. Similar, in the industrial sector, 90 projects with likely cost of more than $1,500 million have been presented. Potential supporters have been found for 74 of these projects including substantial investment in synthetic textiles, fertilizer plants and paper mills.[11]

The development of a network of roads among the SADCC states is a pre-requisite for effective movement of capital goods and peoples among the cooperating states. The effective movement of capital goods and peoples is an important variable in forgoing economic cooperation. Early in 1982, Mozambique and Zimbabwe agreed after months of negotiations on the terms for re-opening the 180 mile pipeline intended to carry all of landlocked Zimbabwe's gasoline and diesel fuel inland from the Mozambican port of Beira. The pipeline was last used before the white minority government in now Harare under Ian Smith unilaterally declared independence in November 1965. The agreement was signed in Maputo, Mozambique on March 7, 1982 by Mozambican finance minister Rui Baltazar and former Zimbabwean Minister for Energy, Simba Makoni.[12] The line can handle about one million tons of liquid fuel a year, more than enough to meet Zimbabwe's annual requirements of 600,000 tons. Its recommissioning marked an important step in Zimbabwe's drive to re-route its import-export trade away from South Africa, and also to relieve congestion of its railway system, which has been bringing in some of the imported fuel through Maputo. But it has suffered serious and repeated attacks by South Africa supported MNR terrorists and has to be guarded by the Zimbabwean army.

SADCC Dependence on South Africa

For the black-ruled states in Southern Africa, their vulnerabilities to the economic dominance of Pretoria and their chronic economic dependence on the racist economy raised crucial questions of their economic survival. It also raises the issue of their freedom in determining their foreign policy options vis-a-vis white-ruled South Africa. This is because, with the possible exception of Tanzania and Angola, the other SADCC states are economically dependent on Pretoria. South Africa is by far the most industrialized and diversified economy in Africa and overshadows its neighbours in respect of production and research and development, etc. Most of the SADCC countries have migrant labour relationships with Pretoria (this is shown in Table 4.1, page 122). In 1981, for example Lesotho had 140,746 migrant workers in South Africa while Mozambique, Zimbabwe and Malawi respectively had 55,811; 19,853 and 39,319 migrant workers in South Africa in 1981. The incomes of these migrant workers constitute a significant proportion of the foreign exchange earnings of the SADCC states. In 1975, remittances from migrant workers from Lesotho totalled

TABLE 4.1
BLACK FOREIGN WORKERS IN SOUTH AFRICA IN 1981

Countries	Angola	Botswana	Lesotho	Malawi	Mozambique	Zimbabwe	Swaziland	Zambia	Other
Agriculture	104	1,088	1,967	4,408	5,925	2,112	608	248	421
Mining and Quarrying	110	16,478	119,429	20,356	46,700	7,379	7,581	160	1,559
Manufacturing	4	1,358	4,012	1,533	835	424	743	68	161
Construction	15	722	5,129	443	339	350	124	31	279
Wholesale and Retail Trade	10	583	1,311	733	373	946	187	68	61
Government Services	11	1,102	3,886	762	694	310	201	50	350
Domestic Services	26	1,005	2,381	2,752	945	6,591	595	153	140
Other	11	864	2,631	1,332	613	1,741	338	140	131
TOTAL	291	22,336	140,746	32,319	55,811	19,853	10,377	918	3,102

Source: A Survey of Race Relations in South Africa (Johannesburg: Institute
of Race Relations of South Africa, 1982), p. 135.

$250 million, a figure more than doubled the gross domestic product of the country. Richard Weisfelder has said that "repatriation of goods and cash transfer by migrant workers plays a major role in offsetting Lesotho's enormous trade deficit, where imports are eight times greater than exports".[13] The importance of migrant workers as earners of substantial foreign exchange is also true in the case of Mozambique. In 1975 alone, the foreign exchange remittances of Mozambican migrant workers in South Africa totalled $175 million - about one-third of the total foreign currency earnings of Mozambique in that year.[14]

The regional dependence of the SADCC states on Pretoria is also reflected in the transport and communications sector where the regional dominance of South Africa is acutely felt. See Map 3 on Southern Africa Principal Railways. Thus, landlocked Botswana depends mainly on South Africa's rail lines for access to the sea. Similarly, 90 percent of the imported trade of Zimbabwe was carried by South African Railways (SAR) in 1980. However, there was a move in early 1982 by the Mugabe government in Zimbabwe to reduce this, and this has led to reduction in its rail transport dependence on South Africa by 65 percent in 1987 and if rehabilitation continues, the figure could rise to 100 percent by 1990.[15] Like Zimbabwe, Zambia also utilizes the South African Railways for the transportation of her copper to the ports of Durban, East London and Port Elizabeth along the coast of the Indian Ocean.[16]

The South African ports like the South African Railways System (see Map 3, page 126) "remain vital for the trade of all the SADCC countries apart from Angola and Tanzania...".[17] In fact, the export and import trade of most of the SADCC states are interwoven with that of Pretoria. Thus, 18 percent of Mozambique's imports, 29 percent of Malawi's, about 66 percent of Botswana's and over 90 percent of Swaziland's and Lesotho's imports originate in South Africa.[18] The imports of the SADCC countries from Pretoria include fuel, maize, canned food, beverages, fertilizer, iron and steel. These are survival products. Their exports to South Africa include sugar, rice, citrus fruits, cotton, cattle, hides and skins, copper, nickel and sulphur.

The economic conditions of SADCC countries are extremely poor and their purchasing power is low. The evidence for this is shown in the basic indicators for the SADCC states in Appendix 5 (page 302). Although the region covers an area of five and a half million square kilometers, rich in mineral resources like uranium, zinc, diamond, copper, nickel, gold, chrome, iron-ore to mention a few, and a total population of sixty-eight million peoples (as of 1980) excluding Tanzania, the region still exhibits a low level of industrialization.[19] This is because of the inability of the poor economies to explore and exploit the mineral resources which would have served as raw materials for industries. In some years the rain is either too long drawn and heavy causing flood or too scanty and short causing drought. For instance, Tanzania had this experience in 1979 and had to resort to getting external aid especially from the EEC and the Soviet bloc to finance its programme of services, chemicals, fertilizers and rural developments. Botswana, Mozambique and Zimbabwe have been going through the same drought agonies since 1981 because of scarcity of rain between the 1981/84 seasons.[20] This had led many of the SADCC states to depend on taking aid from the EEC,

Canada, the United States and the Communist States. We should not forget that a fundamental problem of the SADCC governments is neglect of the rural areas, rural producers, and the production of food crops, all leading to more dependence on external sources of aid for their survival.

SADCC states export primary products such as coffee, cotton, cashew nuts, tobacco, groundnuts, tea, maize, livestock, etc. The quality and quantity to be exported depend largely on weather dictate, and the revenues derived from the exports depend on conditions in the world market. SADCC countries also export mineral resources like diamond, gold, nickel, copper, uranium, etc. but they do not have any control of the prices in the World market. For example, increased diamond production in 1982 did not bring anticipated gains to Botswana because of drop in its price in the World market.[21]

By and large SADCC states depend on South Africa for transport and communications and about three-quarters of them are landlocked states making independence from South African transport and communications almost impossible to achieve, (See Map 3, page 126). Three of the SADCC members are actually or potentially beneficiaries of transit revenues.[22] The three members are Angola, Mozambique and Tanzania. Politically the remaining members have been made to depend on South African ports.

SADCC depends on foreign trade and aid to build and maintain the technical institutions designed to implement its objectives. The foreign financial aid come largely from EEC and Africa Development Bank. Intra-regional trade is minimal within SADCC states relative to trade with the countries in the Western

MAP 3
SOUTHERN AFRICA PRINCIPAL RAILWAYS

UGANDA

KENYA

CONGO

ZAIRE

RWANDA

BURUNDI

ANGOLA

TANZANIA

Dar es Salaam

Luanda

1975

Lobito

ANGOLA

Ndola

MALAWI

Nacala

ZAMBIA

Lilongwe

Namibe

Lusaka

Blantyre

MOZAMBIQUE

Harare

ZIMBABWE

Beira

NAMIBIA

Francistown

1974

Walvis Bay

Windhoek

BOTSWANA

Gaborone

1986

Maputo

Luderitz

Johannesburg

SWAZILAND

SOUTH
AFRICA

Richards Bay

Maseru

Durban

ATLANTIC
OCEAN

LESOTHO

INDIAN OCEAN

East London

Cape Town

Port Elizabeth

SADCC railways
South African railways
Pipeline

Railways and ports of southern Africa

World, and this was shown in the previous chapters. The
bulk of SADCC trade is with South Africa (the Republic
of South Africa's Rand is still legal tender in three of
SADCC countries: Botswana, Lesotho and Swaziland),
United Kingdom, West Germany, U. S., Japan, EEC,
Portugal, Sweden, etc. Tanzania trades with China and
North Korea, and Angola trades with Cuba, Soviet Union
and East Germany, besides the Western countries. The
SADCC countries continued to face stiff challenges from
Pretoria which is increasingly applying economic
policies of "carrot and stick" in Southern African sub-
region. Thus, Swaziland was pressurized by South Africa
to sign a secret non-aggression pact in 1983.
Similarly, the Angolan Government signed a non-
aggression agreement with South Africa in February 1984
and Mozambique followed suit with the Nkomati Accord
with Pretoria in March 1984.[23] The chronic dependence
of the SADCC states would continue to affect their
support for the liberation struggle in Southern Africa.
Already, Botswana, Lesotho, Mozambique, Swaziland and
Zimbabwe have refrained from providing bases to the
guerrilla movements of South Africa - the ANC and PAC.

One other major problem facing the SADCC is the
issue of the capability of Zimbabwe and Zambia to play
their assigned roles in food security and agricultural
development. The problem concerns the sensitive issue
of relations between black political power and residual
white economic dominance in agriculture in the majority
ruled states of Zambia and Zimbabwe. Two-thirds of the
maize production in Zambia is grown on large commercial
farms mainly white-owned. In addition white farmers own
half of the nations' cattle.

The bulk of Southern African States' trade goes on
mostly with the Western World and South Africa, trade

between member states is minimal. An example is shown
in the direction of trade for Malawi in 1979 in Table
4.2 (page 129). Even where member-states diversify the
direction of trade to include the Eastern countries, the
bulk of trade with the Western countries clearly
outweighs those of the Eastern countries. This is
clearly demonstrated on Table 4.3 (page 130) in the
direction of trade in Mozambique for 1979. Also about
19 percent of Mozambique's trade in 1979 was with South
Africa. All SADCC states trade with South Africa to
varying degrees. For instance, trade increased between
Zambia and South Africa from January to September 1979
when Zambia bought $98.8 million worth of goods from
South Africa placing her (South Africa) second to
Britain as supplier of goods to Zambia. Zambia's
exports to South Africa also increased from $40,000 in
1978 to $2.4 million in 1979.[24] About 90 percent of
Swaziland's and Lesotho's trade originated in South
Africa.

Zimbabwe's highly-diversified industrial base is
one of the most sophisticated in the continent of
Africa. But her potential is highly constrained by the
use of antiquated equipment and machinery, and by lack
of foreign exchange for inputs. The greater
responsiveness to availability of currency for inputs
was demonstrated in 1985 when the Zimbabwean government
increased allocations to the sector by 30 percent. By
the end of 1985, as a result of the increased
allocations and sustained export performance - the
manufacturing industry registered a growth in output of
13 percent. Nevertheless, there is greater realization
here that the potential growth of the Zimbabwean economy
cannot continually be pegged on the export of new
commodities.

TABLE 4.2
THE DIRECTION OF TRADE IN MALAWI 1979
(Million U.S. Dollars)

Countries	Exports	Imports
South Africa	7.38	157.00
United Kingdom	91.84	70.43
West Germany	12.57	24.49
Japan	0.50	31.26
United States	18.83	9.22
France	7.55	5.62
Netherlands	15.09	8.48
Zambia	5.84	4.78
Zimbabwe	1.40	7.00
Africa Total	23.07	173.24
World Total	197.12	377.64

Source: IMF Direction of Trade Yearbook (data extrapolated and/or derived from partner countries) in ACR 1980/81, p. B699.

TABLE 4.3
THE DIRECTION OF TRADE IN MOZAMBIQUE IN 1979
(Million U.S. Dollars)

Countries	Imports Value	%	Exports Value	%
Iraq	102	17.7	-	-
South Africa	83	14.4	12	4.9
East Germany	55	9.5	21	8.1
Switzerland	40	6.8	-	-
United Kingdom	31	5.4	16	6.3
West Germany	28	4.9	6	2.2
Portugal	27	4.7	38	14.6
France	241	4.1	8	3.1
United States	21	3.7	61	23.5
Romania	15	2.6	-	-
Netherlands	3	0.6	22	8.5
China	13	2.4	-	-
Soviet Union	5	0.9	3	1.1
EEC	112	19.0	59	22.9
COMECON	89	15.4	24	9.3

Source: "Mozambique" ACR 1980/91 (1981), p. B714.

According to recent studies, manufacturing has the greatest export potential and will remain a significant foreign exchange earner for the next decade and beyond. However, there is great uneasiness here, caused by the situation in South Africa, hitherto Zimbabwe's largest export market. The political unrest there, the subsequent downturn in the South African economy and the fall of the rand have adversely affected local business in South Africa.[25]

For instance in 1984, Zimbabwe exported goods worth Z$232.2 million to South Africa, or over 18 percent of merchandise exports. Imports from South Africa amounted to Z$231.8 million, or 19 percent of total imports. These exports were almost all of manufactures. The figures released in 1986 by the Central Statistical Office in Harare, Zimbabwe show that exports to South Africa during the first eight months of 1985 amounted to only Z$116.6 million, and the figure is not expected to be any bigger when total figures are compiled. This fall which has seen Britain overtake Pretoria as Zimbabwe's largest market has been attributed to the fall of the rand against major currencies, the general depression in South Africa, and possible diversification to other markets by local business.

However, the worrying trend is that while Britain may have overtaken South Africa as the largest market for Zimbabwe, the bulk of the exports to Britain were for raw materials e.g. sugar, tobacco and meat. Clothing exports to Britain from Zimbabwe increased, but the prospects of exports of manufactured goods to Britain or to any other European markets where more competitively-produced goods are available are not good. Zimbabwe's exports to other Southern African countries are also threatened by South Africa. Potential exists for increased exports of manufactures to the SADCC and the PTA Countries (See Table 4.4, page 133) showing Zimbabwe's trade balance with 14 States of the PTA/SADCC Countries), but lack of viable transport links, lack of competitiveness, payment difficulties, protection of domestic industries and the weak rand have hampered larger trade volume to the Southern Africa Sub-region. Meanwhile, South Africa continues to subsidize its manufacturers heavily in order to out-compete Zimbabwe.

Problems of Drought on Agricultural Productions and Food Supply in SADCC States

The Southern Africa sub-region has been haunted by a succession of drought seasons since 1981, which has seriously affected agricultural production and has been one of the most severe constraints to that sub-region's economic development. Drought is not uncommon in the Southern African sub-continent, but this particular drought has been the worst in the history of the sub-region, with about two-thirds of the region especially in Botswana, Lesotho, Swaziland, Mozambique, Malawi and Zimbabwe receiving less than 60 percent of normal rainfall.[26]

The existence of food shortages in Southern Africa, and the region's dependence on food imports had been recognized even before the 1981 to 1984 drought caused a further reduction in food production in the region. This drought has created a severe financial burden for the SADCC states and has jeopardized Southern Africa's financial capacity to revitalize its economies and increase food production. Those projects meant for boosting agricultural production and development that had been started in 1980 have not had a chance to produce results, because financial, physical and human resources have had to be diverted away from these

TABLE 4.4
ZIMBABWE'S TRADE BALANCE WITH 14 STATES OF THE PTA/SADCC REGION, JANUARY TO APRIL 1985

(In Zimbabwe dollars)

Country	Zimbabwe's Imports From	Zimbabwe's Exports To
Angola	368	5,319,175
Botswana	5,825,463	17,867,659
Burundi	0	618,885
Ethiopia	2,332	23,263
Kenya	328,527	178,945
Lesotho	0	87,814
Malawi	1,099,638	6,478,313
Mauritius	2,130	444,971
Mozambique	38,773	7,663,302
Somalia	0	0
Tanzania	184,294	1,373,616
Uganda	0	2,264
Zaire	251	5,807,465
Zambia	10,751,327	12,691,373
TOTAL	18,233,103	58,557,046

Source: Central Statistical Office (Harare, Zimbabwe).

projects towards drought relief and rehabilitation programmes. Also lack of adequate rainfall since 1981 has drastically reduced subsistence production and yields from marketable cash crops and in some areas has resulted in complete crop failures and livestock deaths. The drought has also led to a reduction in the areas under irrigation, devastated available pasture land for livestock, and seriously affected the availability of water for domestic uses.

First because of the importance of agriculture in the economies of most SADCC countries, where about 75 percent of the region's population of about 69 million is directly dependent on agricultural production for income and employment, the ramifications of the drought on the overall performance of the SADCC's economies cannot be fully assessed. The second problem is that some of the effects of the drought are of an indirect nature, and therefore difficult to quantify. These include the long-term effects of reductions in food production, farm incomes, and employment on the nutritional status of the population and on savings for future investment; deterioration of vegetation; and soil erosion. However, attempts have been made in each SADCC state to estimate some of the financial implications of the drought and to give a rough indication of the extent to which the drought has affected the region's economies in the short term. There are two forms of financial losses that are associated with any drought. The first are direct drought-induced financial losses, which result from decreases in crop yields and in the value of crop production per given area, and losses from livestock deaths. The second are related costs incurred through expenditures on drought relief programmes such as feeding programmes, food imports, cattle rescue

operations, distribution of free farm inputs, water
supply schemes and related administrative costs. This
form of expenditure has obviously necessitated the
diversion of funds from normal investment programmes.

The values of losses resulting from reduced crop
yields is calculated by subtracting actual recorded
production from what is assumed to be the average yield
for each crop in a given area in a year of normal
rainfall, then multiplying the difference by the average
price for that crop. However, this method, assumed that
the reduction in yields and in crop areas is attributed
to drought alone, and not to other agronomic factors −
such as pests and diseases or to economic factors such
as low prices. The value of losses attributed to
reduction in crop areas is estimated by multiplying the
total reduction in area planted by the average yield per
crop, and multiplying by the average price. It has been
observed that when farmers are expecting drought
conditions to prevail, they tend to plant less acreage
of food crops such as maize, millets and others, which
are prone to drought. Instead, farmers switch to more
drought-resistant non-food crops such as cotton and
tobacco. This practice usually results in reduced food
availability.

Livestock deaths represent direct losses in income
and wealth, and it is estimated that more than one
million head of cattle have died in the Southern African
sub-region during the 1981 to 1984 drought.[27] Cattle
represents a significant proportion of agricultural
activities since they provide food, draft power, and
manure and are an important source of cash income. The
extent of drought − induced losses and related costs,
calculated on the basis of direct agricultural losses
and drought relief costs incurred is shown in Table 4.5

(page 137) for six of the most affected SADCC countries for 1982-1983. To alleviate famine and other disasters that could have arisen from the drought, the SADCC member governments have had to incur heavy expenditures on emergency drought relief programmes. For the six countries shown in Table 4.5, (page 137) it is estimated that up to $345.5 million was spent in 1982-1983 on food aid, emergency seed supply, cattle rescue operations, water supply schemes and transport and related drought administration costs.[28]

The economic ravages of drought were the main focus of discussion when the SADCC member countries met in Lusaka between 2 and 3 February 1984 for their second annual summit with donors.[29] All SADCC countries except Malawi are now on the United Nations Food and Agriculture Organization's (FAO's) list of 24 African countries facing drought - induced food crisis. "SADCC, on behalf of member governments has already appealed for about $300 million international assistance - the vast majority for short-term relief programmes and for emergency food and seed imports".[30] It has been recognized that the elimination of periodic food crises such as those of 1981 to 1984 experienced the implementation of longer-term projects require that domestic efforts be supplemented by international assistance. Since 1980, SADCC has received $4.4 million for regional food security projects, and in addition $12.6 million has been secured for food security and drought-related projects, excluding food aid.

The SADCC member states declaration "Southern Africa towards economic liberation"[31] on April 1, 1980 defined agriculture as one of the principle areas for regional cooperation and as an important vehicle for reducing economic dependence and fostering economic

TABLE 4.5
FINANCIAL COST AND LOSSES OF THE 1982-83 DROUGHT
(In Million of U.S. Dollars)

Country	Direct Agricultural Losses	Cost Incurred	Total
Botswana	6.8	51.9	58.7
Lesotho	45.0	78.7	123.7
Malawi	–	13.4	13.4
Mozambique	75.1	79.0	154.1
Swaziland	26.4	2.0	26.4
Zimbabwe	360.0	119.6	479.6
TOTAL	513.3	344.6	855.9

Source: SADCC Drought Report (Gaborone, Botswana: January, 1984).

development. Priority was attached to agriculture chiefly because the majority of the people in the region depend on agriculture and livestock for subsistence, and also in view of the fact that food production in most of the SADCC States is currently insufficient. In this regard, Zimbabwe is charged by SADCC with the responsibility of coordinating and working out a regional food security plan as indicated in Appendix 2 (page 297).

The main objective of the SADCC food security plan is to work toward satisfying the basic food needs of the peoples in the member states of the Organization, achieving national self-sufficiency in the supply of essential foods and reducing heavy drains on their scarce foreign exchange imposed by food imports.[32] Apparently the extent to which food production can be increased depends on the measures each member state undertakes according to its own capacity and priorities, although there is a wide range of activities that can be jointly implemented to strengthen the efforts being carried out at the national level. Within this framework, various projects and programmes have been initiated, aimed at reinforcing the national, and regional food research capability; increasing production capacity; improving systems of delivery, conservation, processing and storage of food; and establishing more efficient systems for the prevention of food crises such as those caused by the 1981 to 1984 drought.[33] A series of regional studies aimed at providing the data and analysis necessary to construct a programme tailored to the specific needs of the region has been carried out since 1980 not only with the EEC but also with the assistance of various governments and agencies as indicated in Appendix 3 (page 298).

It has been estimated that during the 1984-85 period, because of the impending food shortages, SADCC will require aid or funds to import grain, particularly maize and wheat valued at more than $1 billion. During the same period the SADCC population of about 69 million will be increased by another two million.[34] Finally, it is important to note that given sufficient incentives, the SADCC states, its farmers and the land can produce positive and tangible results. The SADCC states can produce enough to feed its peoples despite recurrent droughts.[35] Basic incentives that could be given to farmers in the region to boost agricultural production include the provision of adequate input supplies, efficient marketing facilities, appropriate research extension policies and realistic producer prices for their produce.

SADCC Dependence on Transnational Corporations and External Aid

SADCC member-states are economically weak and therefore, they have to rely on foreign aid to implement their projects. The Western countries dominate the granting of foreign aid, particularly financial aid to SADCC states. Romania, Yugoslavia and East Germany represented the eastern bloc and offered, "unquantified" financial support. SADCC organized a two-day conference between 2 and 3 of February 1984, in which discussions were mainly on vital issue. For instance, as unprecedented three-year drought which adversely affected agriculture in Southern Africa (See Table 4.5, page 137) as a result of the wide spread famine and death from starvation,[36] was the focus of the Conference. East Germany, Romania and Yugoslavia attended from the Eastern bloc (Soviet bloc), while many

countries attended from the west. In fact, EEC
identified for self-sufficiency in food, exploitation of
mineral wealth and training of manpower as crucial for
development of the Southern Africa sub-region.
Therefore, in 1984 EEC allocated $140 million to SADCC
for rural development out of $243 million SADCC is
seeking for an international aid to offset the effects
of drought. It has been estimated that $121 million
would be spent externally for the acquisition of
essential inputs, while the total direct cost as a
result of the drought is expected to be $744 million.[37]

SADCC states are very weak, occupying the periphery
of global economy with the possible exception of Angola
and Zimbabwe, hardly can any other Southern African
country do without foreign aid to survive or to
implement basic national objectives. For instance,
Zambia relied on external aid all the year round in
1980,[38] Tanzania also depended on foreign aid especially
in 1980.[39] SADCC member-states also enjoy foreign aid
at the national level, for example, EEC pledged $3
million and $2.5 million to Zambia and Tanzania
respectively during the Lusaka meeting of February 1984.
In view of the severe drought of 1984, to improve food
production Mozambique is already receiving food aid from
the EEC. Sweden is to invest $52 million in different
projects in the SADCC states, and $6.5 million of that
money will be spent on a microwave link between
Botswana, Zambia and Zimbabwe. Sweden spends $242
million annually to finance bilateral projects and
support liberation movements in Southern Africa.[40] It
is necessary here to point out that, the almost
excessive dependence on foreign aid at both the national
and regional levels inhibits autonomy as external

control over projects and trade, will result in a weaker SADCC.

Although SADCC states are politically independent, their economies are mostly dominated by Transnational Corporations (TNC's). One of the reasons for this is that a large percentage of the nationals, of SADCC states lack the necessary skills. For example, about 45 percent of all professional jobs in Botswana are still done by non-Botswanan - that is the co-called expatriates reflecting the drastic shortage of skilled labour.[41] Nevertheless, as the World's fourth largest producer of diamonds, industry accounts for 23 percent of the country's GDP. Botswana's diamond production is in the hands of De Beers Botswana mining Company (Debswana), with equal shares held by the Botswana Government and De Beers Consolidated Mines Limited of South Africa. From the exports of its diamonds Botswana realized $567.8 million in 1981 and $748 million in 1982. Botswana's copper-nickel production is under the control of the Amax Corporation of Louisiana, in the U.S.A.[42]

The colonial legacies of SADCC states have to a very large extent fostered their dependence on South Africa. A very good example of their colonial legacies is the Cabora Bassa Dam, Hydro-electric project on River Zambezi in Tete Province of Mozambique. This is the sixth largest hydro-electric project in the world, but the Portuguese designed it to supply South African needs, while nothing exists to link Maputo directly to Cabora Bassa Dam, therefore the capital of Mozambique is mainly dependent on importing electricity from South Africa. There is possibility for South Africa to impose sanctions by switching Maputo off, anyway, this has been done many times between 1983 and 1984 when the MNR with

the South African collaboration cut-off power supply to
Mozambique.[43]

Angola which is the only oil producing country in
Southern Africa sub-region could supply SADCC needs at
least until 1995, but she does not have a refinery of
its own, while non-oil producing SADCC states like
Mozambique, Tanzania, and Zambia have. The major
problem with these refineries is that, they were
designed to refine Middle-East crude which differs
chemically, from Angolan oil. The Middle East crude is
heavier chemically, while the Angolan crude is lighter
chemically. Once the lighter fuels have been drawn off,
a heavy sludge which is basically heating oil is left,
and the only nearby consumer of the residue is South
Africa. Angolan oil does not produce as much residue,
but major structural changes would have to be made in
the other Southern Africa refineries if they were to
refine Angolan crude,[44] or new ones must be built.

The Southern Africa sub-continent does in fact
possess large quantities of the three modern sources of
power-oil, hydro-electricity and coal. But there are
problems with all of them as pointed out earlier in the
case of oil. There is geological evidence that Angola
may be joined in the future by Mozambique and Tanzania
in oil production. The Ruvuma basin on the border
between Mozambique and Tanzania is geologically
promising, but there is still no definite sign that oil
actually exists there.[45] Angolan oil production is
rising and is certain that it will continue to rise
substantially over the coming decade. Angolan oil
production in 1984 increased by more than 30 percent
from 154,000 barrels per day to over 200,000 barrels per
day, according to figures from the State Oil Company
SONANGOL.[46] Thus, it would seem logical that Angola

should supply the other SADCC states with their needed
oil. When it comes to hydro-electric power, SADCC is a
net exporter. For instance, in 1981, SADCC hydro-
electric production was 17 percent in excess of
consumption. It has been observed that "even with no
further investment in the energy sector, there would
still be on current trends, an 8 percent surplus by
1990".[47] The SADCC energy projects are to be carried
out by Angola with Belgian government assistance. These
projects will involve a detailed analysis of the energy
situation in the region and a review of the energy
development programmes of the member states. A
computerized data base in the SADCC energy technical and
administrative unit, has been established in the Angolan
Energy Ministry. The Norwegian Agency for International
Development (NORAD) has already agreed to help finance
the $236,000 project, with technical help from Sweden
(The Beijer Institute) and the Energy Systems research
group of the United States.[48] For the SADCC member
states, the total national energy demands are shown in
Table 4.6 (page 144) and the percentage breakdowns are
shown in Table 4.7 (page 145). These figures compound
the variations in population with those in per capita
consumption shown in Table 4.8 (page 146) and in
Appendix 5 (page 302). The significance of Zimbabwe and
Zambia in regional commercial fuel consumption is due to
their relatively high per capita income levels (see
Table 4.8 (page 146) and Appendix 5, page 302), while
Botswana and Swaziland despite their high per capita
levels contribute only 3 percent each due to their
relatively low populations.[49]

Angola, Mozambique, Zambia and Tanzania are
comfortably placed for hydro-electric power production
for the foreseeable future. But as for Botswana and

144

TABLE 4.6
1980 FINAL ENERGY CONSUMPTION
AND AVERAGE ANNUAL GROWTH RATE 1980-2000 (%/YEAR)

Country	Grand Total	Commerical Fuels (2) Total	Electric	Coal	Petroleum	Traditional Fuels
Angola						
PJ*	105.5	23.8	2.3	0.0	11.6	81.6
% Year	2.6	23.8	6.3	0.0	4.1	2.0
Botswana						
PJ(1)	22.1	9.7	1.7	3.7	4.4	12.4
% Year	3.3	4.0	4.3	3.6	4.1	2.8
Lesotho						
PJ	24.2	5.2	0.3	1.9	2.9	19.0
% Year	2.4	4.2	6.4	5.1	3.2	1.8
Malawi						
PJ	165.2	9.4	1.3	1.4	6.7	155.8
% Year	1.8	3.8	5.9	3.2	3.4	1.7
Mozambique						
PJ	281.7	30.6	2.5	5.8	22.3	251.1
% Year	2.6	3.9	7.2	3.0	3.7	2.4
Swaziland						
PJ	24.0	9.6	1.6	3.3	4.7	14.4
% Year	3.5	3.9	4.4	4.7	2.9	3.3
Tanzania						
PJ	438.9	37.5	2.3	0.2	35.0	401.4
% Year	3.4	4.1	7.7	3.0	3.8	3.3
Zambia						
PJ	150.8	62.8	20.4	11.2	31.3	87.9
% Year	2.8	3.9	4.1	3.5	3.9	1.9
Zimbabwe						
PJ	244.1	117.2	24.9	65.8	26.4	126.9
% Year	3.4	3.9	4.4	4.1	3.2	2.8
SADCC						
PJ	1456.3	305.9	57.3	93.3	155.2	1150.5
% Year	3.0	4.0	4.7	4.0	3.7	2.6

(1) 1 PJ (peta-joule) = .034 million tonnes coal
    equivalent = .022 Million tonnes oil equivalent
(2) Final consumption only (e.g. coal figures do not
    include coal used for electricity generation).

Source: J.T.C. Simoes (ed.) SADCC: Energy and Development to the Year 2000 SADCC Energy sector in Collaboration with The Beijer Institute and the Scandinavian Instute of African Studies (Uddevalla: Bohuslamingens AB, 1984), P. 16.

TABLE 4.7
COUNTRY DEMANDS AS PERCENT OF SADCC TOTAL

Country	Commercial Total	Traditional Fuels	Fuels
Angola	7.2%	7.8	7.1
Botswana	1.5	3.2	1.1
Lesotho	1.7	1.7	1.7
Malawi	11.3	3.1	13.5
Mozambique	19.3	10.0	21.8
Swaziland	1.6	3.1	1.2
Tanzania	30.1	12.3	34.9
Zambia	10.4	20.5	7.6
Zimbabwe	16.8	38.3	11.0
SADCC	100.0%	100.0%	100.0%

Source: J. T. C. Simoes (ed.), SADCC: Energy and
Development to the Year 2000 SADCC Energy
sector in collaboration with the Beijer
Institute and the Scandinavian Institute of
African Studies (Udevalla: Bohuslauingens AB,
1984), p. 21.

TABLE 4.8
SELECTED PER CAPITA ENERGY USE STATISTICS

Country	1980 Population (millions)	1980 GNP Per Capita (US $)	Annual Per Capital Energy Consumption					
			Total[1] (GH)	Commercial Fuels (%)	Traditional Fuels (%)	Electricity (KWH)	Coal (Tonnes)	Petroleum (Tonnes)
Angola	7.08	400[2]	14.9	22.6	77.4	89	--	.07
Botswana	0.81	910	27.3	43.9	56.1	577	.15	.12
Lesotho	1.34	420	18.0	21.4	78.6	89	.05	.05
Malawi	6.16	230	26.8	5.7	94.3	59	.01	.02
Mozambique	10.47	250[3]	26.9	10.9	89.1	87	.02	.05
Swaziland	0.56	680	42.8	40.0	60.0	815	.20	.18
Tanzania	17.93	280	24.5	8.5	91.5	36	--	.04
Zambia	5.77	560	26.1	41.7	58.3	988	.07	.12
Zimbabwe	7.40	630	33.0	48.0	52.0	943	.30	.08
SADCC	57.52	380	25.3	21.0	29.0	279	.06	.06

Note: [1]GJ (giga-joule) = 10^9 J = .034 tonnes coal equivalent = .022 tonnes oil equivalent.

[2]Total wood requirements (include wood for charcoal production, construction, industrial purposes and losses).

[3]1979 figures, also see Appendix 5.

Source: J.T.C. Simoes (ed.), SADCC: Energy and Development to the Year 2000, SADCC Energy sector in collaboration with the Beijer Institute and the Scandinavian Institute of African Studies (Uddevalla: Bohuslamingens AB, 1984), p. 17.

Swaziland they are certainly very unfortunate in hydro-
electric power production. Thus, they face energy
supply shortage and the Highland water scheme to supply
South Africa and Lesotho. As for coal, there is
certainly plenty of it in the SADCC states. Southern
Africa is one of the richest regions in the world for
the production of coal. Our observation is that
Southern Africa coal will in the long term, when the
supply of Middle East oil begins to tail off, the SADCC
states will find that their coal reserves could become
worth their price in gold. With all these situations,
the numerous handicaps would continue, at least for
sometime to affect SADCC support for the liberation
struggle, and also hinder its economic autonomy in
Southern Africa.

Foreign Aid: Help or Hindrance?

SADCC reliance on foreign aid and investments for
the realization of its objectives is an issue that needs
a critical and careful examination by the organization.
Although, the effect of aid on the economy of developing
countries has been an area which many scholars have
written about in recent times,[50] it is an issue which
features prominently in the development problems of the
Third world countries. It is difficult to believe that
a donor country can give aid primarily to help another
country's economic development. Aid experience has
shown itself self-interested. Donors act essentially
out of economic or political self-interest, in which
case they care little whether or not the aid is
effective.[51]

Most of the Western scholars have argued that aid,
especially from the West and investments in the Third
world countries are for their economic development.

Critically examined however, we find that this is not
always the case. The economic and political returns
received by the advanced countries and their
transnational corporations from the export of capital
and private investments in the Third world are much
larger than their own expenses. The programme of aid to
the developing countries brings the metropolis huge
profit. According to D. K. Leo who has been following
the trend of U.S. investments in developing countries:

> ...the U.S. earns huge incomes from its
> private investments in developing countries.
> For example, in 1980, it is estimated that
> these investments provided almost 37 percent
> of returns on all direct investment.
> Furthermore, it is reckoned that two-thirds of
> U.S. net earning, from services which are
> becoming increasingly important to the
> American economy in relations to manufacturing
> come from developing countries.[52]

The substantial capital that goes to the Third world
from the industrialized capitalist countries is a
perfectly normal phenomenon for imperialism.[53] The view
that credits, loans, participation in international
currency and financial or organization, subsidies,
technical aid,[54] and so on are forms of aid, is also
deceitful. These are ventures motivated by the desire
for profit. These activities have nothing to do with
the economic development of the Third world countries.

For some years development aid has been
increasingly criticized, because living standards have
not improved in many of the developing countries
particularly in Africa, despite more than a quarter of a
century of assistance.[55] As things are now, a majority
of the capital and resources both human and material

will come in form of aid to the SADCC. Going from the above argument that there is no disinterested aid, one can point out the implications of foreign aid in SADCC programmes. It is doubtful if aid and investments which SADCC is seeking from its cooperators would enable it to fulfill its objectives.[56] There is no gain saying that, it will simply detract it from the road to self-reliance. The donors are not philanthropists who would simply continue to tax their own economies in order to carry out a humanitarian mission in Southern Africa.[57]

With very few exceptions, external aid to Africa over the years would seem to have taken the form of commercial transactions, the main difference being that the tag on them reads "aid" and is more expensive. It would be naive indeed to hope for the speedy growth of Southern African countries in particular and African countries in general while they (African countries) have to pay "one out of every eight dollars" of the export earnings on the payment of interest and loan installments. George Woods, former President of the World Bank, was forced to admit that, "to the extent that foreign aid is tied, (it represents help it is clear that they see development) finance as nothing than a disguised subsidy for their exporters".[58] In this way, it is the Southern African countries, indeed the African and the developing countries as a whole, who are assisting the industrial countries more than the latter helping the former. This is the impact of the statement by Reg Prentice, former British Minister of Overseas Development between 1967 and 1969 that:

> ...our aid programme can be seen as an
> investment in our own overseas markets. This
> applies to all donor countries... We provide
> at the moment about 7 1/2 percent of the

> global flow of aid, but we get about 12
> percent of the orders for goods imported by
> the developing countries from the developed
> countries. Our aid programme, being as part
> of an international aid flow, is almost
> certainly a help to our balance of payments...
> Taking into account the indirect effects
> (trade follows aid), and the orders we get
> from other countries' aid programmes, the
> total result is in our favour... So are many
> of the other donors, to a greater or lesser
> extent.[59]

Thus, aid flows to African countries have been
substantial, their effectiveness is open to question.

Peter McPherson, Administrator of the U.S.
controlled Agency for International Development (AID)
could not have been more down to earth (correct) when he
said "U.S. is not an international charity or resource
transfer organization".[60] This reinforces the argument
that there is no disinterested aid. No aid without
strings attached.

More significantly, aid has been set aside by the
developed World to spread ideology. This is an area
where the SADCC will have problems, as I have pointed
out in Chapter Three on the problems of ideology. Since
the majority of foreign aid and investments will come
from Western sources, it goes without saying that the
"gift" will come with an instruction that it be
disbursed under a situation that would be conducive to
free enterprise and individual initiative, key factors
in the capitalist system. There is even a group in the
West which is against government intervention in
economic affairs both at the domestic and international
levels. Their aim is that "...poorer countries be left

to market competition and private enterprise (i.e. the transnationals) or in emergencies (such as Ethiopia or Mozambique) to private charity".[61] For example, the Reagan administration on his part has made it known that in his aid programmes for Africa, funds will be concentrated increasingly on pro-Western countries.[62] One cannot but agree with a development finance expert at United Nations Industrial Development Organization (UNIDO) IV Conference who said that "the U.S. is tying economic assistance to political goal".[63]

The donor's position will certainly over-ride the contention of the SADCC that they reserve the right to decide the extent to which both private and public sector participation will go in their programmes. It will be difficult for the SADCC to dictate to the West or get them to accept its position concerning the development of Southern Africa. As things are now the SADCC has not taken into consideration Thomas Sankara former President of Burkina Faso's assertion that "aid is likely to leave a country worse off than before".[64] For an uncontrolled aid "money distorts the economy and even the philosophy of the people".[65] Burkina Faso's aid experience shows that agricultural aid confused the peasant farmers and made them abandon necessary projects needed for agricultural self-sufficiency for projects that bring quick money.[66]

For when actual aid is examined in practice, it is fairly clear that aid programmes have not been administered in the best interest of the recipient countries, and in a way as to provide dynamizing development input. A large proportion of publicly sponsored foreign assistance is channeled into activities which either are not directly productive or have long gestation periods. By tying a major share of

152

foreign assistance provided capital help in overcoming resource scarcities for establishing modern venture, but usually leave to the African country itself the increasing problem of obtaining enough of foreign exchange to run them at full capacity. Moreover, the aid process is so heavily laden with motives of self-interest on the part of the donor countries that it is not clear "who is helping whom". The situation is not in the least improved by the so-called technical assistance schemes - the scheme which the EEC countries are so much involved in the SADCC case. Doubts have been raised about the quality and appropriateness of the so-called experts provided to (Southern) Africa, and other developing schemes. It is generally agreed, that technical assistance "has been...probably the least efficient segment of all foreign aid"[67] and that Africa seems to have done "less well with it than anybody else". All too often the "experts" provided are men of second-rate ability, especially those on longer assignments. With the capitalists powers' involvement in Southern Africa, a similar situation may likely happen in the case of the EEC experts to SADCC states.

Also, foreign aid extended in the form of direct investment manifested in the operation of Transnational Corporations have also been one of the most powerful impediments to development in Africa, about which much has been written in recent years,[68] and therefore, does not need repetition here. Most of such studies have focused on TNC's impacts upon African countries' balance of payments, export-import structures, employment, income distribution, political sovereignty as well as other economic and political aspects.

Generally, international assistance has been hindering institutional reforms. For a lending country may not accept the wisdom of such changes. Hence foreign aid tends to strengthen the status quo; it enables African leaders to evade and avoid fundamental reforms; it does little more than patch plaster on the deteriorating social edifice. For example, all external assistance poured into Zambia in recent years, both from the west and the east have not helped to ameliorate the economic situation of Zambia.[69] Copper, the country's main export commodity is not doing well in the international markets price-wise. In 1985, the IMF insisted that Zambia needs to generate extra foreign exchange by auctioning Kwazha (the Zambian currency) to local business organizations, as part of a package to help solve Zambia's debt problems.[70] Instead of getting any improvement the Zambian economic situation is deteriorating fast everyday. Even the all important food aid, as the report of the presidential commission on world hunger concluded, has in some cases undermined "the efforts of recipient nations to develop a more self-reliant base of their own" and enabled some recipient governments to postpone essential agricultural reforms, and to maintain a pricing system which gives farmers inadequate incentives to increase local production required for greater self-reliance in basic foodstuffs.[71]

Above all, the growing debt burden of the African countries, the consequent acute balance of payments difficulties, and the severe constraint this imposes on growth, is a major problem of contemporary aid programmes which stems directly from the concentration on loans rather than grants. Between 1970 and 1979 external indebtedness of sub-saharan Africa rose from $6 billion to $32 billion, and debt service (for the oil-importing countries) increased from 6 to 12 percent of export earnings in the same period.[72] By 1982, debt service ratios for Africa had risen from 6.5 percent in 1970 to 28.3 percent.[73] And as repayments grow, they become more of a burden to the indebted African country. In many African countries like Zambia, where the debts have increased beyond the ability of the country to liquidate them, this had led to more in the game of default, namely "rephasing", is aid or international capitalism, then leading to recolonization or a new form of neo-colonialism or dependency?

We believe that Southern African countries in particular, and African countries in general would be less than honest if we were to put the entire responsibility for African countries' failure to achieve a break-through in development at the door steps of donor countries. Indeed the primary responsibility for development rests on the Southern African countries themselves. Aid can be best used only as a supplement to the full mobilization of domestic resources. Thus international assistance should be guided by the priorities laid down by the recipient country.

Dependent or Self-Reliant Development

Although self-reliant development as a strategy designed to redefine the role of foreign aid, and (foreign) western capitalism and all other external linkages in Africa's development process has been formally adopted at the African continental level, its implementation has not yet advanced beyond the stage of theoretical discussions. Specifically, the 1980 Lagos Plan of Action concepts are not yet reflected in country as well as regional development plans, like SADCC as made evident in the 1982 ECA report.[74] Given the entrenchment of neo-colonialism in Africa, and the

extent of diversification of markets and sources of
investment and technology among different metropolitan
countries, the prospects for significant restructuring
of Southern Africa's economy from the short-term frame
point of view are very much limited.

In a long-term perspective, however, self-reliant
strategy of development of the Lagos Plan is a splendid
option, indeed one which would lead Africa as a whole to
overcome its excessive dependence on external
(resources) aid, raise the living conditions of its
people, and assert its position as a major economic unit
within the global economy. But, to emphasize, as an
immediate strategy option self-reliant strategy of
development involving "delinkage" or restructuring of
Southern Africa's economy does not seem to be a feasible
proposition. For it is not likely that there would be
any major changes in SADCC's present strategy during
most of the 1980s.

Transnational Corporations which usually feature
prominently in the aid activities of the West agree that
foreign aid and investments should go to the private
sector in the developing countries. They also agree
that aid should be link to trade and investment policies
in Third world countries which encourage private
enterprise. In fact the U.S. Corporations for instance
prefer aid to be transferred to Third world countries
not through the government but through private
intermediate credit institutions.[75] There is no other
reason for this condition other than the excessive
profit motives of the transnational corporations. All
these boil down to the fact that the economic
emancipation programmes of the SADCC is being built on a
shaky foundation. If the organization continues with
its present insatiable demand for Western investment,

then it had better forget the idea of freeing itself
from the economic bondage of both South Africa and the
metropolis.

Reliance on Western investment will do nothing
other than finding export markets for Western products.
It will also entrench the relationship of dependence
between them (SADCC) and the West. Metropolitan
countries always think of their own economic advantage
first in any venture carried out abroad. Even the
provision of food aid, seen as a humanitarian activity
has to be closely examined. One can conclude that it is
for the entrenchment of Western countries' grip on the
economy of developing countries. United States food aid
programmes in Southern African countries serve no other
purpose other than the expansion of U.S. export markets
and the strengthening of Washington's foreign policy.[76]

Problems of Appropriate Technology for SADCC

A very important phenomenon which the SADCC has
failed to address is the technological requirements for
the Projects being executed by the organization. The
SADCC for now does not have any policy on the technology
that has to be developed. This inadequacy provides an
excellent opportunity for the industrialized countries
to turn the SADCC states into dumping grounds for
unnecessary technology which will not be useful for the
economic development of Southern Africa. The
implication of this is that:

> ...this state of affairs could easily lead to
> a state of technological confusion on the part
> of the SADCC themselves, and enormous wastage
> of resources by the failure of the SADCC to
> get to the understanding and control of any of
> the technologies introduced in the region. At

the end of it all are the donor and investor countries which would have benefited most from the endeavor.[77]

Experience has shown that inappropriate technology deepens dependence on the industrialized countries by developing countries. The SADCC will not be an exception. Economic development in its genuine form does not give room for white elephant or grandiose technology. As far as Southern African countries are concerned, what is needed is technologies that will serve the purpose for which it is needed. Not necessarily must it be sophisticated. For instance, Tanzania is using bamboo in place of pipes to provide potable water for the people. Experts have been able to find out that this system works and is not wasteful.

Another problem the SADCC will face as regards the acquisition of technology for the execution of its various projects is: "...the reluctance of Western companies to allow access to technology, their predilection for surrounding all aspects of technique and technology with rigid and wide ranging patents and their opposition to the training of local personnel".[78] This is all the more reason why the SADCC should go into partnership with countries like India and China who have been able to adopt technology to suit local purpose. It is important for the SADCC to do this because these countries have had the same problems with technology which the SADCC now faces.

India is especially a country that can be of immense help to SADCC's technological needs. The industrial sector in India has been developed through indigenous research and development supported by the selective import of technology.[79] In view of the fact that India was once at a low level of technological development as the SADCC countries are now, they have no alternative than to embrace the Indian interest in SADCC projects. Indian technology is "designed at an appropriate technological level for other developing countries. In other words, the customers are not paying for unnecessary sophistication, and maintenance is within the capabilities of local workshops".[80]

The advantages of technologies that have been adapted to meet local needs is the efficiency and problem free maintenance. This does not give room for unnecessary delays which usually occur when an imported technology breaks down and there is nobody with the expertise to put it back to a functioning state. An expert will have to be flown in. This does not only lead to a drain on scarce foreign exchange, it also leads to the loss of huge amounts at home which could have accrued to government if there had not been any fault in the technology that has been imported.

SADCC must therefore take seriously, its Lusaka declaration which aims at bringing about reduction in economic dependence not only on the apartheid South Africa, but also on any single external state or group of states.[81] The West's aid activities in developing countries have not succeeded in helping any country to "take off" if one is to borrow from W. W. Rostow's theory of the stages of economic growth.[82] Rather, aid and investment have created a cycle of dependence on Western economies and technologies which the developing countries especially African countries now find difficult to break.

SADCC's struggle for economic liberation must be bitterly contested as has been the struggle for political liberation.[83] Even though some SADCC member-states have tried to curtail the dominance of TNCs, for example, Zimbabwe has decided to take control over most of her mineral exploitation and exploration partly through nationally-owned sales agencies known as Minerally Marketing Corporation of Zimbabwe, encouraged programmes to train her own nationals to do skilled jobs rather than rely on expatriates. Zambia sells her copper and cobalt through Metal Marketing Corporation (MEMACO).[84] It is important to note that SADCC's implementation of its programmes are heavily dependent on external aid. Apart from SADCC states having to face stiff challenges from South Africa which is increasingly using her economic and military power to frustrate SADCC programmes. South Africa is also heavily involved in assisting the dissident groups within the SADCC states to destabilize their governments and frustrate SADCC objectives. The most prominent among them are UNITA in Angola and MNR in Mozambique. Despite the Lusaka and Nkomati non-aggression agreements signed on 16 February 1984 between South Africa and Angola, and on 16 March 1984, between South Africa and Mozambique, both UNITA and MNR[85] are still active in their destabilization activities in Southern Africa. The destabilization activities of these two groups - UNITA and MNR will be dealt with in detail in the next chapter.

160

NOTES

[1]SADEX, Vol. 2, No. 3 (May/June, 1980), p. 3.

[2]Michael Wolfers, "SADCC Means Business". West Africa (29 August, 1983), p. 2005.

[3]An address by President Kaunda of Zambia, op. cit., p. 4.

[4]For details on the energy programme of the SADCC States, see SADEX Vol. 2, No. 5, (1980), pp. 4-5.

[5]The Cabora Bassa Dam is the fourth largest hydro-electric scheme in the World, see Southern Africa: The Continuing Crisis, op. cit., p. 82.

[6]For full details see Organization of African Unity, Lagos Plan of Action for the Economic Development of Africa, 1980-2000 (Geneva: International Institute for Labour Studies, 1981).

[7]For details see, Olayiwola Abegunrin, "The Southern Nine", Current Bibliography on African Affairs, Vol. 14, No. 4, (1981-1982).

[8]SADEX, op. cit., p. 2.

[9]Africa, No. 113, op. cit., p. 25.

[10]Michael Wolfers, "SADCC Means Business". West Africa (29 August, 1983), p. 2005.

[11]Ibid.

[12]"Zimbabwe, Mozambique agreed in Pipeline" Daily Sketch (Ibadan), March 9, 1982, p. 12. After the death of Arthur Blumeris, in 1984, Simba Makoni was appointed the new Executive Secretary of SADCC.

[13]Richard Welsfelder, "Lesotho: Changing Patterns of Dependence", in G. M. Carter and P. O'Meara (eds.) Southern Africa: The Continuing Crisis, (Bloomington: Indiana University Press, 1979).

[14]Tony Hodges, "Mozambique: The Politics of Liberation", Southern Africa: The Continuing Crisis, op. cit., p. 181.

[15]For the percentage of the Import Trade of Zimbabwe that goes Through South African Railway, see _African Business_ No. 4, (January 1982), p. 13. See also "Fresh Tracks in The Limpopo Corridor", _SOUTH_ (July 1988), p. 47.

[16]"Mozambique: Threat to SADCC Strategy" _Africa Now_, No. 9 (London), December 1981, pp. 19-21.

[17]"Realistic Route to Self-Reliance", _The Times_ (London), August 9, 1982, p. 5.

[18]Kenneth W. Grundy, "Economic Patterns in the New Southern African Balance", _Southern Africa: The Continuing Crisis_, op. cit., p. 295.

[19]See O. Abegunrin, op. cit., p. 332.

[20]"Southern Africa's Drought: Natures' Curse, Man's Folly", _The Economist_ (London), February 11, 1984, pp. 70-71.

[21]Stan Winer, "Botswana Prepares on SADCC Role", _Africa Now_ 11 (March 1982), p. 112.

[22]R. H. Green, "SADCC: From Dependence and Poverty Towards Economic Liberation", _Africa Contemporary Record 1981/82_ (London: Africana Publishing Company, 1982), p. A. 108.

[23]See, Banji Adeyanju, "Racists Subdue Frontline States" _Sunday Concord_ (Ikeja, Lagos) 29 April 1984, pp. 12-13.

[24]"Zambia" in _ACR 1980/81_, p. B. 905.

[25]"Kingdom of Lesotho: International and External Reapproachment", _ACR 1980/81_, p. B 682. See also Andrew Rusinga, "Zimbabwe Survey", _African Business_, (May 1986), pp. 52-55.

[26]Denis R. Norman, "Food Security for Southern Africa", _Africa Report_, Vol. 29, No. 4 (July-August 1984), pp. 15-21.

[27]Ibid.

[28]Ibid.

[29]Sue Turner, op. cit.

[30] Ibid.

[31] Amon J. Nsekela, op. cit.

[32] Sue Turner, op. cit.

[33] Kenneth Hackett, "Africa's Drought: Will the Tragedy be Repeated", Africa Report Vol 29, No. 4 (July-August 1984), pp. 19-23.

[34] Sue Turner, op. cit., pp. 2-3.

[35] Ibid., pp. 3-4.

[36] Sue Turner, "SADCC: Lusaka: Food Security Emerges as the Key Issue" Africa Economic Digest (Longon), Vol. 5, 27 January, 1984, pp. 2-4. For adverse effects of drought in Southern Africa see Senator Denis R. Norman, "Africa's Drought: Food Security for Southern Africa" Africa Report, July-August 1984, pp. 15-18.

[37] Ibid.

[38] For details on Zambia's reliance on foreign aid see "Zambia" in ACR 1980/81 pp. B 910-911.

[39] "Tanzania" ACR 1980/81 pp. B 348.

[40] For details on foreign aids at the national level for SADCC States see "SADCC: Lusaka Meeting" New Africa March 1984, p. 49.

[41] "Botswana: Development in the Face of Dependence Africa Now, September 1983, p. 101.

[42] Ibid, p. 102.

[43] For details on South Africa-MNR Collaboration to Destabilize Mozambique see Jonathan Bloch and Andrew Weir, "Pretoria's dirty trick army:, Africa Now (October 1982), pp. 9193. See also Glenn Frankel, "South Africa - backed Rebels Weaken Mozambique" in The Washington Post, (8 October, 1984), pp. 1 & 36.

[44] Paul Fauvet, "Energy Meeting Generates Heat and Light", Africa Now, September 1983, p. 79.

[45] Ibid.

[46]Mark Doyle, "Angola: The Cost of Defending Independence", West Africa 7 January 1985, p. 16.

[47]Paul Fauvet, op. cit., p. 80.

[48]"Energy Planners Face Difficult Policy Choices" Africa Economic Digest, Vol 5, No. 4 (January 27 - February 2, 1984), p. 3.

[49]J. T. C. Simeos (ed.) SADCC: Energy and Development to the Year 2000, SADCC Energy sector in Collaboration with the Beijer Institute and the Scandinavian Institute of African Studies (Uddevalla: Bohuslaningens AB, 1984), p. 20.

[50]Gunder Frank is one of the scholars who has debunked the idea that foreign aid and investment is for Third World economic development. His argument can be found in Sociology of Development and the Under-development of Sociology Catalyst, No. 3, 1967, pp. 34-37.

[51]"ACP-EEC File": West Africa (February, 1985), p. 370.

[52]See D. K. Leo, "The Politics of Aid" Africa (March 1985), p. 42.

[53]E. Utkin, "Socialism and Third World Economy" Communism 4, Questions and Answers (Moscow: Progress Publishers, 1976), p. 147.

[54]Ibid.

[55]"ACP-EEC File": West Africa (February, 1985), p. 371.

[56]E. J. Kinsanga, op. cit.

[57]Ibid.

[58]The Guardian (Manchester) 1 August, 1967.

[59]For details see Reg Prentice, "More priority for Overseas Aid", International Affairs, Vol, 46, No. 1 (January 1974), pp. 5-6.

[60]D. K. Leo, op. cit., p. 43.

[61]"On Course of Catastrophe", South (February 1985), p. 37.

[62]"Famine in the age of plenty" Ibid., p. 33.

[63]Tunji Oseni, "UNIDO IV, UNCTAD VI: Different Fora, same outcome", The Guardian (Lagos), 24 September 1984, p. 9.

[64]Frank Barton, "African Aid Results not Encouraging", Daily Times (Lagos), 11 March 1985, p. 3.

[65]Ibid.

[66]"Magic Aid" South (February 1985), p. 61.

[67]Philip M. Allen, "The Technical Assistance Industry in Africa: A Case for Nationalization", International Development Review, No. 3 (1970), p. 8.

[68]Transnational Corporations in Africa: Some Major Issues, Economic Commission for Africa Secratariat, E/ECA/UNCTC/21 (13 January 1983).

[69]See Makwapatira Mhango "Devaluation Chaos in Zambia " New African (December 1985), p. 50.

[70]"Zambia to Auction Foreign Exchange", New African (November 1985), p. 15.

[71]Report of the Presidential Commission on World Hunger, Overcoming World Hunger: The Challenge Ahead (Washington, D.C., 1980), p. 140.

[72]IBRD, Accelerated Development, op. cit., p. 3.

[73]World Development Report 1983 (London: Oxford University Press, 1983), p. 21.

[74]See Economic Commission for Africa, Critical Analysis of the Country Presentations of African Least Developed Countries in the Light of the Lagos Plan of Action and the Final Act of Lagos, Dec. No. ST/ECA/PSD.2/31 (ECA, Addis Ababa, 1982).

[75]Ibid.

[76]"Famine in the age of plenty" op. cit.

[77]E. J. Kinsanga, op. cit., p. 38.

[78]"COMECON Connection", South (February 1985), p. 64.

[79]Bob Adams, "Focus on Africa and India: A well qualified partner for Development", African Business (March 1985), p. 58.

[80]Ibid.

[81]Roger Leys and Arne Tosten, "Regional Cooperation in Southen Africa: The Southern African Development Coordination Conference", Review of African Political Economy, No. 23, 1982, p. 69.

[82]See Walt W. Rostow, The Stages of Economic Growth: A Non-Communist Manifesto (Cambridge, MA: Harvard University Press, 1961).

[83]SADEX, Vol. 2, No. 3, op. cit., p. 20.

[84]"Zimbabwe Plans to takeover Metal Sales", Africa Now, (March 1982), p. 106.

[85]"Mozambique: MNR still Active", Africa Report (July-August, 1984), p. 50.

CHAPTER 5

SOUTH AFRICA'S POLICY OF DESTABILIZATION
IN SOUTHERN AFRICA: A THREAT TO SADCC

In relations with its neighbouring countries South Africa, having lost the insulation of nearby former Portuguese colonies and the friendship of a like-minded, white-minority controlled (former Rhodesia) Zimbabwe, has undertaken a campaign to destabilize the neighbouring countries - the SADCC States through tactical programmes combining assassination, economic leverage, military invasion and undeclared war; with the ongoing material support for dissident groups within these countries. South Africa is waging an undeclared war in the Southern African sub-region and especially in Mozambique and Angola. Its main weapons in the area are the Mozambique National Resistance (MNR or RENAMO) in Mozambique, and the National Union for the Total Independence of Angola (UNITA) in Angola.[1]

South Africa's threats and support of the MNR and UNITA have two interrelated objectives: first to destabilize the whole of the Southern Africa sub-continent, particularly Angola and Mozambique, and to delay the Namibian settlement and prevent the South West African Peoples Organization (SWAPO) from coming to power after Namibian independence. Second to sabotage

SADCC's objectives. The SADCC objective is an integrated regional economic alliance of the Southern African States, forged to break Pretoria's economic hegemony in Southern Africa.[2] To SADCC member-states, their economic liberation is as vital as their political freedom. Thus, South African assistance to the MNR and UNITA rebel groups cannot be separated from its heightened economic and military pressures against Botswana, Mozambique, and Zimbabwe, its increased attacks and daily military raids on Angola, its assassination activities in Lesotho and its efforts to seduce Swaziland with the Kangwane Bantustan and the Ingwavuna piece of barren land.[3] Viewed from this regional perspective, the MNR (activity) in Mozambique, the Lesotho Liberation Army in Lesotho, and UNITA in Angola since 1975, are all valuable political weapons for the South African white minority regime to keep the area divided and in turmoil.[4]

This chapter will examine and analyze the threat posed by these anti-government bandits - the MNR and UNITA in Southern Africa and particularly their serious threat on SADCC. Our assessment in this chapter is set within the wider framework of South Africa's relations with its neighbouring states, and the collaboration of certain foreign powers to aid these two anti-government rebel groups in their efforts to keep the Southern African sub-region destabilized.

The Threat from South Africa to SADCC

In the past few years, and particularly since 1980, the SADCC states have all felt the direct or indirect effects of South African policies of military and economic destabilization. In particular, the 1983-1984 military attacks on Angola and Mozambique,[5] and the continuing failure of the talks on Namibian independence[6] are supposed to produce calls from the Western Powers, especially the U.S. and Britain to exert pressure on South Africa. Yet, as in the past, they are just expressing ordinary sympathy but minimal and no real action at all.

Clearly, the most significant threat to SADCC's ability to expand its options is South Africa. Moreover, South African actions have not escaped the attention of the SADCC member-states, many of whom have been the targets of its policy of destabilization. An increasingly belligerent South Africa, with stepped up attempts at undermining the SADCC through subversion and destabilization is currently in progress. Destabilization may consist of either covert or overt acts, or combine both covert and overt acts, but is short of a full scale war. However, at times, the conflict may assume the proportions of a full scale but undeclared war. This is the kind of war South Africa is waging against its neighbours. The phenomenon of destabilization is nothing new in international politics. But its sophisticated form, which now poses a threat to peace and international order and thus to the survival of mankind, is a direct product of capitalism and its greediness in the form of monopoly capital and finance capital.[7] This is the reason why Lenin has described finance capital as a "decisive force in all economic and in all international relations", because of its capacity to subdue under its control even countries that have political independence.

Karl Marx said, that the state is an organ of class rule, an organ of the oppression of one class by another; it is the creation of "order" which legalizes and perpetuates this oppression by moderating the conflict between classes. Therefore, in the opinion of the petty bourgeois - capitalist, order means the reconciliation of classes, and not the oppression of one class by another: to alleviate the conflict means reconciling classes and not depriving the oppressed classes of exact means and methods of struggle to overthrow the oppressors. Engels pointed out that:

> As the state arose from the need to hold class antagonisms in check, but as it arose at the same time in the midst of the conflict of these classes, it is, as a rule the state of the most powerful economically dominant class which through the medium of the state becomes also the politically dominant class, and thus, acquires new means of holding down and exploiting the oppressed class.[9]

Lenin added his own views by saying that "finance capital is such a great, and such a decisive force in all economic and in all international relations that is capable of subjecting and actually does subject to itself even states enjoying the fullest political independence..."[10]

The above quotations show the political and economic power of a ruling class which it expresses in "the establishment of a public power which no longer directly coincides with the population organizing itself into an armed force defends the interests of the majority - the working people. The "public power" - that is that "special bodies of armed men having prisons...and institutions of coercion of all kinds..."[12] are there only to safeguard the interests of a ruling class against the oppressed classes. In capitalist countries this "public power" also facilitates the acquisition and holding of territory in imperialist ventures, or the control of property in the colonies and neo-colonies. Consequently, this "public power" is indispensable for imperialism in safeguarding their monopoly capitals around the world.

The desire on the part of one government to actively and openly seek the overthrow of another government stems, from that government's dislike for the other government's policies. South Africa's destabilization policy against the SADCC member-states has a racial, class and ideological basis. In other words, destabilization has become a weapon for the defense of the immediate interests of the Boer dominated South African ruling class, and of the international bourgeoisie (capitalism) in their attempts to safeguard their social privileges, and economic interests. And it is ipso facto anti-independent development, anti-socialist and anti-liberation. Destabilization of the Southern Africa sub-region is therefore, clearly an imperialist policy. South Africa regime's hegemonistic policies in Southern Africa serve both South Africa's own political and economic interests, as well as those of imperialist powers led by the United States and Britain.[13] Therefore, we surely would expect joint destabilization actions by the Western imperialist powers and South Africa.

The South African and United States policy in Southern Africa is more than just a response to the specific liberation movements in South Africa and Namibia or just one country, but an imperialist strategy responding to the whole struggle in the Southern Africa sub-continent, for social transformation aimed at eliminating neo-colonial domination and exploitative social and productive relations. The South African Foreign Minister, Pik Botha, confirmed this when he stated that "South Africa's sphere of influence", extended to all its neighbours in the Southern Africa sub-region.[14]

The intensity of South Africa's destabilization measures against the SADCC states and the degree of support or collaboration it received from its imperialist allies for such measures are in direct proportion, in the first instance. The second instance, is that the Pretoria racist regime's perceptions of the SADCC states' support for the Liberation Movements in South Africa and Namibia and, to the Western imperialist perceptions of the SADCC States' commitment to the fundamental transformation of production relations towards liberating their national economies from the clutches of transnational monopoly capital.

The South African policy of destabilization was hatched between 1967 and 1975[15] - during the periods of the National Liberation Struggles in Angola, Mozambique and Zimbabwe. From 1967 to 1975, there were over 4,000 South African troops with armoured cars, helicopters and planes supporting Ian Smith's illegal minority regime in (the former Rhodesia) Zimbabwe, and over 1,000 South African soldiers to bolster the Portuguese colonial forces in Mozambique. And in Angola, the South African regime, and the dictatorship regime of Salazar in Lisbon signed an agreement setting up a joint command to direct South African air reconnaissance and moved troops against MPLA in Angola and SWAPO in Namibia.[16] All these arrangements were underwritten by the U.S. Central Intelligence Agency (CIA). Thus, the aggressive and interventionist policy of the racist regime in South Africa have been adjusted since Mozambique, Angola and Zimbabwe were independent.

South Africa has developed a "siege mentality" because it does not feel secure any more, amongst its African majority-ruled independent neighbours. The existence of the apartheid system is being threatened and its collapse is imminent.[17] Thus, it has modified its policy of destabilization into a "carrot and stick" strategy - that is those South African neighbouring states that accept the South African wishes of not allowing any Liberation groups that are anti-White policy (ANC and SWAPO) will be accepted and even offered economic aid, and treated as allies and friends of South Africa. While those South Africa neighbouring African states that are harbouring the nationalist movements are regarded as enemies and are being whipped by South Africa.[18] The "carrot" approach adopted by South Africa was the Constellation of Southern African States (CONSAS) (for full details about CONSAS see Chapter One in this book). The "stick" aspect of the policy adopted was the aggression tactics or "the total strategy" - the strategy of destabilizing its neighbours to force them to submit to its wishes.

To justify its attacks against African majority-ruled neighbouring states, South Africa has invoked all sorts of arguments, including quite surprisingly the tactics of "self-defense" and even that of "hot pursuit". The director of the South African Defense Force (SADF) General Viljoen said that "South Africa will not employ hot pursuit and pre-emptive strikes against bases, training centres, logistics and leadership cadres of the terrorist movements".[19] The invasion of Angola and ruthless massacres of over 800 defenseless Namibian women, old people and children refugees at Cassinga refugee camp by South African troops on 4 May 1978:[20] the invasion of Mozambique and

174

the cold-blooded massacre of 13 ANC refugees in Matola on 31 January 1981, and on 23 May 1982,[21] the assassination of Joe Ggabi, the ANC representative in Zimbabwe by the South African hit squad in Harare in August 1981;[22] the merciless killing of 5 Mozambican citizens and one South African refugee in the same Matola refugee camp; the invasion of Lesotho on 9 December 1982, and the indiscriminate killing of 42 South African refugees and Lesotho citizens, were not acts in self-defense nor as a result of hot pursuit.[23] The Namibian and South African refugees had not been caught in hot pursuit after committing any offenses in their countries. They had fled their countries because of the repression and atrocities of murder, rape, torture and illegal imprisonment committed by racist South African security forces. Besides, none of the places attacked was a military base or a training centre. For instance, the refugees in Maseru were "refugees living openly in the town suburbs with their Lesotho neighbours".[24] The May 1983 attack on a suburb of Maputo was an attack on genuine homes of Mozambican civilians, both black and white, which were shattered by cannon and rocket fire of racist troops.[25]

The invasions of neighbouring countries by South Africa have two objectives that are quite unrelated to any threat to South Africa's territorial integrity nor to threatened attack by its neighbours. Its first objective is to destroy communications, economic infrastructure, and to demoralize the population and thus subvert and undermine the gains already made towards the Liberation and economic cooperation of the SADCC States. Secondly, the attacks are also part of South Africa's policy of genocide against the African people. The combined effect of those attacks is supposed to beat the SADCC into political and economic submission so that they can stop supporting the Liberation Movements on the one hand, and give up attempts to form a separate economic cooperation (SADCC) different from the one initiated by South Africa (the Pretoria Constellation) Southern African economic constellation.[26] All these objectives are tacitly supported by the U.S. and other Western capitalist countries which are constantly trying to make it appear that South Africa is being attacked by neighbouring states. The Reagan administration's policy of "Constructive Engagement" in Southern Africa is nothing but an insulting shame. We are yet to see any U.S. purposeful engagement in Southern Africa. All we have seen is more frenzied construction of political and economic devices that are facilitating more repressions. Reagan refuses to strike a blow for freedom in Southern Africa and instead, he is threatening the Africans that the U.S. would send troops to South Africa if the white supremacists there come under destabilizing threat.[27] To buttress Reagan's assertion in an interview on one of the Nigerian Television Stations on 9 December 1984, the U.S. Chargé d'Affaires in Nigeria, Herbert Gilbert confirmed Reagan's threat that, "it would be foolhardy for any African country to show hostility towards the apartheid regime in South Africa"[28]

UNITA-South African Collaboration

Jonas Malheiro Savimbi, an assimilado from Bie Province in Southern Angola tried to join the MPLA in 1960 before joining the Union of the Angolan Peoples' Organization (UPA). It was not clear just why things did not work out for him to join MPLA.[29] The UPA played a prominent role in the Revolutionary Government of

Angola in Exile (GRAE) formed in April 1962, and led by Holden Roberto. But on 16 July, 1964, while in Cairo attending a Summit Meeting of the OAU, Savimbi announced his resignation as the Foreign Minister of the GRAE.[30] Professor Soremekun, an authority on the history of the nationalist struggle in Angola has pointed out that:

> of all the three nationalist movements UNITA appeared to have been the one which evoked the tightest ethnic cohesion. This has been so because it was too late to arrive as a party and hence the leadership had to evoke unquestioned loyalty, and partly because the Ovimbundu (Savimbi's tribe) had developed a certain belief that they were being "wronged by the other groups in the country who they charged looked down on them, and regarded them as stooges to the white man".[31]

The Portuguese had always tried to play off one ethnic group against the other, thereby attempting to split Angolans. The strategies were calculated to make each Angolan elite group think only of its own ethnic interest. To achieve their aim, the Portuguese portrayed the Southerners (Savimbi's people) as loyal and northerners (Roberto's and Neto's people) as trouble-makers. Therefore, the northerners saw the southerners as uneducated, illiterate "collaborators", while the Southerners saw the northerners as assimilated mesticos (Mulatos) who have lost their African roots. The consequences of all these were bound to affect nationalist efforts sooner or later in Angola, just as such strategies had affected African nationalism in Nigeria, Sudan, Chad, Zaire etc., African states where an erstwhile colonial power encouraged tribalism as a diversionary strategy against African nationalism. "It was probably that this was one of the reason why Savimbi broke with Roberto in 1964".[32]

On 12 December 1964, Savimbi, including 20 other Angolans, published a "Manifesto of the friends of Angola" (Amangola) in which he proclaimed his willingness to cooperate sincerely with all political-military formations of Angolan patriots within and outside Angola, given the fact that "a good Angolan never kills another Angolan".[33] According to its Manifesto the aim of the "friends of Angola" was to promote an active struggle to isolate Portuguese colonialism. It declared its willingness to prepare the whole country to forge a permanent spirit of struggle, the only guarantee for the creation of popular power after the democratic revolution.[34]

On 13 May, 1966, in the Southern part of Angola Savimbi launched a new movement, known as the National Union for the Total Independence of Angola (UNITA). The document circulated by UNITA's Central Committee stated that its guiding principles were:

> the systematic mobilization and organization of the peasants inside the country, as a main force of struggle. Integration of intellectuals and military cadres inside and outside Angola in the struggle, side by side with the broad masses. Refusal to rely on military camps created in neighbouring countries for the sake of external propaganda. Active participation of all the people from both rural and urban areas in the general resistance against foreign domination. Refusal to be led by big foreign powers. Faith in unity and cooperation of all Angolans in this phase of national liberation.[35]

178

It is both funny and ironical that since UNITA had
been formed in 1966 its leader Jonas Savimbi has always
been a collaborator with the foreign imperialist powers
especially with Portugal, the U.S. and the racist regime
in South Africa which he (Savimbi) was accusing the FNLA
and MPLA leaders of collaborating with in the 1960s and
1970s. Most especially Portugal is here regarded as the
most imperialist European country because she (Portugal)
kept Angola as her colony for almost 500 years - 1482 to
1975. Portugal is the last European imperial power to
grant independence to her African colonies. Portugal
was even forced-out of her African colonies by the
nationalists, because Portugal was never ready to grant
them independence anyway. Today, Savimbi has become a
pawn in the hands of those imperialist powers. The
worst of all, he and his UNITA reactionary group is
collaborating with the racist regime in South Africa to
destabilize Angola and destroy the efforts of the SADCC
States to achieve their economic liberation from South
Africa. According to certain sources, UNITA, led by
Jonas Savimbi started collaborating with imperial
Portugal under Salazar regime against the Angolan
national interests as far back as 1971. Evidence
abounds to prove that the leadership of UNITA in the
person of Savimbi has always been a traitor and a sell-
out of the Angolan liberation from the imperial rule.

Savimbi in 1972 served as an agent of the
Portuguese and of their politics whatever the
difficulties. In any case, the Portuguese had always
regarded Savimbi's people Ovimbundu as loyal to them and
therefore, "good Angolans". This had made the other
Angolan tribes (the northern peoples) see Savimbi as a
leader of the southern collaborators and therefore, an
agent of the imperialist Portugal. On 26 September,

1972 Savimbi wrote a letter to General Marcel Caetano in Lisbon through General Luz Cunha - the then Commander-in-Chief of the Portuguese armed forces in Angola. In the letter Savimbi accused the MPLA of being the principal obstacle to peace in Angola. In the same letter Savimbi requested that General Luz Cunha should furnish him with 1,500 rounds of 7.62 ammunition to be used against the MPLA and FNLA.[36] Savimbi was also secretly passing confidential information about the MPLA and the FNLA liberation activities inside Angola to the dictatorship regime in Lisbon through the Portuguese Governor General in Angola. The fascist Salazar regime specifically regarded "MPLA as its number-one enemy in Angola until 1975, which UNITA led by Savimbi was given the task to destroy".[37] Therefore, there is no gainsaying to see Savimbi collaborating with the fascist South Africa regime and the U.S., since the MPLA has come to power in Angola.

Jonas Savimbi has described his movement as Pretoria's ally and said, "I do not hide my ties with South Africa".[38] Savimbi is not a true and committed nationalist. John Stockwell, a former chief CIA Task Force in Angola has described him (Savimbi) as a confused man who when the moral stakes were highest would choose imperialism rather than his own country - Angola. Stockwell's description of him was quite apt. "Savimbi is a man without profound ideology. He was neither Marxist nor capitalist nor even a black revolutionary. He was an Angolan patriot fighting for the freedom of the Ovimbundu people. He had accepted North Korean training for his men, and Chinese money and arms. He liked Americans. If South Africa would give him the help he needed he would accept".[39] This description shows that the UNITA leader is a diehard tribalist who was mainly concerned about his sectional tribal interest and not the national interest of the Angola nation. He is a sell-out of the cause of the Angolan struggle - total independence from imperialism and neo-colonialism.

UNITA has had its national and regional objectives so inextricably linked with those of South Africa and the West, particularly the Reagan administration in the United States. Since the MPLA has come to power in the People's Republic of Angola in 1975, Jonas Savimbi has become a willing tool in the plunder and pillage of the country and people he claimed to be fighting for their liberation. UNITA has been described by the former Angolan Foreign Minister, Paulo Jorge as "the foremost group on the Frontline of South Africa's policy of destabilization".[40] In October of 1975, during the Angolan second war of national liberation, an expeditionary force of South Africa invaded Southern Angola with the collaboration of the UNITA forces. With the assistance of its true allies, the Cubans and the Soviet bloc, the MPLA repelled the South African forces and defeated both the UNITA and FNLA, expelling them from all the cities and villages they occupied.

UNITA is a force to be reckoned with in Angola provided its leadership in the person of Jonas Savimbi is a true and committed nationalist, but he is not as stated earlier on. During the cause of this research, in all the discussions had with the Angolan officials, and non-officials I was told and reminded that the MPLA will not, and will never negotiate with Savimbi as long as he continues to collaborate with South Africa, and the foreign powers, particularly the U.S. under the Reagan administration. An Angolan official categorically confronted me by saying that "how can we (the MPLA) negotiate with Savimbi - a reactionary element, a friend of number one enemy of the Angolan Peoples and the African Peoples as a whole-South Africa; not now".

With the new situation in Southern Africa, a situation which is changing so fast, and very volatile, in which Namibia has become the Vietnam of South Africa. This new situation has led South Africa to sign a disengagement pact with Angola on 16 February, 1984 non-aggression (Nkomati) agreement with Mozambique on 16 March, 1984 (see Appendix 2, page 297) and now South Africa has started talking directly with SWAPO leaders as a move to find a peaceful solution to the Namibian problems.[41] After the Angolan-South African disengagement truce, Presidents Dos Santos of Angola and Fidel Castro of Cuba met and outlined three main conditions under which the Cubans might leave Angola. First, demand for the withdrawal of all South African troops in Southern Angola. Second, demand for South African acceptance and implementation of the United Nations Resolution 435 of 1978, calling for the withdrawal of the racist regime army from Namibia, and full independence for the territory. The third condition is an end to South African invasion of Angola and its support for UNITA. The two leaders said that, "on their own decision and exercising their sovereignty, Angola and Cuba shall implement the gradual withdrawal of Cuban troops as soon as the conditions are satisfied".[42] The 16 February, 1984 Lusaka "agreement" between Angola and South Africa is not an agreement as such, but an understanding reached between the two governments covering those three demands above. In addition a Joint Monitoring Commission (JMC) was set up, comprising Angolans, South Africans and Americans.[43]

The commission is responsible to detect, investigate and report alleged violations of the parties' commitments to halt the conflict between Angola and South Africa in Angola; and the withdrawal of the South African troops inside the Angolan territories.

Savimbi was deported from Zambia in 1968, and that deportation seriously demoralized his UNITA rebel group. In his own assessment "Angolans, Zairians and Zambians were bound by geographical conditions to live together and their destinies are the same".[44] The same Savimbi who believed in the same destinies of these Southern African neighbouring countries is at the same time working against and threatening the national interests of those countries. Since the creation of SADCC in 1980, UNITA has been bombing and blowing up the 700 miles Benguela rail line which is one of the life-lines of the SADCC transport system. It is through this railroad that Zambia transports its copper which is the main source of Zambia's revenue and foreign exchange to the port of Benguela in Angola to be shipped to the outside world. It is also through this same railroad that Zaire transports most of its products to the port of Benguela on its onward shipment to overseas countries. UNITA has made it difficult for the MPLA Government in Angola to govern the Southeastern and the Southern Provinces as efficiently as it could. Without political stability and peaceful internal environment, the natural and human resources of a nation cannot be geared towards the economic development and progress of that nation. The UNITA-South Africa collaboration against the MPLA Government in Angola is adversely affecting the political stability of that country and its economic development.

It has been argued that the Soviet Union on behalf of the MPLA capitalized highly on the South African involvement in Angola in support of UNITA-FNLA coalition. A number of African countries which hitherto remained neutral at the beginning of the Angolan second war of national liberation in 1975 threw their weight behind the MPLA after South Africa's intervention, a good example is Nigeria.[45] And since the end of the Angolan conflict in March 1976, the FNLA has disintegrated and some of its leaders have fled to Zaire, to North Africa and many of them are scattered all over Europe. UNITA in its own case has regrouped into the bush with Savimbi vowing to fight to the finish. According to Savimbi's information Secretary, Fernando Wilson, UNITA's forces number about 10,000 regulars and 20,000 militia fighting the MPLA government forces since 1976. The rebel forces operate mainly from the Southeastern and the Southern parts of Angola bordering the Namibia northern border.

South African Defense Forces (SADF) and UNITA attacks on Angolan territory have concentrated on localities of economic or public relations value. The tactics are to hit bridges, trading centres and the all-too-vulnerable Benguela railway, which runs through the centre of the country and is very important for SADCC. Savimbi and the SADF collaborator have in this way created a sense of insecurity in some regions, but certainly not in the capital, as some reports have suggested, and also in disrupting the economy.

Part of the South-eastern, Ovimbundu-dominated area of the country is in fact the scene of regular UNITA attacks. Western diplomats and a few journalists, whose dream is of a truly pro-western Angola (Western stooge), for the potential wealth of the country is enormous, even talk of "control" by the so-called UNITA in this part of Angola. But this is misleading, for the fact that the South-eastern section is thinly populated and certainly of limited economic value for Angola. The fact of the whole situation is that Savimbi's public relations network particularly in the western capitals is far more effective than his military capability.[46]

The UNITA-South Africa collaboration is a strategy which works this way; South African troops come in, capture Angolan town or village, lease it to UNITA guerrillas who are invariably driven out by the MPLA government forces. An example of this strategy is the case of Cuando Cubango province Central town of Mavinge (where an estimated 1,500 people attended a UNITA Congress in July 1982) which was captured by the South African troops and handed over to the UNITA rebel group early in 1982. By September 1982, the town has been re-captured by the MPLA government forces.

The implementation of development projects in the South-eastern, and Southern parts and especially the rural areas of the southern provinces of Angola has been curtailed by the UNITA activity. UNITA has sabotaged urban installations in Benguela and Lobito provinces. At the end of 1981, UNITA claimed responsibility for the partial blowing up of the huge oil refinery in Luanda in collaboration with South African troops.[47] The 700-mile Benguela Railway operates only at a tenth of its capacity and irregularly, because of sabotage by UNITA dissidents.

Much of this activity depends on the mutual support that the South African government and UNITA render each other militarily. With the collaboration of the UNITA group, South African troops have infiltrated and occupied about 150 miles inside Southern Angolan territories, supporting UNITA with 5,500 South African troops.[48] From their near-permanent bases around Ngiva and Xangongo north of the Cunene in Southern Angola, South African troops supply UNITA forces with arms, food and medicines. The South Africans and the UNITA group also plan joint military activities and exchange intelligence information on the Movements of the SWAPO nationalist freedom fighters and Angolan government troops - Peoples Armed Forces of the Liberation of Angola (FAPLA). South African bases in northern Namibia and in the Caprivi Strip in the east provide useful facilities for the UNITA group to train their forces in preparation for movement into the eastern and central areas of Angola. "UNITA needs South Africa in its fight against the Luanda government, and South Africa needs UNITA in its fight against SWAPO. It is a marriage of military necessity".[49]

In the MPLA Congress of 1977, Angolan society was transformed into a Marxist-Leninist state and the Party-MPLA transformed into a Marxist-Leninist Party. The New Action Programme of the MPLA leaders, considering the intentions of external forces trying to impose neo-colonial domination on Angolan (MPLA) leadership was obliged to embark upon the road to "scientific socialism". This meant adopting, the socialism of Marx, Engels and Lenin - scientific socialism that explicitly entails the ending of exploitation of man by man.[50] Inspired by an internationalist world view, Angolan leaders rejected regionalist notions of African socialism or Pan-Africanism as diluted and constricted approaches to the goal of collective human liberation. Angola under the MPLA leadership is committed to the liberation of the remaining Southern African territories under white domination. For example Angola is committed

and is sacrificing the lives of her citizens for the
liberation of Namibia.[51]

Considering the current South African policy of
destabilization in Southern Africa, from both the
economic and political points of views, Angola is
Pretoria's prime target. South Africa has reason to
fear Angolan development in the future. Firstly, the
ruling MPLA party's commitment to socialism is firm.
Secondly, Angola's potential wealth in natural
resources, which unlike other Frontline states could be
developed independently of South Africa, is the greatest
of the nine SADCC states; and is the only country that
produces oil abundantly and for export in Southern
Africa. If there is peace and political stability in
Angola, it will challenge South Africa in terms of
economic development. Therefore, from Pretoria's view
point, Angola must be stopped in its development
efforts.

Political Necessity

Politically, South Africa has utilized UNITA for
its own advantage in attempts to forge a Namibian
solution consistent with its interests, while UNITA has
backed South Africa to make a Namibian settlement
conditional upon the withdrawal of Cubans from Angola.
Therefore, UNITA is behind the South African white
regime making the Cubans withdrawal from Angola a
precondition for finding solution to the Namibian
independence issue. A SWAPO-ruled Namibia alliance with
an MPLA Government in Luanda would mean the military
demise of Savimbi, and this would be unacceptable to
white South African authority. The argument is that,
with the Cubans gone, South Africa could still throw its
military weight behind Savimbi until Angola agrees to

accommodate him politically. Thus South Africa needs UNITA not just only to destabilize Angola but also to delay Namibian independence, and even to paralyze the SADCC's objectives.

The South African policy of destabilizing Southern Africa is failing. This is the reason that has led Botha to sign non-aggression agreements with Swaziland in 1983, Mozambique and Angola in 1984, and his visit to eight European countries in June 1984. The aim of Botha's visit to Europe was three-fold. First, to secure international acceptance for South African apartheid. Second, to secure financial and economic aid from the European governments and banking institutions. Namibia has become the Vietnam of South Africa and is causing the apartheid regime lives and too much money to continue that illegal war. It has been estimated that the war in Namibia is costing Pretoria over $1.36 billion a year - about 10 percent of the South African budget. President Botha has confessed openly in Parliament that the war in Namibia is straining the South African economy.[52] The worst side of the situation is that the number of South African white soldiers dying in the Namibian war is increasing daily, morale is declining, and young Afrikaner soldiers are deserting the South African Army.[53] Third, South Africa wants to unify and harden western opinion on Namibia.

In a wider context, Savimbi has cast UNITA as an important element in the Frontline against Soviet expansion in the Southern Africa sub-region. According to Savimbi, "the West's frontline against the Soviet Union runs through Southern Angola".[54] The voices criticizing the United States intervention in Angola have continued to decrease and weaken before the former President Carter left the White House in 1980. A number of influential private American Organizations have been promoting the cause of the UNITA rebel group in Angola. One such organization, the conservative, New York based Freedom House sponsored an America tour of UNITA leader Jonas Savimbi in November 1979. During Savimbi's trip to the United States, he met with many American leaders, including former Secretary of State Henry Kissinger, the late Senator Henry Jackson (Democrat from Washington State), Senator Daniel Moynihan (Democrat from New York) and the American Labour leader Lane Kirkland.[55] UNITA has opened an office in Arlington, Virginia a suburb of Washington, D.C., and run by Marcos Sambondo as its Washington representative. Besides, South Africa, the U.S. and Morocco, Franz-Joseph Strauss, the former Bavarian leader in West Germany are close allies of Savimbi and UNITA has an office in Munich.[56] The London Observer reports that a secret $18 million fund was given to UNITA jointly by South Africa, Iran, Saudi Arabia, Morocco and France in their efforts to destabilize Angola.[57]

The Reagan Factor

The Reagan administration repealed the Clark Amendment in 1985, channeled financial and military assistance to UNITA and encouraged the formation of opposition groups, such as the Military Committee for Angolan Resistance (COMIRA) to replace the defunct FNLA.[58]

A great controversy has surrounded the Clark Amendment. The Reagan administration argues that the amendment improperly ties the President's hands in formulating and conducting foreign policy. It blames the measure (amendment) for the failure of the Ford and Carter administrations to dislodge the Soviets and

Cubans from Angola. Although the Reagan administration has succeed in getting the U.S. Congress to repeal the amendment, it has extended recognition to UNITA to force a political showdown in Angola by creating a military stalemate. In January 1982, in Rabat, Morocco, Savimbi said, "material help is not dependent on nor limited by the Clark Amendment. A great country like the United States has other channels".[59] These and like comments tend to lend credibility to allegations of United States subversion made by the Angola News Agency (ANGOP). In March 1982 ANGOP reported that COMIRA was formed in close collaboration between the Reagan administration and UNITA as a replacement for the FNLA and was training 2,000 men in northern Angola.

Southern Africa has again become an area of East-West competition and President Reagan has offered an open endorsement of covert U.S. aid to UNITA rebels fighting the MPLA Government in Angola. Before Jonas Savimbi's January 1986 visit to Washington, Mr. Reagan remarked that, "we all believe that a covert operation would be more useful to us (America) and have more change of success right now than the overt proposal that has been made in the Congress".[60] Both Caspar Weinberger the Secretary of Defense and George Schultz, the Secretary of State and William Casey the Director of the CIA now favour covert military aid to UNITA rather than overt assistance. George Schultz has argued that, "such an approach (covert military aid) would allow the U.S. to follow a two-track policy of continuing to seek a negotiated settlement of the Namibia dispute and the withdrawal of Cuban troops from Angola".[61] The Reagan administration is also pressuring the MPLA Government in Luanda to include Savimbi in a government of national unity, as a quid pro quo to help hasten a Namibian settlement. The Reagan administration has gone to the extent of pressuring Chevron oil company to pull out of Angola.[62] Chevron's subsidiary, the Gulf Company has been a major operator in Angola's offshore oil fields for the past 30 years, generating some $2 billion a year for Luanda.

Receiving Jonas Savimbi into the White House on the 31 January 1986, President Reagan remarked, "we want to be supportive. We are seeking a way to be of help".[63] This was in reference to Savimbi and his rebel UNITA group waging a guerrilla war against the MPLA Government in Angola. On the same day while meeting the American news media, Mr. Savimbi categorically declared, "I consider Botha as my friend. It may shock you or not, but I consider him my friend".[64]

It is unthinkable what Reagan wants to accomplish by getting America involved in a second adventure into Angolan conflict after its defeat and humiliation of 1975 to 1976, when it supported Holden Roberto's defunct FNLA. Actually, America's second intervention in Angola is predicated on Reagan's belief that to stop Soviet expansionism in the World and need to avoid "handing over all of Southern Africa to the Soviet Union". The fact is that intervention this second time around cannot bring about a "Pax Americana" in Angola, and Reagan ought to have learnt from the Vietnam experience of 1958 to 1975. Any U.S. second intervention in the Angolan conflict would be dangerous and risk serious damage to America's stature in international affairs. In fact there would be no moral justification for United States intervention in Angola to unseat (the MPLA) a legitimate regime (as Mr. Reagan has been doing in Nicaragua since 1984),[65] and at the same time accusing the Soviet Union of promoting regional instability around the World. Is

Mr. Reagan's covert aid to rebels in Angola, Afghanistan and Nicaragua stabilizing these countries? The Reagan adminstration has tilted the U.S. support away from SADCC by providing aid to UNITA. The Reagan administration's funding of Savimbi (UNITA) runs counter to American professions of friendship and cooperation with the independent states of Southern Africa. This places the Reagan White House in league with South Africa in fomenting instability in the region.

America's second gamble in Angola would have serious economic, diplomatic, political and military implications. For these reasons, it would be better for Mr. Reagan to exercise restraint, because the Angolan situation coupled with the Reagan's so-called policy of constructive engagement towards South Africa will lead to a zero-sum game for the U.S. in the Southern Africa sub-region. Economically the U.S. is Angola's number one trading partner with an annual trade total of over $1 billion as of 1985. American would be the loser as the American oil installations of the Gulf oil Corporation in Angola would be confiscated, possibly without compensation.[66] Diplomatically, the U.S. would suffer a serious blow in the international community as it would invariably be regarded that America has openly declared itself a bedfellow with fascist South Africa in Pretoria's sworn determination to destabilize the SADCC States. The consequence of the current marriage of convenience between the U.S. and the UNITA will increase the CIA covert activities in the Southern Africa sub-region, and will buy U.S. disaster in Africa. Although, against the Defense Intelligence Agency's confidence in UNITA's prospects, "the CIA and the State Department Bureau of Intelligence have apparently concluded that the UNITA led by Jonas Savimbi cannot win militarily against the Angolan Government and has little prospect of ever forming a coalition government with the MPLA".[67]

However, in Africa as a whole, no such role as to include in the MPLA government is envisaged for UNITA. UNITA is of no threat to the MPLA government in Angola without the collaboration of the South African and American (the Reagan administration) authorities. Many of the African countries which supported UNITA during the Angolan second war of national liberation between 1975 and 1976 have normalized their relations with Luanda. For example, Zaire normalized its relations with the Angolan Government in 1978, while Senegal and Gabon did the same in 1982. Only the Government of Morocco riveted to the American perception of UNITA. The Moroccan government is one of the foreign collaborators helping UNITA in the training of its guerrillas. Just like South Africa, the Moroccan government's aircraft are flying American weapons into the UNITA occupied areas of Southern Angola. King Hassan has been a defender of the French and U.S. interests in Africa, as shown most starkly by his dispatch of Moroccan troops to Zaire in the 1977 and 1978 crisis in Shaba Province.[68] Morocco's role in the Shaba crisis of 1977-1978 was that of French and American surrogate. King Hasaan has continued with his anti-African Liberation activities by helping fly American weapons to the UNITA rebel group in Angola.

The Soviet involvement in Angola is positive, and very important to the survival of Angola since its independence in 1975. The Soviet assistance to Angola is not only in the military aspect. For instance, just as Cuba's assistance to Angola was invaluable in coping with the post war break in technical services so also the Soviet help was very crucial to the MPLA survival since 1975. The Cuban doctors, dentists, nurses, medical technicians, education experts and agricultural specialists were "joined by an influx of technical personnel from the Soviet Union and Eastern Europe, in the Angolan battle of national reconstruction".[69] From a reliable source by an Angolan official, the Soviet Petroleum technicians are assisting in the mining of the Angolan oil; and many Soviet fishing specialists are working in the fishing industry in Angola. There are also Soviet doctors and teachers assisting in the Angolan reconstruction.

The Soviet Union is interested in the success of SADCC. To show its interest, Moscow has delegated East Germany to sit in SADCC sessions as surrogate, and even to offer unquantified financial support.[70] The Soviet Union does not want to get directly involved in SADCC because of the prominent Western role in SADCC. Secondly, the Soviet Union always claims that the West was responsible for the poor condition, the inhuman treatment and many years of colonial domination and oppressive situation of Southern African and African peoples as a whole. One of the major aims of SADCC states is to integrate their economic development and the need for devising a collective economic strategy to lessen and cut their economic dependence on Pretoria. To this end, SADCC member states hope that reduction of economic dependence not only on the white racist regime in Pretoria, but also on any single external state or group of States.[71] J. A. Shaw, South African chargé d'affaires in Blantyre, Malawi has characterized the economic links between South Africa and its neighbours with these statements:

> Though South Africa is saddened at the
> artificial division of the subcontinent, it

> welcomes the SADCC efforts to improve their
> own economic situation and circumstances... If
> conditions improve and go well around us, then
> the same will apply to South Africa itself...
> If these states are successful, all the
> regional states will become more interdepende-
> nt until a stage is reached where it will be
> to cooperate... Nor do we see SADCC as a
> deliberate move to isolate South Africa.[72]

In any case, President Jose Eduardo dos Santos has categorically ruled out any possibility of a purported "coalition government with UNITA and insisted that this question will not be discussed at any negotiating table".[73]

American foreign policy is designed to serve American interests. The Reagan administration has defined these interests in the Southern African sub-region as the promotion of peace, and regional security and the support of those regimes ideologically sympathetic and supportive of the U.S. policies in the sub-region. Given the fact that these terms are defined in anti-liberation movements and anti-Soviet terms, the pre-occupation with and support for the racist South African regime is the Reagan administration's objective. Thus, there are two conflicting views of the Southern African sub-region as far as the Reagan administration is concerned. First, by linking all political-economic activities in the SADCC states, the Reagan administration is taking the historical and colonial view which accepted South Africa as the regional centre through which most economic transactions took place. Second, the Reagan administration's Southern African policy places any foreign aid programme towards the

SADCC states in a distinctly secondary role within its overall policy framework.

Moreover, the ultimate goal of the Reagan administration's so-called "constructive engagement" in Chester Crocker's words is to "end South Africa's polecat status in the world" and to lead to the "greater acceptance of South Africa within the global framework".[74] This is an irony that the U.S. - the so-called self-proclaimed holder of the torch of human rights and human freedom, a country that is eternally self-righteous about its motive, closes its eyes to, and make money out of the apartheid system which at heart is tantamount to the gradual genocide of the black people of South Africa.[75] According to Howard Wolpe (Democrat from Michigan), Chairman, House Foreign Affairs Sub-Committee on Africa, the fundamental issue as far as the Reagan administration's Southern African policy is concerned is that:

> unless the U.S. and the Western allies make
> the issue of South African aggression outside
> of South Africa itself and make the issue of
> South Africa's economic harassment of the
> neighbouring countries much more of a centre-
> piece of our own (American) diplomacy, South
> Africa will continue to engage in
> destabilizing activities. The only way that
> the cost of that kind of activity can become
> real for South Africa is by a very tough kind
> of diplomacy from America and the European
> allies. I frankly see the present (Reagan)
> administration moving in precisely the
> opposite direction. Indeed, much of the
> recent activity by South Africa with respect
> to the invasions of Angola and with respect to

the harassment of Zimbabwe can be interpreted
precisely to be a result of South Africa's
conclusion that this present (Reagan)
administration is not about to engage in any
kind of overt resistance to such moves. I
think that is very dangerous and very
destructive ultimately of regional stability
and it's destructive of American interests
within the area.[76]

MNR-South African Collaboration:

The Origins of the Mozambique National Resistance
rebel movement have been kept in secrecy since its
formation around 1974-1975.[77] Unlike most of the
nationalist liberation groups in Africa, the MNR was
created by former white Rhodesian intelligence officials
under Ian Smith's minority settler regime, founded by
defeated (European) Portuguese businessmen who had fled
Mozambique after Frelimo took power. Also unlike other
African Liberation Movements, MNR was born not in the
African bush, but in the capital of former white
minority-ruled Rhodesia under Ian Smith.[78] According to
the available sources, Orlando Cristina, a white
Portuguese who was an aide to Jorge Jardim, one of
Mozambique's wealthiest businessmen who fled Mozambique
after Frelimo came to power in 1975, and Andre
Matzangaiza and Alfonso Dhlakama, two former Frelimo
soldiers were the first leaders of MNR. When the MNR
was formed initially, it was kept small, manageable,
clandestine and African.[79] In the words of the former
Rhodesia's intelligence director, Ken Flowers, who was
very instrumental to the creation of the MNR, the
movement "never exceeded 500 men and that was done
purposely. We are not interested in mercenaries, and we

did not want anyone to be able to say this thing had been created by us, so we kept it small".[80]

The Mozambique National Resistance was formed because analysts for the former Rhodesian Central Intelligence Organization wanted to keep close watch on the more than 500 miles of border Zimbabwe shared with Mozambique. Secondly, the former Rhodesian Intelligence Security Forces needed information about Frelimo and about Zimbabwean National Liberation Army (ZANLA) who have launched their war of liberation against the settler-minority regime of Ian Smith. Thirdly, the former Rhodesia Central Intelligence Organization found Portuguese intelligence capabilities inadequate, thus, they decided to create the MNR and established on a farm near the city of Mutare in Zimbabwe and later a clandestine radio station known as the "Voice of Free Africa" was set up, and operated from the Zimbabwe side of the border.[81]

The MNR's Rhodesian connection faded away in 1979, when the Ian Smith rebel regime was finally forced to negotiate with the Zimbabwean nationalist freedom fighters at the Lancaster House talks in London. The MNR were ordered to get out of Zimbabwe with three conditions. One, to bury their arms and return to Mozambique; two, to leave Mozambique through Zimbabwe and settle elsewhere; and three, to get ready to go to work for the South African Boer regime who had become interested in taking over the MNR operation. "The majority of the MNR chose to accept South African control".[82] After the election victory of ZANU-PF in March 1980, and the attainment of the Zimbabwean independence under the leadership of Robert Mugabe on 18 April, 1980, the MNR operation was taken over by the South African military intelligence security. The South

African Military Intelligence regrouped the MNR rebels,
brought in fresh supplies and arms and expanded it with
white former Portuguese secret police and military
personnel who had fled to South Africa from Mozambique
after Mozambican independence. Alfonso Dhlakama, a
former Frelimo soldier with full support and financial
assistance from Jorge Jardim, was made the field
Commander of MNR, after Andrea Matzangaiza was killed in
1979 by the Mozambican forces.[83]

Recruitment into the MNR

Most of the recruits into MNR have been coerced
into joining the group. According to Sara Muchalima, a
26-year old woman who was kidnapped by the MNR, "The
rebels came to my house and told my parents I had to go
with them. My father refused, but they beat him up,
tied my hands, and with a gun to my head took me to
their base at Garangua".[84] Another eyewitness by John
Burlson, a British ecologist held captive by the MNR
bandits for several months in 1982, observed that those
forcibly recruited were kept under armed surveillance
until they participated in their first raids. The
recruits were usually warned that if they fled and were
captured by government troops, they would be killed as
terrorists.[85] Because of fear of retribution, most of
the recruits feel that they have no choice but to stay
and participate in MNR activities, although a number of
these recruits have managed to escape. Secondly, the
MNR has appealed to tribal sentiments, by skillfully
manipulating tribal divisions and appealed to
"traditional" Shona values to gain support. Like the
Portuguese colonial regime, MNR propaganda claims that
Frelimo is dominated by Southerners, and that it has
systematically discriminated against ethnic groups

living in Manica and Sofala provinces, especially the Shona-speaking Ndau and Manica. Most of the MNR military commanders come from these two ethnic groups and this adds credibility to the claim that if Mozambique is regained from the Frelimo government by the MNR, the situation will be reversed. The MNR embraces the traditional chiefs and seeks to enshrine itself in the Shona past in order to enhance its legitimacy. These positions also appeal to the region's "traditionalist" who are dissatisfied with the government's attacks on such traditional practices as bride-price, polygamy, and ancestor worship, which are considered to be reactionary and exploitative. Thirdly, many of the recruits were former Frelimo soldiers who had grown disenchanted with the government's Marxist socialist orientation and who in some cases had run foul of Frelimo's tight code against corruption. Fourthly, the economic problems plaguing Mozambique since its independence make MNR recruitment easier. For instance, the droughts which started since 1980,[86] the Frelimo government's failure to provide sufficient support for the family farming sector, and the lack of consumer goods in the country, especially in Manica, Sofala and Inhambane Provinces provide fertile ground for MNR overtures.[87]

Whatever, the initial attraction of MNR appeals to economic dissatisfaction and ethnic traditional sentiments, wide-scale plundering and increasing terrorism is eroding its support and alienating the rural population which, above all else, wants to be left alone. A captured MNR rebel, Raque admitted that he and his compatriots were ordered to rob and terrorize the rural population in order to discredit the Frelimo Government. "We cut off many peoples ears, and we sent them off and said, now go to Frelimo and say that we have been here".[88]   Another MNR guerrilla said "those whom we did not initially kill were locked in their houses, which were set afire".[89]   According to some reports from Inhambane Province:

> the MNR murdered people and stuffed them in
> wells in order to poison the water, and in one
> of its most violent actions, terrorists
> stopped a packed train on 9 August 1982, and
> raked it with machinegun fire, killing 14 and
> wounding 50 others.[90]

According to documents captured by Mozambican forces in December 1981 South African military advisers and instructors were working with MNR at their Gargua base before it was captured by the government forces. The South African sets up military bases at Zoabostad in the Transvaal Province, trains MNR guerrillas, provides foods, arms and logistical assistance.   Their South African military instructors even participate in raids inside Mozambique with the MNR rebel group, the same way they participate with UNITA in Angola.[91]

By 1983, MNR was conducting a kind of coordinated campaign against the Frelimo government.   For instance, buses, and trains were sabotaged, food supplies from Maputo to remote rural areas were cut off.   Rural peasants who refused to cooperate with them had their ears, lips and noses mutilated.   The oil pipeline between the Mozambican port of Beira and Zimbabwe was blown up several times.   Twenty-four Soviet mining technicians were kidnapped and held for several months. In August of 1982, MNR also kidnapped six Bulgarians working near the Malawi border on a road project[92] sponsored by the SADCC which aims at lessening transport dependence on Pretoria.   MNR activities in Morrumbala district were blamed for delaying a $20 million cotton project funded by France and the African Development Bank.[93] According to reliable sources in the Mozambican capital, Maputo, the South African Boer regime deeply regret Malawi's cooperation ' with the independent Southern African states in joining SADCC. To show its opposition toward Malawi joining SADCC, following the November 1981 SADCC Summit, Pretoria directed MNR bandits to sabotage Malawi's transport routes through Mozambique.[94]

The MNR guerrillas operate in well coordinated units, using sound military tactics. They often appear well-armed and well-fed guerrillas. But unlike other African Liberation Movements, the MNR has never developed its own ideology nor articulated a political alternative to the Marxist Frelimo government it seeks to overthrow. Nevertheless, the MNR is an important arm and has played a significant role in Pretoria's undeclared economic, political and psychological war against Mozambique and its SADCC allies. By the end of 1983, MNR rebels were operating with the full backing of the South African troops in most of Mozambique's eastern provinces, and at times, even in the suburbs of Maputo. The Mozambican government estimated that between 1975 and 1982, the MNR campaign had cost the country $3.8 billion.[95] Combined with drought of 1981 to 1984, and unsuccessful government economic policies, the rebel campaign has pushed Mozambique into an economic mess, that was a key factor in persuading President Machel to negotiate the 1984 Nkomati agreement with South Africa, (see Appendix 6, page 303) for full text of the Nkomati Accords signed on 16 March, 1984 between Mozambique and South Africa.

The Nkomati Accords

The origin of the Nkomati Accords can be traced to Deinde Fernandez, a Nigerian business tycoon based in Geneva, Switzerland and Connecticut, United States. It was Deinde Fernandez, who arranged a secret meeting near New York City in June 1982 between former American Defense Secretary Melvin Laird and Mozambican Foreign Minister Joacquin Chissano.[96] At the time, Maputo wished to renew dialogue with Washington and Mr. Fernandez who has been a close friend of Samora Machel turned out to be the best link man. Through business contacts Fernandez has known Barry Shihito, Melvin Laird's assistant when the latter was Secretary of Defense under former President Nixon. Following a series of meetings held at Fernandez's suburban home in Connecticut late in 1982 and early 1983 Melvin Laird introduced the representatives of Mozambique to the U.S. State Department officials,[97] who in turn connected them with the Reagan administration.

Prior to 1982, Portugal because of its own economic interest in Mozambique has been trying to bring South Africa and Mozambique to a negotiating table. The U.S. did not lose the opportunity in further exploring the groundwork already laid by the Portuguese, and saw in Mozambican economic plight a chance for shaping the regional events in its perceived interest. The Reagan administration believe that resolving the differences between South Africa and its neighbours will help to reduce Soviet influence in Southern Africa sub-region, which the American believes thrives only in conflict situations. Acting in concert with Portugal, the Reagan administration offered Mozambique and South Africa its good offices to enable the two states to resolve their differences. Indeed, the extent of the U.S. involvement in the Nkomati Process entailed all the categories of third party intervention.[98]

According to a reliable source, the first major contact between South African officials and their Mozambican counterparts took place at the border town of Nkomati port in late 1982 and middle of 1983.[99] Nothing concrete came out of these meetings. After the return of President Machel from his European tour in October 1983,[100] it was reported that Mozambican and South African officials held a meeting in Swaziland. The exact agenda of the talks were not known, given the air of secrecy that the talks were essentially preliminary, defining the scope and form future negotiations were to take.

Subsequently, parallel discussions were held in Maputo and Pretoria. As in the previous contacts, no information was available besides the cryptic remark of a South African spokesman that "matters of mutual interest were discussed". Indications about the existence of diplomatic negotiations between Mozambique and South Africa became public knowledge when President Machel acknowledged in an interview granted in Guinea Bissau that the "talks" with Pretoria were "essential to find a modus vivendi with South Africa". Another meeting at ministerial level in Muabane, Swaziland in December 1983 between the two countries set up a number of working groups. These groups · were to examine specific thorny issues. Among others, these issues were security, economic relations, tourism and the Cabora Bassa Dam.[101]

These working groups deliberated in guarded secrecy and alternated their meetings between Maputo and Pretoria. In February 1984, a one day meeting was held in Maputo to examine the reports of the different study groups. A joint communique issued at the end of the talks said that the two parties had agreed in principle to sign a "non-aggression and good neighbourliness treaty". A Joint Security Commission the communique continued was to be set up to oversee the treaty implementation. The culmination of the series of those secret negotiations between South Africa and Mozambique was the signing of the Nkomati Accord on March 16, 1984.[102] An eleven article accord, and essentially a non-aggression and good neighbour agreement between the two states.[103] The Nkomati Accord between Mozambique and the South Africa Boer regime is the first and most spectacular break-through (besides the ones signed with Malawi and Swaziland) in South Africa's regional diplomacy since the Boer-dominated National Party has come to power in 1948. The Reagan administration as a close ally of the apartheid regime in South Africa was very instrumental to the negotiations that led to the signing of the 16 March, 1984 Nkomati Accord. The Nkomati River Accord was a pact of non-aggression between Mozambique and South Africa.[104] Under the Nkomati agreement, Mozambique agreed to curtail sharply the activities of the ANC of South Africa operating against the Pretoria regime from Mozambican territory, in return for a South African Commitment to eliminate its support for the MNR. Mozambique fulfilled its own part of the bargain by expelling most of the ANC freedom fighters living in Mozambique,[105] (See Appendix 3, page 298, on the Communiqué of the Arusha Frontline States Meeting). But the South African MNR backed rebels continued to function inside Mozambique without apparent impediment.[106] Some sources have claimed that, South African military operatives, aware that Pretoria was about to make a deal with Frelimo, rushed in enough supplies and arms to maintain the MNR for at least a year, after the agreement might have been signed. The same sources also claimed that MNR is receiving funds independent of Pretoria from Portuguese businessmen in South Africa and Lisbon.[107]

In signing the Nkomati Accord, Mozambique believed it was taking a step which could ensure its own self-preservation from the Marauding and destabilizing activities of the MNR guerrillas. Addressing a rally in Maputo a day after signing the Nkomati agreement, President Machel said, "we have closed the tap from which they drank".[108] As it has now turned out, President Machel has misread the Pretoria's intentions. From the Pretoria regime's own perspectives, Nkomati was not a deal designed to relieve the Frelimo government in Maputo of the menace of the MNR guerrillas. On the contrary, it was a calculated strategy at the ANC, the successes of whose freedom fighters inside South Africa was becoming increasingly worrying and threatening to the racist regime. As a base from which it could launch effective guerrilla strikes against the Boer regime in South Africa, Mozambique, as Tanzania had been to Frelimo, was an invaluable rear base for the ANC. It has also become a great and serious threat to the apartheid regime.

Apparently, Nkomati was used by the apartheid regime in South Africa to remove the ANC threat. In what must have been a painful move to demonstrate its sincerity about living up to the letter and spirit of the Nkomati Accord, the Frelimo government in Mozambique has asked the ANC to leave its territory, except for a diplomatic mission of only ten staff in Maputo. The racist South African regime, on the other hand, did very little, if anything to curtail the destructive activities of the MNR guerrillas. The Boer authority in Pretoria pretended that it was unable to control the MNR, and finally in 1985, admitted continuing to supply the MNR guerrillas.[109] The South African racist president even talked of "considering giving military aid to Mozambique if asked to do so publicly by the the West and the Mozambique Government".[110]

Since the Nkomati agreement has been signed in March 1984, South Africa has been trying to negotiate a cease-fire agreement between the Mozambican government and the MNR. The South African apartheid regime for whom the Nkomati accord marked a critical breakthrough from its international diplomatic isolation and political ostracism is eager to see Frelimo and the MNR sign an agreement that will end the war in Mozambique.[111] However, with the South African moves to bring Mozambican government and MNR to the same negotiation table, the MNR, like the UNITA in Angola is seeking an agreement that will grant them a role in a new, non-Marxist Mozambican government, a concession Frelimo leaders insist they will never make. However, barring such a deal with the current situation inside Mozambique, and in Southern Africa as a whole the war to sabotage SADCC efforts and the Mozambique agony may continue for some time.

NOTES

[1] "Assassination as an Extension of Politics" _Africa Now_ No. 18, (October 1982), pp. 91-93.

[2] For details see Layi Abegunrin, "Southern African Development Coordination Conference: Politics of Dependence" in Ralph Onwuka and Amadu Sesay (eds.) _The Future of Regionalism in Africa_ (London: Macmillan Press, 1985), pp. 351-371.

[3] "ANC, Tutu and Buthelezi oppose land handover to Swaziland" _Sowetan_ (Soweto) 15, 16 and 22 July 1982. See also David Robbins "Swaziland: The South African Land Deal", _Africa Report_ November-December 1982, pp. 18-22.

[4] Holger Jensen and Peter Younghusband, "Southern Africa: The Zone of Instability", _Newsweek International_ 6 September, 1982, pp. 20-21.

[5] "SADCC: South African aggression threatens our existence", _Africa Now_ September 1983, pp. 34-35.

[6] For details on the political issues surrounding the Namibian independence questions see Peter Katjavivi, "Namibia: 100 Years of Occupation" _West Africa_, 1 October 1984, pp. 1987-1993. See also Suzanne Cronje, "U.S. Moves against Namibia", _West Africa_, 5 December 1983, pp. 2791-2792.

[7] See Ann Seidman and Neva Seidman Makgetla _Outposts of Monopoly Capitalism: Southern Africa in the Changing Global Economy_ (London: Zed Press, 1980).

[8] V. I. Lenin, _The State and Revolution_ (Moscow: Progress Publishers 1981), p. 11.

[9] Frederick Engels, _The Origin of the Family, Private Property and the State_ with an introduction by Evelyn Reed (New York: Path Finder Press, 1972), p. 160.

[10] V. I. Lenin, _Imperialism, the Highest State of Capitalism_ (Peking: Foreign Language Press, 1973), p. 97.

[11]V. I. Lenin, op. cit., p. 12.

[12]Ibid., pp. 12-13.

[13]See M. M. Noube "The U.S. South Africa and Destabilization in Southern Africa", Journal of African Marxists Issue 6, October 1984, p. 18.

[14]See Aziz Pahad, "Apartheid Terror: How Pretoria Wages War on Africa", Sechaba March 1983, p. 21.

[15]Origin of South African Policy of Destabilization can be traced to its "outward-looking policy" which involved interference and involvement in the domestic affairs of neighbouring states. See Kenneth W. Grundy, Confrontation and Accommodation in Southern Africa: The Limits of Independence (Berkeley: University of California Press, 1973), pp. 250-275.

[16]Aziz Pahad, op. cit., p. 24.

[17]H. E. Newsum and Olayiwola Abegunrin, United States Foreign Policy Towards Southern Africa: Andrew Young and Beyond (London: Macmillan Press, 1987).

[18]Horace Campbell, "Total War and Total Failure" Zimbabwe Herald (Harare) 9 December, 1983.

[19]Morning Star (Johannesburg), 5 March 1983.

[20]"South Africa: The Total Strategy Policy", ACR 1979/1980, pp. B 766-767. See also Moto (Zimbabwe), February, 1983.

[21]On Mozambique Menace by the apartheid South Africa see Marcelino Komba "Mozambique's return to arms" Africa, June 1981, pp. 52-62. See also "Mozambique-South Africa: Diplomacy and Destabilization", Africa, March 1984, pp. 34-36.

[22]"South Africa: Underground War heavier and nastier" Africa Now October 1981, p. 42.

[23]"Botswana, Lesotho, Swaziland: trapped in Pretoria's net", Africa Now, October 1982, pp. 95-96. See also AIM (Maputo), No. 83, April-May 1983, pp. 1-4 and Janice Turner, "Rising tide of vengeance", South July 1983, pp. 18. See also "Pretoria's midnight raid in Newsweek International, 20 December 1982, p. 16.

[24]The Rand Daily Mail (Johannesburg) 14 January 1983. See also "Lesotho: More Killings" Africa Now September 1982, p. 34.

[25]On South African bandit-style operations in the Frontline States and destabilization of its neighbours as a major foreign policy element see Jonathan Bloch and Andre Weir, "Pretoria's dirty tricks army", Africa Now, October 1982, pp. 91-93. See also Sowetan (Soweto) 7 July 1982.

[26]"South Africa: Constellation of Southern African States", ACR 1979/1980 (1980), pp. B 772-773.

[27]Editorial Comment, "U.S.: The evil Empire?" Daily Sketch (Ibadan) 11 December, 1984, p. 2.

[28]Ibid.

[29]See Fola Soremekun, ANGOLA: The Road to Independence (Ile-Ife: Obafemi Awolowo University Press, 1983), p. 8.

[30]Ibid., p. 7.

[31]Ibid., pp. 7-10.

[32]Ibid., p. 19.

[33]Ellen Ray, William Schaap et al. (eds.) Dirty Work 2: The C.I.A. in Africa (Secaucus, NJ: Lyle Stuart, 1979), p. 221.

[34]Ibid.

[35]Africa Yearbook and Who's Who 1977 (London: Africa Journal Limited 1976), pp. 240-241.

[36]Proof of Compromising Connection between UNITA and Portuguese Secret Police Policia Internationales de Defesado Estado (PIDE), emerged when the PIDE files were made available by the Portuguese army in Lisbon for inspection by journalists in August of 1982. For details see "Savimbi and PIDE: File discovered" Africa Now September 1982, p. 32.

[37]Ibid.

[38]"Angola: Savimbi's rebellion" Africa, September 1982, p. 15.

[39]Fola Soremekun, op. cit., p. 148.

[40]"Angola: Savimbi's rebellion, op. cit., p. 15.

[41]Since December 1983, the representatives of SWAPO and South African government have been meeting in Cape Verde Islands, See "NAMIBIA: SWAPO will fight on" in West Africa, 6 August 1984, p. 1606.

[42]Banji Adeyanju, "Racists Subdue Frontline States" Sunday Concord (Ikeja, Lagos), 29 April, 1984, p. 12.

[43]"Racist Troops still in Angola", Daily Sketch (Ibadan), 6 June 1984, p. 6.

[44]ACR 1968/1969, (1969), p. 390.

[45]Oyeleye Oyediran (ed.) Nigerian Government and Politics under Military Rule 1976-1979 (London: Macmillan Press, 1979), p. 155.

[46]"ANGOLA", West Africa, 26 September, 1983, pp. 2220. See also Mark Doyle, "Southern Africa: Boers on the Offensive", West Africa, 17 October, 1983, pp. 2397-2402.

[47]"Angola: Refinery Sabotaged", ARB Vol. 18, November 15-December 14, 1981, p. 6240.

[48]See Joseph Hanlon, "Hostage to apartheid: Frontline Angola", South (London), June 1983, pp. 12-13.

[49]"Angola: Savimbi's rebellion" op. cit., p. 16.

[50]John Marcum, "Angola: Perilous Transition to Independence", in G. M. Carter and Patrick O'Meara (eds.) Southern Africa: The Continuing Crisis (Bloomington: Indiana University Press, 1979), p. 192.

[51]See "Angola-South Africa: War and Blackmail" Africa, March 1984, pp. 37-39.

[52]Colin Legum, "Cease firing, start talking: South Africa counts the cost", New African, March 1984, pp. 12-14. See also "Namibia: Pulling a fast one" South March 1984, p. 30.

[53]See "South Africa: Whites Against War" and "Namibia: The Silent War", Africa, April 1983, pp. 22 & 32-33.

[54]"Angola: Savimbi's rebellion", op. cit.

[55]See The Washington Post 20 November, 1979.

[56]"More about Savimbi's friends" West Africa, 15 October 1984, pp. 2071-2072.

[57]The Observer (London), 26 March 1978.

[58]H. E. Newsum and O. Abegunrin, op. cit., p. 94.

[59]Alexandre Mboukou, "An African Triangle" Africa Report (New York) Vol. 27, No 5, September-October 1982, p. 40.

[60]David B. Ottaway, "Covert Angolan Aid Encouraged: Reagan sees more chance of success than in open Assistance" The Washington Post, 23 November 1985, p. 4.

[61]Ibid.

[62]"Oil firm Resists Pullout Pressure", Daily Sketch (Ibadan) 31 January 1986, p. 8.

212

[63]"Savimbi Meets Reagan", Daily Sketch (Ibadan), 1 February, 1986, p. 8.

[64]Ibid.

[65]See Rita Cauli "U.S. Raising the Stakes in Nicaragua", Africa-Asia (Paris), January 1986, p. 25.

[66]See Layi Abegunrin, "Angola and the U.S. Since 1975", Lusophone Areas Studies Journal, No 4. (June 1985), pp. 51-82. Some of the U.S. Companies involved in Angola include Boeing, General Tire and Rubber, Mobil, Lockheed and Conoco. Chevron has $600 million in Angolan assets and is by far the largest American investor in Angola, the U.S. being Angola's largest trading partner.

[67]"ANGOLA: CIA Admits Savimbi Cannot Win", West Africa (February 17, 1986), p. 378.

[68]Tony Hodges Africa Report, Vol. 27, No. 4, July-August 1982, p. 10.

[69]John Marcum, "Angola: Perilous Transition to Independence" op. cit., p. 1983.

[70]Douglas Anglin "Economic Liberation and Regional Cooperation in Southern Africa: SADCC and PTA" International Organization, Vol. 37, No. 4 (1983), p. 698.

[71]SADEX (Washington, D.C.) Vol. 2, No. 3, May-June 1980, p. 3.

[72]Financial Times (London), 20 November, 1982, p. 4.

[73]"Angola: No Compromise with UNITA", West Africa, 7 January, 1985, p. 39.

[74]Bernard Magubane "Constructive Engagement or Disingeneous Support for Apartheid" ISSUE: A Journal of Africanist Opinion Vol. XII, Nos. 3/4 (Fall/Winter 1982), p. 10.

[75]Ibid.

[76]Howard Wolpe "U.S. Economic Assistance, SADCC and Southern African Development: A Trans-Africa Forum Seminar" in Trans-Africa Forum, Vol. 1, No. 1 (Summer 1982), p. 32.

[77]Horace Campbell, "Nkomati, before and after war, Reconstruction and Dependence in Mozambique" Journal of African Marxists, Issue 6 October, 1984, pp. 51-52.

[78]Glenn Frankel, "South African-backed Rebels Weaken Mozambique" The Washington Post, 8 October 1984, p. 1.

[79]Ibid., p. 36

[80]Ibid.

[81]Ibid.

[82]Ibid.

[83]"Mozambique: Dissidents by Proxy" Africa, September 1983, p. 20.

[84]Allen and Barbara Isaacman, "Mozambique: South Africa's Hidden War" Africa Report, Vol. 27, November-December 1982, p. 6.

[85]Ibid.

[86]See Senator Denis R. Norman, former Zimbabwean Minister of Agriculture's report on "Africa's Drought: Food Security for Southern Africa", Africa Report, Vol, 29, No. 4, July-August 1984, pp. 15-18.

[87]Voice of America Radio report on "Mozambique's Drought and MNR in Inhambane Province", 29 December, 1984.

[88]Allen and Barbara Isaacman op. cit., p. 6.

[89]Ibid.

[90]Ibid., pp. 6-7.

[91]For Comprehensive reports of South Africa's acts of aggression and its involvement in the killings of the citizens of the SADCC States see ministry of External Relations, People's Republic of Angola, White Paper on Acts of Aggression by the Racist South Africa Regime Against the People's Republic of Angola: 1975-1982 (Luanda, 1982).

[92]The Guardian (London) 20 August, 1982.

[93]Zimbabwe Sunday News (Harare) June 27, 1982.

[94]David Ward "Malawi: Sabotage by South Africa", Africa, November 1982, p. 28.

[95]Glenn Frankel, op. cit., p. 37.

[96]For details on Mr. Deinde Fernandez's close association and friendship with Presidents Samora Machel of Mozambique and Eduardo dos Santos of Angola see Le Matin de Paris (Paris) 1 October 1984, pp. 14, see also The Guardian (Lagos), 23 December 1984, p. 9.

[97]Ibid.

[98]See Africa, March 1984, pp. 22-26.

[99]Ibid.

[100]Ibid.

[101]"Squaring the Circle", Africa Now, March , 1984, pp. 35-38.

[102]See the "Text of the Nkomati Accord in Appendix 2.

[103]Ibid.

[104]Ibid.

[105]See "Communiqué of the Arusha Frontline States Meetings: Arusha, Tanzania: 29 April 1984 Final Communique", in Appendix 3.

[106]"A Promise Botha Won't Keep" Africa, June 1984, pp. 36-37. See also "Mozambique: MNR Still Active", Africa Report July-August 1984, p. 50 and Mohammed Musa Mawani "Nkomati's False Dawn", New Africa, October 1984, pp. 14-15.

[107]Glenn Frankel, op. cit., p. 37. See also Mark Doyle "Mozambique: The Nkomatic Process" West Africa, 15 October, 1984, p. 2074.

[108]AIM, the official News Agency of Mozambique Reports (Maputo), January 1985.)

[109]"Failure of Non-aggression Pact: Machel Blames South Africa", Daily Sketch (Ibadan), 22 March 1985, p. 6.

[110]"Botha Pledges Military Aid to Mozambique", Daily Sketch (Ibadan) 19 March, 1985, p. 6.

[111]Allister Sparks, "South Africa Announces Truce by Mozambique and Rebels", The Washington Post, 4 October 1984, pp. 1 & 26.

CHAPTER 6

SOUTHERN AFRICA AFTER THE NKOMATI ACCORD

Political analysts are divided over what exactly
are the objectives of the South African white regime in
signing the Nkomati Accord. This is a controversy which
has been further compounded by South Africa's disclosure
of a similar pact it has secretly signed with Swaziland
(in 1983) a year earlier, and the unrelenting effort of
Pretoria to force Botswana and Lesotho into signing an
Nkomati styled unequal treaty.

SOUTH AFRICA'S POLITICAL, ECONOMIC AND SECURITY OBJECTIVES IN NKOMATI ACCORD

One school of thought[1] believed that South Africa's
motive for friendship treaties with its neighbours of
which the Nkomati Accord is just one manifestation was
borne out of its belated realization of the futility of
its destabilization strategy. According to this
argument, South Africa has realized the weakness of its
much vaulted military brawl. Consequently, it needed
some breathing space given the immense material and
human toil its wars of aggression against the Southern
African Liberation Movements (the ANC and SWAPO), Angola
and Mozambique are wrecking on its economy. This is
clearly put that:

> The cost of destabilization has been for South
> Africa both human and financial. Too many
> young white South Africans have been returning
> from the regime's wars in coffins. According
> to the man who should know, Defense Minister
> Magnus Milan, 738 South African soldiers died
> in action over the past year. This is not
> good for white morale. With prospect of a
> major military defeat in Angola, and with many
> more white conscripts losing their lives, the
> South Africans have had to negotiate with the
> Marxist neighbour they once despised.[2]

This argument though strong on the surface cannot
explain the totality of South Africa's regime objectives
in signing the Nkomati Accord. The fact that Pretoria
had signed a similar accord with Swaziland in 1983, and
is putting severe pressure on Botswana and Lesotho to
sign a similar accord did show that her objectives
transcend (military) security calculation alone implicit
in the forgoing argument. This conclusion derived from
the fact that Lesotho and Swaziland are known not to
harbour any ANC military infrastructure in their
respective territories.

Another argument[3], comprising mostly the apologists
of South Africa's apartheid policies, saw the Nkomati
Accord as the objection of South Africa's friendly
disposition towards its black-ruled neighbouring
countries. Racist white-ruled South Africa, it is held
as the most industrially advanced state in Southern
Africa sub-region in particular and in African continent
as a whole, has a higher stake in the preservation of
peace in (the region) Southern Africa. Thus, South
Africa's peace endeavours, the argument goes, has been

frustrated in the past by the rabid unremitting hostility of its neighbours.

This argument coming as it were from the South African Press is too self-serving to warrant any attention. At any rate, South African relations with its neighbours had been characterized by the recurrent theme of the wholesale employment of bullying tactics as the instrument of diplomacy.[4]

Yet another argument viewed South Africa's objectives in mainly economic terms. This economic centred explanation of Pretoria's objectives in the Nkomati Accord has two dimensions. The first which is encapsuled in a liberal mode of explanation, points at South Africa's rising unemployment put at over 3 million, rising inflation that stood at 11 percent, dwindling capital inflow from the west and rising military budget of $3.16 billion for 1984,[5] among others as compelling necessity which disposes South Africa towards greater regional accommodation.[6] All these put together simply, show that South Africa signed the Nkomati Accord so as to resolve its nightmarish security problems, and to enable her to give greater attention to her economic problems.

Whatever attraction this argument may have, it is obviously too simplistic to explain the totality of Pretoria's possible motivations. For instance, why did Pretoria with its economic problems give military and logistical support to the MNR rebel groups, whose activities cut off between 8 and 10 percent of her electricity requirement which came from the Cabora Bassa Dam in Mozambique?

Another related economic-centred argument[7] employing a political economy mode of analysis saw the Nkomati Accord as South Africa's attempt to resolve the contradictions inherent in what Timothy Shaw described as "South Africa's sub-imperial standing" within the international capitalist system.[8] Furthermore, the west view the entire Southern Africa sub-region as "a single political economy" with the centre of "accumulation in South Africa". In signing the Nkomati Accord, South Africa was not only seeking to resolve its economic problems but also enhancing its value to western capitalism as she is creating a conductive condition with such an accord to facilitate international capital penetration of the Southern Africa sub-region.

This argument looks very sound logically, especially if the disinterested role of the U.S. in the Nkomati Process is taken into account. However, like a similar attempt at a monocausal explanation of so complex a phenomenon as state motivation, it is open to the objection that it cannot explain the totality of Pretoria's objectives. However, it would be more appropriate to analyze South African objectives within the framework of national interest.

Joseph Frankel defines national interest as being "the sum total of a nation's interest".[9] While Donald Nuechterlein defines it as "the perceived needs and desires of a sovereign state which constitute its external environment".[10] He went further to categorize these "needs" and "desires" in a descending order of priority into:

1. The protection of the nation-state and citizens from the threat of physical violence by another country, and/or protection from an externally inspired threat to the national political system.

2. The enhancement of the nation state's well-being in relation with other states.

3. World order interest in the form of the maintenance of an international political and economic system in which the nation state can feel secure, and in which its citizens, and commerce can operate peacefully outside their borders.

4. The protection and furtherance of a set of values which the citizens of a nation-state share, and believe to be universally good.[11]

The Nkomati Accord could be analyzed within these interest rankings. Therefore, from the point of view of South Africa's white regime, the Nkomati Accord is a diplomatic master-stroke designed to achieve substantial part of the interest highlighted above within its subordinate environment in particular.[12]

THE NKOMATI ACCORD AND THE PRESERVATION OF THE APARTHEID SOUTH AFRICA

A commentator once said,

The Republic of South Africa is the classic case of a country whose foreign relations are determined largely by its domestic policy of apartheid. That unique system of government which requires that skin colour (sic) shall be the crucial factor in daily lives of the nation's twenty-two million people.[13]

In unique case of South Africa, the preservation of the nation (the Afrikanernation) is synonymous with the preservation of the values of apartheid. The goal of South Africa's foreign policy is therefore, to preserve this core interest. Evidently, this interest is under an unprecedented challenge from both within and without. Since the military component of the challenge in the shape of the ANC guerrilla activities inside South

Africa represented for Pretoria the greatest threat, its objectives in the accord is primarily to neutralize the threat posed by the ANC. Article Two of the Nkomati Accord (See Appendix 6, page 303) which forbids the signatories from allowing their respective territories as a base by any "organization or individuals" to commit "acts of violence", is instructive in this regard. Given the ubiquitous nature of South Africa's intelligence outfit, the importance of Mozambican territory as sanctuary for ANC freedom fighters cannot be overemphasized.

Another important dimension to the self-preservation goal of the accord is discernible from the sequence of events that followed the signing of the accord. It is worth noting that there has been a half-hearted attempt by P. W. Botha to reform what some analysts called "petty apartheid". Today the black majority in South Africa do not want reform but negotiation for democratic majority rule. The so-called "constitutional reforms", which gave a deceptive semblance of power sharing with the coloured and Indian community,[14] and the glib talk about the abrogation of the mixed marriage Act of 1949, one of the legal underpinnings of petty apartheid are some of the measures being designed to win the confidence of South Africa's so-called non-violent opposition. In essence, the Nkomati Accord is a cleverly designed subterfuge by Pretoria to buy time to initiate superficial domestic reform of apartheid so as to ensure the preservation of South Africa's dominant white structure.

More importantly, there is evidence that South Africa is trying to create a cordon sanitaire of black ruled states reminiscent of the white buffer offered by the former Rhodesia and the Portuguese colonies of

Angola, and Mozambique before 1975. This is clearly discernible from the all out treaty-making spree embarked upon by Pretoria. Creating a network of friendly states in its northern borders fits well into South Africa's traditional defense assumptions that saw the Limpopo river as its natural defense limit.[15]

It is also possible that Pretoria believed that an appearance of having a semblance of friendly relations with the neighbouring states in general, and the Marxist FRELIMO government of Mozambique in particular will blunt the revolutionary appeal of the latter and have a profound psychological telling effect on her oppressed black majority. South Africa stands to gain immensely in terms of security if the oppressed black majority relapses into apathy because of the tremendous limitations the accord had placed on the military activities of the anti-apartheid forces.

Admittedly, an unwitting outcome of the Nkomati Accord, and the agreements between South Africa and Swaziland on the one hand, and Angola on the other is that these countries have been subtly enlisted in Pretoria's devilish battle to have security. The lack of which has caused in the first instance its repugnant apartheid policies. Significantly, in line with its obligation under article three of the Nkomati Accord, that forbids the presence of "any organization or individuals that plan acts of aggression against the other", the Mozambican leadership has terminated the ANC military presence in Mozambican territory.

Pretoria must have been relishing the prospect of an Nkomati Accord inspired peaceful South Africa, as Africans are treated to the agonizing spectacle of a joint Mozambican and Swaziland security hunt down of ANC nationalist fighters under the supervisory eye of a joint Mozambican-South African Commission.[16]

However, whatever security gains Pretoria envisaged seemed to be transient. This conclusion is clearly supported by the increasing security nightmare, the unabating wave of black unrest had created. As Sam Nolutshungu rightly observed, "South Africa might succeed too well externally and not sufficiently at home".[17] Implicit in this is the fact that Pretoria's goodwill must never be taken for granted, Nkomati Accord notwithstanding.

THE NKOMATI ACCORD AND BOTHA'S NOTION OF A CONSTELLATION OF SOUTHERN AFRICAN STATES

The Nkomati Accord could be seen as an attempt by Pretoria to realize its historic economic objectives in the Southern Africa sub-region. Since the early 1960s when South Africa formulated its so-called "outward policy";[18] Afrikaner (Boer) nationalists[19] have argued the case for the relentless pursuit of what Professor Huam aptly described as South Africa's "sub-regional manifest destiny".[20] Translated into practice, this policy urges on South Africa a role parallel to that of the U.S. in the Americas. As succinctly put by Innes, "our economic and political objectives in Southern Africa are to harness all natural and human resources from Table Mountain to the border of the Congo river".[21]

Significantly, P. W. Botha had resuscitated this old dream when he explicitly compared his country's role in the sub-continent to that of the U.S. in the Western hemisphere, citing "special responsibility" in the region similar to the Monroe Doctrine in the "promotion of stability and strengthening of democratic forces against communist subversion in the region".[22] A major snag to Pretoria's imperial dream has been the tenacious opposition to South Africa's hegemonistic design and its apartheid policies by the SADCC states and this has become a confrontation between SADCC and apartheid South Africa. An opposition further reinforced by the substantial shift in the regional balance, emerged in the wake of Zimbabwe's independence which enhanced the prospect for greater cooperation between the independent black-ruled Southern Africa states (SADCC states).

Given the failure of the alternative of military coercion thus far to create a "moderate leadership" network that is patterned after Malawi in the sub-region. South Africa had merely altered its strategy to call into existence, a pliable leadership in the SADCC states that would be favourably disposed towards maintaining a clientage relationship with her through such dubious peace accords. A regional economic order, implicit in the Pretoria sponsored "constellation of Southern African states", which envisaged a close economic union between racist South Africa and its "spinoff statelets" (Bantustans), the "captive states" of Lesotho and Swaziland, Angola, Botswana, Mozambique, Zambia and Zimbabwe will create the conditions for uninhibited South Africa penetration of these countries.

A further security oriented economic consideration is also discernible from the Nkomati Accord. South Africa hoped that working for regional accommodation will enhance her value to the west. It is instructive to note that western capitalism views the entire sub-region as one economic unit with the centre of accumulation in South Africa.[23] Pretoria also hopes that new western investment would make for a more buoyant economy. This will enable her to put into motion the newly conceived counter-insurgency strategy which emphasizes the need to win the hearts and minds of the black population through elite accommodation.[24] Since this strategy is more concerned with class alliances within South Africa as against the time-honoured doctrine of state racism, South Africa's intention is to create an urban black bourgoisie with vested interest in the preservation of the racist state in the long-run.

The same logic dictated that South Africa will somehow have to end its perpetual border wars sooner or later. Evidently, these wars impose a fiscal crisis that dries up the funds needed to reward collaboration and to effect the amelioration that is intended to "win the hearts and minds" of the black population.[25]

This economic and security dimension of the Nkomati Accord is aptly reflected by Lieutenant-General Dutton, South African Chief of Staff Operations when he said:

> The military role in national security can no longer be confined exclusively to the employment of armed force. It is broadened to contributory roles, virtually every other sphere of strategic action and specifically in the psychological, economic and political sphere.[26]

A significant event since the signing of the accord is the follow up series of economic agreements between Mozambique and South Africa. This trend could only reinforce Mozambique dependence on Pretoria in the long-run. Whatever the short-term gains of economic cooperation with Pretoria, an economically penetrated Mozambique given its importance to Zambia, and Zimbabwe in terms of rail and Port facilities will have a profound negative impact on the objectives of the SADCC states.

THE NKOMATI ACCORD AND SOUTH AFRICA'S QUEST FOR REGIONAL AND INTERNATIONAL RESPECTABILITY

In the contemporary international political system, nation states according to Harold Laswell pursued "trinity of political goals-deference, income and safety".[27] For a pariah state like South Africa, the goal of winning acceptability and respect within the comity of nations cannot be overstressed.

One of the objectives of Pretoria in the Nkomati Accord was to break out of the isolationist shell, adopt African diplomacy, and moral weight of world opinion imposed on her. Pretoria doubtlessly calculated that striking a deal with a radical regime could enable conservative African states to deal with her more openly. This prospect would thus undermine the OAU position that frowns at any kind of intercourse with the racist regime in South Africa. Africa Now noted that, "photos of South African ministers shaking the hand of Samora Machel will doubtless make a major contribution to the regime's attempt to break out of its international isolation, arms embargo, disinvestment, sports boycott and calls for economic sanctions".[28]

Beyond this, South Africa also hoped to use the false image of a peace loving state the accord unwittingly conferred to end what M. Ncube described as South Africa's "polecat status in the world".[29] Louis Nel, South Africa's Deputy foreign minister argued that:

> The talks with Mozambique meant that there was now a stable order in South Africa, and it was useless for people in the west to try to overturn this. If the Marxist government in Mozambique is prepared to accept us as legitimate negotiating partners, then why would anyone else try to boycott us?[30]

Pretoria's assumptions in this regard were hardly a wide gamble given the red carpet reception accorded Pieter W. Botha during his eight-nation Western European tour, that followed shortly after the signing of the Nkomati Accord.[31] In the same vein, the accord did provide justification for the authors of "constructive engagement" in the U.S. to intensify cooperation with the white minority regime in South Africa.[32] Undoubtedly, the current orchestrated campaign over the so-called new "direction of reform" that P. W. Botha is said to be leading South Africa towards, immensely benefited from the Nkomati Accord.

It is significant to note that Botha's speeches during his European tour in his whistle stops dealt with the issue of western aid for Mozambique.[33] There could be no greater challenge to African diplomacy than the arch-priest of the evil apartheid system posing as the solicitor of aid to an African state. It is instructive to note at this juncture that there was an increasing debate in the west and in U.S. in particular, on the merits of continuing the United Nations embargo against Pretoria, now that South Africa has become a "respectable member" of the international community – thanks to the Nkomati Accord. It is worth recalling that, though the west and north America had honoured the U.N. sanctions against South Africa more in the breach, they have nevertheless had an enormous impact on Pretoria. More importantly, the sanctions remain a symbolic gesture of world moral disapproval of the conscience-assailing practice of apartheid.

Timothy Shaw[34] aptly surmised, that the international respectability of South Africa is dependent on co-existence in Southern Africa. Already the accord is being cited as justification for cultural, and sporting contacts with South Africa. Julian Amery, a British Conservative member of Parliament once remarked, "if South African and Mozambican ministers can dine together in Maputo, who is to say that the MCC (England Leading Cricket Authority) should not play in Johannesburg".[35] The same argument is being raised by racist inclined sporting groups in New Zealand and the Caribbean to justify their sporting flirtation with apartheid South Africa. Within conservative leadership circles in Western Europe; and North America, that have only reluctantly accepted the necessity of South Africa's isolation; there is now open advocacy of a more closer cooperation with Pretoria citing its alleged strategic and ideological importance as an ally in the East-West competition in the Southern Africa sub-continent.[36]

That the Nkomati accord had enhanced the image of South Africa beyond what P. W. Botha could possible have thought is beyond questioning. What remains to be seen is how long the euphoria of peace created by the accord will continue to influence the false image of a peace-lover, that Botha enjoyed after the Nkomati Agreement in the west. Perhaps, more shockers could be in the offing as events continue to unfold. It is only hoped that a dreaded scenario painted by an African foreign minister while addressing the U.N. General Assembly that, "Tomorrow, maybe we shall see Pretoria asking for membership of the OAU, what do they want us to do (referring to the Mozambican leadership)... Welcome Botha to Addis Ababa with applause and hugs Nkomati-style".[37] This will not come to pass. However, the fact that such a prospect is contemplated at all testifies to the negative effect of the accord to Africa

in general.   Herein lies its implication to both the
frontline states and African diplomacy.

NKOMATI ACCORD AND MOZAMBICAN SECURITY

The Nkomati Accord between Mozambique and South
Africa is the first and most spectacular breakthrough in
South Africa's regional diplomacy since the Afrikaner
(dominated) National Party came to power in 1948. This
is obviously clear from the foregoing analysis that
Pretoria's aims in the accord are at cross-purpose with
the goals and aspirations of Mozambique.   Moreover,
given the zero sum nature of the diplomatic game which
underlined the conflict between South Africa and
Mozambique, any diplomatic gain by Pretoria must be
presumed as a corresponding loss to Mozambique. What
are the potential setbacks of the Nkomati accord to
Mozambique and Southern Africa? I shall seek to answer
this question through the analysis of the implications
of the accord to Mozambique, Liberation struggle in
South Africa, Namibia and SADCC.

What in retrospect seemed an over-sanguine
assessment of the anticipated gains from the accord, was
claimed by Joaquim Chissano, the Mozambican Foreign
Minister when he told a United Nations General Assembly
that the Nkomati agreement was an "instrument for the
defense of Mozambique's national sovereignty and created
conditions for economic development and building of a
Socialist State of Mozambique".[38] To evaluate Joaquim
Chissano's assertion we should use the following working
definitions of national security as analytical base.
According to Walter Lippman:

> A nation is secure to the extent that it is
> not in danger of having to sacrifice core
> values, if it wishes to avoid war, and is able

if challenged to maintain them by victory in
such war.[39]
And Arnold Wolfers believed that security is the absence
of "threat to acquired values such as traditional
sovereignty and independence, socio-economic interest as
well as political traditions".[40]

Examining the above working definitions of national
security, it is evident that the Nkomati accord cannot
bring security to Mozambique as claimed by the
Mozambican leaders. Apparently, only a flawed
assessment of the true designs of Pretoria could
possibly have fed such naive optimism that a pact with
the Boer dominated South Africa could advance the
security of Mozambique, or any of the SADCC States (see
Appendix 8, page 317, on the ANC response to Nkomati
accord).

The Nkomati accord as stated in its clauses
envisaged the reciprocal mutual termination of military
aid and assistance to "dissident elements" within their
respective states. It was for this understanding that
Maputo expelled a number of African National Congress
(ANC) members from Mozambique. As a quid pro quo for
this, South Africa was expected to end its military and
logistic assistance to the Mozambique National
Resistance (MNR or Renamo). Therefore, on balance the
Nkomati agreement looked like an equal and a reasonable
deal from the point of the security interests of both
signatories. However, the test of the fairness of the
agreement could be more meaningfully assessed not just
on paper, but on the ground of the actual political
operations. Here, South African motives are obviously
clear since that accord was signed in 1984. South
Africa, at any time, never owned up to her sponsorship
of the MNR, a fact that made Pretoria's bona fides

questionable in the first place. Furthermore, the MNR had never once attacked ANC military bases in Mozambique, but had rather concentrated on the destruction of vital economic and social infrastructures. This has proved that Pretoria's motives transcend more than ANC military presence in Mozambique. This is a very significant point because it has explained why South Africa had failed to honour her obligation under the terms of the Nkomati accord. See Appendix 6 (page 303) on the text of the Nkomati Accords.

In fact two of the main objectives that led South Africa to sign the Nkomati accord are first, to gain a new bridgehead for the white regime in Pretoria in its desperate "efforts to undermine the unity of the frontline states, destroy the SADCC and replace it with a so-called constellation of states, and thus transform the independent countries of Southern Africa into its client states".[41] Secondly, to use the prestige of the frontline states in the campaign to reduce the international isolation of the white regime in South Africa, and to lend legitimacy to its colonial and fascist policy.[42] Just like South Africa "Israel is one of the de facto supporters of the MNR".[43] Besides, aid from the white South Africa regime, Portuguese businessmen in South Africa and Lisbon;[44] MNR is also being assisted financially and materially by some Arab countries. The Arab aid to MNR is being channeled through the Seychelles (Islands) in the Indian Ocean into the rebel held areas inside Mozambique.

The problem of dissidents is one of the tasks the SADCC countries will face in their march towards economic emancipation. If a solution is not found the situation might degenerate into a stage in which the

SADCC builds infrastructures for the development of the region which the dissidents are preoccupied with destroying. A situation like this will lead to chaos and waste of huge amounts of capital and other important resources. It might even portray Africans as being unable to solve their problems by themselves. This is usually an excuse for superpower or regional power intervention in Southern Africa's affairs. For instance the Reagan administration's support to UNITA in Angola.

It is a measure of the naivety that had dogged the Mozambican leadership from the start that it never made a vigorous protest of Pretoria's deceit when it was evident that South Africa had reneged on the implementation of the Nkomati accord. The Mozambican leadership hoped that by not accusing Pretoria directly of violating the accord but ascribed such violations to "certain elements with nostalgia for colonialism" some real or imagined faction within South Africa would persuade Pretoria hardliners to honour the accord. The price of this diplomatic blunder was that South Africa had successfully manipulated itself as an "honest broker" between Mozambique and the MNR which South Africa was treated to the bizarre scene of Mozambican ministers sitting with the bands of South African sponsored rebels with Pretoria playing a dubious mediatory role to the hilt.[45]

South Africa's Dishonesty

For the time being the Mozambican leadership will have to content itself with the melancholy reprise of Pretoria's declarations of her intention to see that Mozambique's security improves.[46] In a re-enactment of an even more bizarre show of Pretoria's deceit while the MNR (Renamo) continues to spread its destructive mayhem inside Mozambique, and P. W. Botha in a Press conference categorically declared "I do not deny that there might be elements within South Africa and further a field from where individuals take or plan actions in support of the MNR".[47] Here, Botha openly admitted assistance to the MNR from the racist South African regime while at the same time pleading his inability to restrain the movement that it nurtured.

In September 1985, the white racist regime in South Africa was forced to admit to violations of the Nkomati Accord with Mozambique, as a result of documentary evidence captured by Frelimo following a raid on the headquarters of MNR inside Mozambique.[48] The documents discovered in the Gorongosa base known as Casa Banana Camp – the main headquarters of Renamo, located in central Mozambique suggested that not only was Pretoria guilty of violations, but it had no intention of honouring the Nkomati agreement. The captured documents consisted of a handwritten diary and notes apparently left behind by the MNR leaders during an attack by the Frelimo forces on the Gorongosa base in August 1985. The documents showed that beginning as from December 1983, almost four months before the signing of the Nkomati Accord, South African military had started supplying the rebels (Remano) inside Mozambique with food, medical equipment and ammunition. In addition, South African military instructors were training 100 instructors and 200 soldiers for Renamo in conventional warfare in the Zambezia province of Mozambique.[49] Even as far back as February 1984, just a month before the agreement was signed, plans for the reorganization of South African military support for the MNR efforts to destabilize Mozambique continued.

All these actions as revealed in the documents
found in Casa Banana base provide evidence of flagrant
violations of agreements between Maputo and Pretoria.
The so-called "gentlemen's agreement" reached in talks
between the two governments in December 1983 prior to
the signing of the Nkomati agreement on 16 March 1984,
and constantly reaffirmed in subsequent meetings held
variously with South African Defense Minister Magnus
Malan, with the Head of Police, General Coetzee and
President P. W. Botha, established that neither country
would use this period to infiltrate men or equipment
into neighbouring territory.[50] As had become evident
since the accord was signed, peace will continue to
elude Mozambique as long as she builds her hope on the
possibility of the Pretoria authorities playing in
accordance with the terms of the accord. This
reinforces the argument that South African duplicity
"reaffirmed the wisdom that dealing with the apartheid
devil requires a very long spoon".[51] We cannot agree
less.

The South African foreign minister Pik Botha has
admitted that despite the signing of the Nkomati accord
with Mozambique, Pretoria was still giving material
support to the Mozambican rebels. Pik Botha's admission
of Pretoria's support to the MNR, followed his visit to
Maputo in October 1985, where President Machel had
presented him with evidence, in a diary belonging to a
senior aide to Renamo leader, Alfonso Dhlakama. The
document presented showed that since signing the accord
South Africa had systematically violated it by building
an airstrip inside Mozambique for the MNR.[52] South
Africa was also supplying, what Pik Botha called very
"limited quantities of arms to the rebels, providing
submarines to infiltrate the MNR guerrillas into

Mozambique, and has transported Deputy Foreign Minister Louis Nel into the MNR base at Gorongoza on three separate occasions".[53] In all his three visits to the Casa Banana base meeting with Dhlakama, Louis Nel was transporting medical supplies and ammunition to the MNR. This was another violation of Nkomati accord and the entry laws of a sovereign nation.

The South African Foreign Minister had made an attempt claiming that Pretoria's violations of the Nkomati accord were only "technical and did not amount to serious developments in relations with Mozambique".[54] This view was rejected by the Mozambican government, which arranged a follow up meeting with Pik Botha at Komati-port, where the Foreign Minister was given further evidence of South African direct help for the MNR rebels, and further evidence of the Frelimo government's anger at the discovery of Pretoria's dishonesty. Pik Botha had made a baseless excuse to put part of the blame for the Nkomati accord violations on Mozambique by alleging that the ANC still had a presence in Mozambique after signing the accord with South Africa.[55]

Just as South Africa has openly admitted its support to the UNITA in Angola, a group the South African Defense minister spoke of being allied with was aimed at preventing the so-called "Marxist infiltration and expansionism".[56] This was paralleled to the South Africa's military support of the MNR to continue to destabilize Mozambique; and its public admissions that it broke the Nkomati accord is that Pretoria never had any intention of paying more than lip service to the Lusaka agreement with Angola on 16 February 1984 and the Nkomati accord with Mozambique. General Malan's statement on aid to the UNITA made it very clear that whatever else may happen in Southern Africa, the white authority in Pretoria has no intention of giving up its efforts to destabilize SADCC states.

Nkomati Accord and Mozambican Economy

Another important question that arose in the wake of the Nkomati accord is the question of the future course of Mozambique development. This question is all the more important especially when we take into consideration that one of the reasons why Maputo signed the Nkomati accord besides her security needs, was the anticipated windfall of Western aid and capital investment. It has been demonstrably shown in this chapter that security continues to elude Mozambique almost three years after the Nkomati accord. Given the dialectical relationship between security and economic development, it is obvious that the prospect for increased Western aid and investment is inextricably tied to the Mozambican security situation.

So far, the campaign to win foreign aid and investment with such attractive concessions as uninhibited repatriation of profits and low level state intervention had only attracted minimum response from the West.[57] Apart from the 60,000 tonnes worth of grain granted to Mozambican drought victims in 1984, and a loan of $10 million at 3 percent annual interest rate for the purchase of American grain. The pre-accord promises of the Reagan administration to help Mozambique to its economic feet had come to naught.[58] It is also worth noting that though Peter de Vos, the U.S. Ambassador to Mozambique signed an agreement with Mozambican officials providing for guarantees to be given U.S. investors for any of their investment in Mozambique under the aegis of the Overseas Private

Investment Corporation (OPIC), nothing concrete is yet to come out of this.[59] As the Egyptians learned later after the much criticized Camp David accords, the Mozambicans will sooner or later learn that aid pledges from the U.S. do not just fall like manna, the more so when the underlying motive is the winning of the hearts and minds of the recipients.

While the dream of Western and American-fueled aid and capital boast to the Mozambican economy remain dreams, more tangible economic results seem to have resulted at the bilateral level from South Africa. A number of bilateral economic agreements had been struck between Pretoria and Maputo. For instance, Mozambique and South Africa signed a new contract for the supply of electricity to South Africa from the Cabora Bassa dam at a new rate of 1.10 cents per kilowatt, which doubled the old rate for the next thirty-two years.[60] A number of Mozambican state farms have been placed under the management of South African based multinationals, and "large tracts of farmland leased to South African agrobusiness concerns".[61] Judging from the recent pro-western and South Africa politics of Maputo, Mozambique may sooner or later return to its pre-independence vassal-like status as a service sector for South African economy.

For Machel's government the fruits of Nkomati Pact are now proving to have a bitter taste. President Machel saw the Nkomati accord as a last chance for survival, but little has been achieved if anything at all, since the Nkomati accord was signed almost three years ago. The war is intensifying and spreading like wildfire inside Mozambique, and the promises of South African aid to boost the Mozambican economy remain dreams. The current Mozambican economic situation is rapidly worsening and is eroding FRELIMO's internal and external supports.[62] The international aid expected after the Nkomati accord was signed is no more forthcoming, and it is unlikely it will ever come. Potential investors and donors are pressuring the Machel government by making it clear to Maputo that they are waiting for a cease fire between MNR and FRELIMO before they can commit their money.

The national elections scheduled for 1985 have been postponed for what President Machel characterized as "elections need mass involvement and organization, and conditions are not appropriate at the moment".[63] The Finance Minister Rui Baltzar in his 1985 budget speech reported that exports fell by 22 percent for 1984 fiscal year. This was so, probably owing to the effect of MNR activities on transportation. The growth rate for 1985 is targeted for 5 percent. The government intends to increase exports by 21 percent, imports by 9 percent and rail receipts for international cargo by 38 percent, while the other sectors could expect a decrease, including domestic air travel.[64] The government has also decreased the budget for health and education for the first time since independence by 15 percent in 1985. The Finance Minister has signaled a wary attitude to Mozambique's growing links with international financial institutions, by implication - the World Bank and the International Monetary Fund (IMF), which the country joined in 1984.[65]

The FRELIMO army is generally poorly prepared and ill-motivated for battle in the war being waged against the MNR. However, the army is being used to protect main production centres, large development projects and principal transport areas. The Zimbabwean government is providing 10,000 of its troops and military aid to help the Mozambican government combat the MNR. The troops will also help in guarding Zimbabwe's road, rail and oil pipeline routes through Mozambique. This President Mugabe has declared that "if those routes ceased to function in toto, the alternative is for us to divert our goods through South Africa, and that alternative we just cannot countenance".[66] The Tanzanian government has also provided an unspecified troops and military assistance as parts of its contributions as a SADCC member to help Mozambican government alleviate the MNR activities in the country.

Another important economic dimension of the accord is renewed South African interest in the Mozambican tourist industry. Already, the South African based hotel and resort group - Sun International had dispatched a team of its development and investment experts to inspect potential hotel sites in Mozambique. For this reason, Mozambique has initiated a series of agreements with Sun International chief executive, Sol Kerzner.[67] Certainly, all this has important economic and political implications for the future of Mozambique and SADCC.

In fact one can safely predict that sooner or later, the colonial practice of South African whites flocking into Mozambican beaches, and other tourist attractions, for prawns, beer and prostitutes will be re-enacted on a larger scale.[68] Admittedly, Mozambique will earn substantial foreign exchange from this source. However, there is the obvious danger that the price of unrestrained South African domination of Mozambique's tourism could be very high in the long run. In the final analysis, a fistful of South African rands cannot compensate for the effective reduction of a supposedly independent Mozambique to a "pleasure periphery" of racist South Africa.[69]

For sure, Mr. P. W. Botha, like the master player that he is continues to dangle its appetizing economic carrots to aid-and investment-hungry Mozambique. On the other hand, the Mozambican leadership had remained enmeshed in the apparently faulty thinking that only cooperative economic relations with South Africa, could revive its depressed industries and infrastructure, and develop its productive forces upon which the hopes of building a socialist economy rest.[70] One obvious question that must be raised is how the Mozambican leadership could regulate aid and capital investments from the capitalist West and South Africa, given her weak bargaining position vis-a-vis the dominant Western and South African Multinationals?[71] Perhaps, only the future can answer this question.

However, it could be authoritatively asserted that history affords us no example so far, of how Western aid and investment or international capital had been utilized to develop a socialist economy in any country. On the contrary, greater incorporation into the world capitalist system and creeping neo-colonialism of such states has invariably been the outcome of such experiment as the Latin American experience had shown. Herein lies the danger of flirtation with the apartheid South African capital for Mozambique. Mr. Botha had hoped that the accord he signed with Maputo would clear the way for South African increased trade not only for Southern Africa but with the whole of the African continent.[72]

The Nkomati Accord and Mozambique's Standing in the Comity of Nations

The Nkomati Accord as pointed out earlier boosted the image of South Africa. The same cannot certainly be said of Mozambique. While, the argument that the imperatives of survival that drove Mozambique into signing the accord is more important than the vague notions of states ego sounds attractive, it is difficult to disagree with the superior opinion that the ability of a state to maintain her image formed an important component of its survival.[73]

Against this background, the circumstances that drove Mozambique under Pretoria's arm notwithstanding, her image no doubt has suffered considerably at the bar of progressive world opinion. As AfricAsia rightly put it:

> For a regime which had prided itself as the source of inspiration to all the peoples in Southern Africa to abandon sacred principles by reaching a tactical accommodation with apartheid South Africa is bad enough. For the same regime to enter into negotiations with counter-revolutionaries such as the MNR is inexcusable.[74]

Even if some reservation is held over the above contention, for the obvious reason that "the blood of survival is thicker than the waters of national prestige", it must be conceded that, the principle of negotiating with a tiny band of counter-revolutionaries evident in the abortive South African mediated contacts between the MNR and FRELIMO officials is fraught with dangers of far reaching consequences. There is no doubting the fact that it could embolden South Africa to set up more MNR's or even mercenary bands in other Frontline states to pressure them to succumb to its diktat.

This danger inherent in the Mozambican precedent in the sub-region is best captured by the statement credited to Mario Soares, the Portuguese Prime Minister, to the effect that, "the example set by the Mozambican government could persuade Angola to be more realistic and not to retreat into ideology".[75] This is a veiled suggestion that the MPLA government in Angola should enter into negotiation with UNITA. Indeed, an American State Department official even suggested to the Angolan Government less than innocently that "you have but to do the same as Maputo".[76]

Another important dimension is that the accord has raised a whole lot of moral questions, especially when it is recalled that Tanzania took an unprecedented hammering from the Portuguese airforce for offering material aid and sanctuary to the Mozambique Peoples Liberation Force (FPLM) during its Liberation Struggle. This position is without prejudice to the impeccable record of Mozambique during the liberation struggle of Zimbabwe. What is being emphasized, is that the accord is an indelible dent on the moral record of Mozambique as regarding its obligations to the liberation struggle in South Africa.[77]

While the Nkomati Agreement may be accepted as a "disagreeable act of necessity", the toll in terms of international prestige for a state that has gone full circle from a radical Frontline state, to that forming joint military commission with apartheid South Africa is bound to be high. In the light of this, President Machel tongue in cheek declaration after the accord, that "we will do everything that brings respect and dignity to our people, and we won't consult with anybody about it", sounds like a plain Orwellian "double speak".[78]   The Nkomati Accord did not certainly bring honour and dignity to Mozambicans.

The Nkomati Accord and the Liberation Struggle in South Africa and Namibia

Another important question that has arisen in the wake of the Nkomati Agreement is its potential consequence for the liberation struggle in Southern Africa.   For the purpose of this analysis, liberation struggle is being used to refer to both the struggle of the ANC and SWAPO against South Africa and the effort being made by the SADCC states to reduce their dependence on Pretoria.

By and large the liberation struggle in Southern Africa had traditionally employed the dual strategy of armed confrontation and political/diplomatic pressures. The Nkomati Accord is meant by South Africa to weaken the liberation struggle in Southern Africa, but this is not so, judging from what has been happening inside South Africa since September 1984.   If a measure of military pressure in the form of a protracted guerrilla war against Pretoria, as had come to be widely accepted is important in the dismantling of apartheid, the Nkomati accord no doubt represented an important set-back.   As already stated earlier, Mozambique has terminated the use of its territory as a sanctuary and infiltration route for the ANC guerrillas in accordance with the provisions of the accord.   Furthermore, it has also banned ANC political and military leaders from visiting Mozambique-based South African refugee camps which was a useful source for ANC military recruitment.[79]

Admittedly, the prospect for a military defeat of South Africa looks remote even if the ANC had not been denied the external sanctuary hitherto offered by

Mozambican territory.[80] However, military analysts believe that the utility of a guerrilla warfare in the context of South Africa lies in the fact that it is the best way of driving the point home that Pretoria is in a no win situation.[81] In addition, a protracted guerrilla warfare against South Africa could whittle away at her strength bit by bit, and this is bound to make a psychological impact in the long run.[82]

Undeniably, the refusal of the valuable rear base, which the Mozambican territory hitherto offered presents immense organizational and logistical problems for the ANC in its struggle against the apartheid regime.[83] It may be very difficult militarily for the ANC to organize within the apartheid enclave given the ubiquity of Pretoria's intelligence outfit. The ANC aptly reflected the forgoing point of view when it declared that, "of all the valuable acts of international aid our movement has received from many countries, the facilities accorded us by Mozambique in the past have been amongst the most important".[84] It is significant to note that reports of Umkonto We Sizwe (the ANC military wing) spectacular military actions such as the SASOL and South Africa's airforce headquarters bombings of 1982 and 1983 respectively had become increased since the September 1984 uprising in South Africa.

At another level of analysis,[85] some analysts argue that unless South Africa is sufficiently pressured through a guerrilla warfare, any hope of the voluntary dismantling of apartheid will not come to pass. The authors of this argument stressed the potential negative effect of a prolonged guerrilla war on the economy of South Africa in terms of escalating military budget and possible plight of Western capital. This, it is held coupled with sustained diplomatic pressure could in the long run move the apartheid leadership into a course of dismantling of apartheid. The Nkomati Accord could strengthen the apartheid military machine because of the breathing space from ANC guerrilla attacks it gave her and to that extent a significant setback to the Liberation struggle. Beyond all the obvious military setback, highlighted in the forgoing analysis, the Nkomati Agreement also adversely affected the political component of the liberation struggle.

Most analysts argue that the political dimension of the struggle for decolonization is as important as the military. This realization must have informed the diplomacy of the Frontline states to create a cordon sanitaire of "isolation" which Kenneth Grundy described as "a conscious effort to resolve a conflict situation by physically sealing off the actor regarded as the cause of the problem",[86] around South Africa. The Nkomati Agreement thus marks the breaking of that cordon.[87]

In addition, the action of Mozambique represented the first overt breaking of the political solidarity of the SADCC states which has been an effective component of the struggle against South Africa. On the other hand, the accord had strengthened the political standing of P. W. Botha, and by implication the apartheid state, at least to some European states. Botha's eight-nation European tour, an unthinkable event before the Nkomati Agreement, and the hilarious declaration by Dr. Koornhof, Minister for Cooperation and Development, on Botha's triumphal return that "you have ended forty years of isolation during which South Africa had been the punch ball and scapegoat of the world",[88] attest to the above point.

In political terms, the accord thus ranked in significance with the so-called Botha's "constitutional reform" that sought to break the solidarity of the United opposition against apartheid through the granting of limited superficial power to the Indian and coloured communities.[89] Whatever might have been the intentions of the Mozambican authorities, the Nkomati Agreement had made them accomplices in the military and political preservation of the apartheid state. This no doubt is an ironical outcome for a nation that had declared several times that "the aims of the struggle of the people of South Africa are aims for which all mankind fights".[90]

If the accord had a negative impact on the liberation struggle in South Africa as had been demonstrated clearly from the forgoing analysis, it must necessarily have a similar bearing in the struggle for Namibian independence given the dialectical relationship between the two struggles. As already mentioned, the agreement has accorded South Africa some measure of relief from ANC guerrillas. This would only permit South Africa to divert more resources to its wars of aggression against SWAPO in Namibia and Angola in order to maintain its illegal occupation of Namibia.

It is also possible as reported in the New Nigerian[91] that Pretoria merely wanted to neutralize the ANC through the Nkomati Agreement before consenting to any settlement on Namibia – a potential ANC sanctuary if that territory becomes independent. This however, is a moot point. What is beyond debate if some measure of inspired guesses is brought to bear on the interpretation of South Africa's actions is that the Pretoria regime is merely stalling for time. With the Nkomati Agreement and the disengagement agreement with

Angola, Pretoria hopes to build up the multi-party Conference (a grouping of anti-SWAPO internal political parties in Namibia) with the hope of fostering a neo-colonial solution in Namibia and to counter-poised SWAPO.[92]

This line of thought is evident in the statement credited to the South African appointed illegal administrator-general of Namibia to the effect that, "if SWAPO should succeed in taking control, it would necessarily destroy South Africa's strongman image in Southern Africa, stimulate radical groups working for black power in the republic.[93]

In the light of the above analysis, "a Luta Continua" as far as the ongoing liberation struggle in Southern Africa is concerned. Being that as it were, one cannot agree less with Mohamed Buba's assertion that a "metamorphosis of gigantic proportions has occurred in Southern Africa in which constructive engagement (the foster father of the Nkomati Accord) has been transformed into a destructive engagement",[94] one only hopes that the retreat would be temporary.

The Nkomati Accord and SADCC

An important question raised by the Nkomati Accord is whether it would enhance or negate the goals and aspirations of the Southern African Development Coordination Conference. The Lusaka declaration is also a continuation of Black Africa's continuous search for total economic freedom through intra-continental development and cooperation in the economic field. The SADCC Countries view their programme of action as part of the Liberation struggle in Southern Africa which, with the independence of Zimbabwe, will shift its focus on Namibia and on South Africa itself. Thus, SADCC will erode the constraints that South Africa's established regional dominance has sought to perpetuate as a means to divert the attention and energy of the Southern African states from the Liberation struggle.[95]

Mozambique because of its strategic location along the Indian Ocean, and its natural Ports of Beira, Nacala and Maputo has been assigned responsibility for the Southern African Transport and Communication Commission (SATCC) in the SADCC programme of Action. Maputo has been chosen as the headquarters of SATCC. SATCC is "fully recognized within the international community, as a permanent and effective institution...for the coordination and development of the region's transport and communication programme".[96]

The Nkomati accord had adversely affected the military and political component of the liberation struggle in South Africa and Namibia. In the light of this contention, it can be argued that the accord cannot possibly have excluded the economic dimension of the liberation struggle as represented by SADCC. This is so for the obvious reasons noted by President Machel that:

> our countries' dependence in relation to South Africa was conceived as an instrument to strengthen and defend the apartheid regime. Consolidating the independence of the free states of the region means weakening the racist.[97]

South Africa's aim in the Nkomati accord must be seen as a diversionary attempt to weaken the commitment of Mozambique to the objectives of the SADCC. This is clearly apparent, when it is noted that shortly after the accord was signed South Africa offered to increase its contribution to the Southern Africa Custom Union made up of Botswana, Lesotho and Swaziland if these reduce their commitments to SADCC.[98] Taken together with the promise of South African economic aid, and capital flow to Mozambique, it will not be wrong to conclude that South Africa was employing the strategy of selective inducement to undermine the Southern African States' commitment to SADCC objectives.

The foregoing position is supported by the speech of Julius Nyerere at SADCC's fifth summit shortly after the signing of the Nkomati accord:

> South Africa is trying to force SADCC members into a new form of expanded cooperation with which it could weaken the anti-apartheid struggle, as well as the real independence of our sovereign states by using a combination of threats and promises to get SADCC members to chase after the mirage of economic prosperity.[99]

Given the centrality of Mozambique to the SADCC states' objectives of the development of their own transport and communications systems, so as to reduce their continuing dependence on South Africa's. A Mozambique that is economically dominated by South Africa would make the objectives of the Maputo based Southern African Transport and Communication Commissions (an agency of SADCC),[100] very difficult to attain in view of the landlocked nature of most of SADCC states.

More important, South Africa has shown no inclination to put an end to its military support for the MNR. Rather, it continues to aid the MNR albeit, covertly in its effort to undermine the objectives of the SADCC states through a sustained attack and destruction of the infrastructural linkages between Mozambique and the other landlocked SADCC member states.[101] Arising from this analysis, it would be reasonable, to conclude that the Nkomati accord and the penchant of the SADCC for foreign assistance from the capitalist West, and racist South Africa could only undercut SADCC attempts to break Pretoria's hegemony of the Southern Africa sub-region.[102] Given the importance of the politics of the Southern Africa sub-region to the Western sources from whom assistance is being sought, as well as SADCC's own objectives, it is doubtful whether the West would want to see a situation which would make the independent black states in Southern Africa strong enough to pose an economic and military threat to South Africa, which is still considered to be a vital link in the West's strategic and economic thinking. Thus the problems of funding of SADCC programmes and the dependence on the West for international capital remain interconnected and interchangeable.

Whatever might have been the circumstances that led to the signing of the Nkomati accord, it is inherently detrimental to the interests of Mozambique, the SADCC States and Africa as a whole. My argument in this wise is not to contest the sovereign right of Maputo to make treaties, it deemed necessary for survival even if at cross-purpose with the larger interest of SADCC states. What I have attempted to do in this chapter is to point out the flawed premise on which the Mozambican leadership exposition on the accord was based. For instance, the claim by Jose Luis Cabaco, the Mozambican Minister of Information that, "the Nkomati accord is part of Mozambique's policy of defending its national sovereignty, and independence and promoting peace and development".[103] This could not be right. So also is the belief that accommodation with South Africa could end MNR's destructive activities which is but an arm of Pretoria's destabilization strategy in SADCC states.

The problem of South African destabilization of Mozambique which the Nkomati accord was meant to solve from the point of view of Mozambique is rooted in the conflict inherent in the inner workings of the apartheid system inside South Africa. The destabilization strategy of South Africa is therefore, a partial manifestation of that conflict. In a nutshell, the conflict in the SADCC states in general and Mozambique in particular is a spill over of the larger conflict which has its roots inside South Africa itself.[104] However, South Africa must be seen to be playing only the Israeli game in the Southern Africa sub-region[105] - the game of grabbing Arab land and asking the individual Arab States to negotiate for this land, thus, side-tracking the substantial issue of Palestinian national self-determination. South Africa is using the destabilization strategy as forte for trade-off bargaining between the African sanctuaries of the ANC and its armed bandits - the MNR to divert attention from the substantial issue of its apartheid policies, the Casus belli of instability in the Southern Africa sub-region, and inside South Africa itself.[106]

Therefore, if South Africa could not escape the inevitability of increased nationalist pressure, Nkomati accord or not, no SADCC could hope to gain a respite from separate peace with Pretoria either. This is more so, when the logic of their (nationalist) radicalizing and revolutionary presence will continue to engender widespread militancy by the oppressed blacks inside South Africa. The nationalist revolutionary activities inside South Africa have been intensified tremendously in the past few years, especially since the Nkomati accord has been signed in 1984.[107] Moreover, a stable Angola and Mozambique, according to Nolutshungu, would reduce the role that "South Africa could play on behalf of Western interests there (in Southern Africa), since its own interest might be in competition with those of Western states".[108] Some western observers of the Southern Africa politics have also projected that South Africa would pursue the dual policy of the gradual "Malawianization" of the SADCC states, and elite accommodation inside South Africa. One piece of evidence to prove this was the rush of South African capital into Mozambique after the Nkomati accord. Another move in this direction was the suggestion by elements within South African ruling class, on the need for development of a black capitalist (elite) stratum that would have vested interest in the apartheid system.

All we have seen from the South African ruling authority behaviours and policy since the Nkomati accord was signed, for Mozambique and any other SADCC states for that matter with desire to hold fast to its chosen course must look beyond separate accommodation with the racist South African regime. A good beginning is an urgent need by the Mozambique leadership to return to the call of AmilCar Cabral that Africa could place on the agenda one very essential item which is not usually discussed "the struggle against our own weakness".[109] While the factor of South African destabilization policy against SADCC states, and natural disasters confronting them are very significant, the internal policies of the Mozambican leadership, such as excessive collectivization of agriculture, and the obsession with doctrinaire rigidity cannot be isolated in analyzing the hunger complex and shortage of essential items in the rural areas, and the general crisis of the Mozambican economy that drove President Machel into South Africa's arms.[110]

The Mozambican leadership's penchant for branding any critic or opposition with the stigma of "reactionaries" and "counter-revolutionaries" only serves the interest of the racist regime in Pretoria. In fact, some of the real and psychological victories scored by the MNR originated in the context of the political errors of the Mozambican leadership.[111] A far reaching programme of internal reforms and reassessment of certain military and political policies such as the transformation of the army from a "people's army" as it was during the period of the liberation struggle, to an elite force with rank insignia, and the excessive centralization of power is not desirable in this regard. Besides this, the SADCC states and the OAU as a whole must come to the aid of Mozambique. It has been admitted that one of the main reasons that drove Mozambique to sign the Nkomati accord was a grant of $5 million by Tiny Roland's Lonrho group of companies.[112] In fighting against apartheid South Africa, SADCC states and the African states as a whole must have to stand together as a unit or go under individually. Apparently, the balance of advantage for Mozambique and the Southern African states lies in abrogating the Nkomati accord.

NOTES

[1] See Nduka Uzuakpundu, "Any chance for detente in South Africa", National Concord (Ikeja) March 19, 1984.

[2] Africa Now, April 1984, pp. 27.

[3] Chris Freimond, "Africa given time to experience Soviet reality: South Africa armed raids, Basis for Peace", Rand Daily Mail, (Johannesburg) April 12, 1984.

[4] A. E. Ekoko, "South Africa Defense Strategy in Africa 1932-66: A Study in Dream of Empire" Mimeo, Department of History, University of Ibadan, 1984.

[5] World Military Expenditures and Arms Transfers 1972-1982 (Washington, D.C.: U.S. Arms Control and Disarmament Agency, April 1984), p. 44.

[6] Phillip Van Niekirk, "Message for Pretoria" South January, 1985.

[7] Horace Campbell, op. cit.

[8] Timothy Shaw defines a subimperial state as a "client-state that is able to exert dominance in one region while it is in turn dependent on a greater metropolitan power", Timothy M. Shaw, "Kenya and South Africa: Subimperialist State", ORBIS, Vol. 21, No. 2 (Summer 1977), pp. 375-389.

[9] Joseph Frankel, National Interest and Foreign Policy (London: Pall Mall Press, 1970).

[10] Donald E. Nuechterlein, "The Concept of National Interest: A Time for new approaches", ORBIS, Vol. 23, No. 1 (Spring 1979), p. 75.

[11] Ibid.

[12] See Michael Brecher's classificatory model cited in Olajide Aluko, "Necessity and Freedom in Nigerian Foreign Policy" An Inaugural Address University of Ife (17 March, 1981), p. 15.

[13]John de St. Jorre, "South Africa: Up against the World" Foreign Policy, No. 8 (Fall 1977), p. 53.

[14]See David Ferreira, "South Africa: Botha's Constitutional Minefield", AfricAsia, June 1984, p. 26.

[15]A. E. Ekoko, op. cit.

[16]Peter Enahoro, "The Looming Tragedy" Africa Now, May 1984, p. 2.

[17]Sam C. Nolutshungu, "South Africa and the Transfers of Power in Africa: A Preliminary Outline", Conference on the Transfer of Power in Africa (Harare, Zimbabwe, January 1985).

[18]For details on South Africa's "Outward Policy" see Sam C. Nolutshungu, South Africa in Africa: A Study in Ideology and Foreign Policy (Manchester: University Press, 1975), p. 114.

[19]A good example of Afrikaner nationalist is Eschel Rhoodie, a former South African Director of Information Department.

[20]See Hyam, R. The Future of South African Expansion 1908-1948 (New York: A. P. C. Press, 1972), p. 2.

[21]See Alex Callinicos and John Rogers, op. cit., p. 77.

[22]Jennifer S. Whitaker, "African Beset" Foreign Affairs, Vol. 62, No. 3 (1982), p. 765.

[23]Horace Campbell, op. cit.

[24]Sam Nolutshungu, "Conference on the transfer of Power in Southern Africa, op. cit., p. 22.

[25]Ibid., p. 23

[26]Alex Callinicos and John Rogers, op. cit., pp. 102-103.

[27]Harold Laswell, Politics: Who Gets What, When and How cited in F. S. Northedge, International Political System (London: Faber and Faber 1976), p. 19.

[28]Africa Now, March 1984, p. 37.

[29]M. M. Ncube, op. cit., p. 37.

[30]Africa Now, op. cit.

[31]Onome Osifo-Whisky, "South Africa: Botha's Wild Gamble", Daily Times (Lagos) July 3, 1984.

[32]Michael Manley, "The Poison in Pretoria's Heart", South (May 1985) p. 37.

[33]Marc Frons, et al. "Botha's Failed Overtures" Newsweek International (June 18, 1984), p. 18.

[34]Timothy Shaw, "Discontinuities and Unequalities in African International Politics", International Journal Vol. XXX, No. 3 (Summer 1975), p. 381.

[35]Africa Now, April 1984, p. 28.

[36]Chester Crocker, "The African Dimension of Indian Ocean", ORBIS, Vol. 20, No 3 (Fall 1976), pp. 644-666.

[37]Simon Malley, Mozambique: An Easy Prey for Pretoria", AfricAsia (November 1984), p. 19.

[38]See Andrew Akporuga, "Is Nkomati non-aggression Pact Concluded?" The Guardian (Lagos) October 7, 1984, p. 2.

[39]Walter Lippman, U.S. Foreign Policy: Shield of Republic (Boston: Little Brown and Company 1943), p. 72.

[40]Arnold Wolfers, Discard and Collaboration: Essays on International Politics (Baltimore: John Hopkins University Press, 1979), p. 150.

[41]For details see "Nkomati Accord - ANC Response" and "Communique of the Arusha Frontline States meeting of 29 April 1984" in Appendices 7 and 8.

[42]Ibid.

[43]"Malawi: Mozambican rebels seek sanctuary", Africa Now (London) August 1985, p. 21.

[44]Glenn Frankel, "South African-backed Rebels Weaken Mozambique", The Washington Post October 8, 1984, p. 1.

[45]See "Somalia gives bases to South Africa" Africa Now (February 1985), pp. 22-23. See also "Mozambique: Double-crossed?" Africa (London) March 1985, p. 10.

[46]Mr. Louis Nel, South African Deputy Foreign Affairs Minister, in an interview on March 28, 1985, declared that "our (South African) priority now is to help Mozambique get rid of the MNR, and to work with the international community to block the MNR's supplies" Africa Research Bulletin Vol. 22, No. 3, April 1985, p. 7564.

[47]Ibid., p. 7493.

[48]Karin Monoteiro, "Secret Documents Reveal South Africa's Nkomati Fraud", New African (London) December 1985, p. 25.

[49]Ibid.

[50]Ibid.

[51]The Guardian (Lagos), January 23, 1985, p. 2.

[52]Keith Sommerville, "ANGOLA/Mozambique: Old Loyalties die hard", New Africa, November 1985, p. 24.

[53]Ibid.

[54]Ibid.

[55] "MOZAMBIQUE: The Storming of Casa-Banana Africa Now (London), October 1985, pp. 35-36.

[56] New Africa, op. cit., p. 23.

[57] See "Mozambique new investment code" Africa Research Bulletin, Vol. 21, No. 8, September 1984, p. 7415.

[58] "Scrap Nkomati" The Guardian (Lagos) January 23, 1985, p. 8.

[59] "Mozambique: Politics of Investment" Africa, October 1984, p. 32.

[60] "Mozambique's new deal for Cabora Bassa Power", Africa Now (London), June 1983, p. 55.

[61] Muhammed Musa Muwani, Mozambique: Renamo ruins the economy" New Africa, May 1985, p. 33.

[62] Olayiwola Abegunrin, "Nkomati Accord: Botha's Betrayal" Daily Sketch (Ibadan) July 22, 1985, p. 5.

[63] Lois Browne, "Mozambique: New budget bites the bullet" African Business (London) August 1985, p. 27.

[64] Ibid.

[65] Ibid., p. 28.

[66] "Zimbabwean troops to fight MNR" Daily Sketch (Ibadan) August 9, 1985, p. 6.

[67] See Africa Research Bulletin, Vol, 21, No. 9, October 31, 1984, p. 7439.

[68] "South Africa: Carrots?" Africa Confidential Vol. 25, No. 2, January 18, 1984.

[69] For an incisive analysis of pleasure periphery, See Jonathan Cruch and Paul Welling "Southern Africa Pleasure Periphery 1966-83", Journal of Modern African Studies, Vol, 21, No 4, 1983.

260

[70]For a criticism of this view see Edwin Madunagu and Kayode Komolafe. "Mozambique: Beyond Nkomati" The Guardian (Lagos), March 16, 1985, pp. 9-10.

[71]Horace Campbell, "Nkomati, Before and After War, Reconstruction, and Dependence in Mozambique", Journal of African Marxists, Issue 6, October 1984, p. 67.

[72]Marc Frons et al, "South Africa: Botha's feuled overtures" Newsweek International (18 June, 1984), p. 18.

[73]Francis Pym, "British Foreign Policy: Constraints and Opportunities", International Affairs, Vol. 59, No. 1 (Winter 1982/83).

[74]See Simon Malley, op. cit.

[75]Ibid.

[76]Ibid., p. 19.

[77]"Why Mozambique Signed Accord with Racists" New Nigerian (Kaduna) 23 March, 1984, p. 8.

[78]George Orwell, Nineteen Eighty Four (London: Heinemann, 1984).

[79]"What the Nkomati Accord Means for Africa", The African Communist No. 98, (3rd October, 1984).

[80]For the Military Balance see Africa (May, 1985) pp. 20-24.

[81]Mao-Tsetung, On Guerrilla Warfare cited in R. Pfaltzgraff and J. Doherty, Contending Theories of International Relations (Philadelphia: J. B. Lippincott Co. 1971), p. 193.

[82]For an analysis of the psychological impact of guerrilla warfare see John W. Spanier Games Nations Play (New York: Preager Publishers 1972), p. 173.

[83]Bernard Fall, Street Without Joy (Hannsburg: The
Stackpole Co. 1966), p. 16.

[84]See The African Communist, op. cit.

[85]Nduka Uzunkpundu, "Nkomati: A Futile search for
peace", National Concord (15 March 1983), p. 3.

[86]Kenneth Grundy, Confrontation and Accommodation
in Southern Africa: The Limits of Independence
(Berkeley: University of California Press, 1973),
p. 296.

[87]The African Communist, op. cit.

[88]Africa Research Bulletin, Vol. 21, No. 6 (15 July
1984), p. 7291.

[89]David Ferreira, "South Africa: Botha's
Constitutional Minefield", AfricAsia (June 1984),
pp. 26-27.

[90]"Mozambique/South Africa: Diplomacy and
Destabilization", Africa March 1984.

[91]"Of Nkomati Discord", New Nigerian (Kaduna), 11
January 1985.

[92]South Africa announced in May 1985 that it is
setting up an international multi-parties administration
in Namibia, but this has failed.

[93]Ross Halstaff, "Namibia: South Africa Stalls for
Time", South (March 1981), p. 23.

[94]See Abdul Rahman Mohammed Buba, "Portugal's New
Empire:, Africa Now, (June 1984), p. 43.

[95]Layi Abegunrin, "Southern African Development
Coordination Conference: Politics of Dependence" in R.
I. Onwuka and A. Sesay (eds.) The Future of Regionalism
in Africa (London: Macmillan Press, 1985), p. 190. See
also O. Abegunrin, "Southern African Development
Coordination Conference: Towards Regional Integration
of Southern Africa for Liberation"   A Current

Bibliography on African Affairs, Vol. 17, No. 4, 1984-85, pp. 363-384.

[96]Communiqué of SADCC Summit Conference held in Gaborone, Botswana, July 22, 1982, p. 2.

[97]See "Surviving a Cold Shoulder: from the North" South February 1981, p. 53.

[98]"News Commentary" External Service of Radio RSA, January 1, 1985.

[99]Africa Research Bulletin, Vol. 21, No. 3, July 31, 1984, p. 7327.

[100]See Christopher Hill, "Regional Cooperation in Southern Africa" Africa Affairs, Vol. 82, No. 327, April 1983.

[101]For instance, Zimbabwe which depended on the port of Beira was forced to sign a contract for the supply of fuel from South Africa, a month after the MNR blew up 34 oil storage tanks at Beira.

[102]O. Abegunrin, "SADCC-EEC Cooperation: Politics of Aid or Imperialism?" Conference paper on International Aid and Development in Africa (University of Ife, May 1985).

[103]Jose Luis Cabaco, "Mozambique-South Africa: The Nkomati Accords", Africa Report Vol. No. (May-June), p. 24.

[104]Thomas G. Kavis, "Revolution in the Making: Black Politics in South Africa" Foreign Affairs, Vol. 62, No. 2, Winter 1983/84, p. 379.

[105]Samuel Tarka, "Message from Nkomati", Nigerian Forum May/June 1984, pp. 123-127.

[106]"Apartheid in Crisis" West Africa (London) August 19, 1985, p. 1683.

[107]"Loss of Faith in Apartheid" New African August 1985, pp. 24-25.

[108]Sam Nolutshungu, "South Africa and the Transfer of Power in Africa: A Preliminary Outline" Conference on the Transfer of Power in Africa, Harare, Zimbabwe, January 1985.

[109]Horace Campbell, op. cit., p. 50.

[110]Lois Browne, "Mozambique: New budget bites the bullet" African Business, August, 1985, pp. 27-28.

[111]It is not surprising that it is within the rank of this officially tagged "reactionary and counter-revolutionary elements that the MNR mostly find willing recruits.

[112]Revealed at the "International Conference on Foreign Aid and Development in Africa" University of Ife, Ile-Ife, Nigeria, May 1985.

CHAPTER 7

SADCC AND THE FUTURE OF SOUTHERN AFRICA

Whatever political goals the SADCC may pursue in the future, particularly in Namibia and South Africa, it must confront not just South Africa's minority government with its heavy war machine but also the Western capitalism which benefits most from the apartheid socio-economic and political arrangements in South Africa. It is at this level, that economic dependence would mediate concrete moves to make meaningful political gains. Considering the Angolan question, we observed that, if Cuban troops leave Angola, which the Reagan administration and South Africa are demanding,[1] the non-existent OAU Defense force even any of its (OAU) usual ineffective peace-keeping forces would be unable to guarantee Angola's security. The protracted nature of negotiation over Zimbabwe's independence between 1965 and 1979,[2] is a pointer to the intransigence and interests of the West and South Africa. SADCC cannot pretend not to be aware of the huge political tasks ahead, if it regards itself as a liberation movement; well-worded treaties and ordinary verbal statements of unity, which are characteristics of the Third World cooperative schemes must begin to give way to concrete and action-oriented moves to mobilize, disengage and act decisively. As Seretse Khama succinctly put it while down-playing ideological differences and highlighting the congruity of political and economic interests that:

> the five frontline states have already shown that cooperation is possible among the independent states of Southern Africa regardless of their different ideologies and economic systems. We have been working harmoniously together to solve common political problems, and I see no reason why we cannot work together harmoniously to solve common economic problems[3]

In so far as there is a common political problem or a common enemy, ideology can play a secondary role, but when it comes to making sacrifices, initiating strategies and tactics for confrontation and disengaging from existing alliances and relationships, ideology in all its ramifications is bound to become very useful. Perhaps, the struggle in Namibia and South Africa will have to be resolved through violent confrontation. Again as Seretse Khama noted, in Angola, Mozambique, and Zimbabwe, the "nationalist movements found themselves faced with no alternative but to respond to the violence of repression with the violence of liberation".[4] In choosing this alternative, the nationalists received solidarity and support from the independent states of the region that was intensive, coordinated and sustained, and "in Namibia, SWAPO's struggle continues to command the same support".[5] This has to be extended to the ANC, for as R. H. Green has noted, that SADCC is a Liberation Movement which is "anti-racial in principle and anti-white dominance in practice".[6] In extending

similar levels of sustained intensive and coordinated
support to SWAPO and the ANC, SADCC member-states must
be fully aware of the implications and possible
confrontation with South Africa and its supporters. As
SADCC presently stands, it had neither the economic nor
military power to achieve these political goals.

The most imposing structural characteristic of
Southern African affairs is the complete unchallenged
economic domination of South Africa. This, more than
any other single fact, has shown in foregoing chapters,
(especially in Chapters Four and Six), has determined
the economic, military, and diplomatic networks that are
being constructed in the sub-region. This domination,
or imbalance is evident in a comparison of gross
national product data for the Southern African states
shown in Table 7.1 (page 268). Similarly, South Africa
is the most industrialized country in the Southern
African sub-continent;[7] given the situation as it is,
the future for any meaningful self-reliance is very
bleak without first breaking the South Africa domination
of the region, and SADCC has to instill a level of
discipline into its members if there are going to be any
useful strategies toward promoting intra-regional trade
and economic cooperation.

Balance of Political Forces in Southern Africa

The declaration following the 1980 Lusaka
conference by SADCC states noted that "while the
struggle for genuine political independence has advanced
and continues to advance, it is not yet complete".
Therefore, taking a position on the issue of political
liberation, the Lusaka declaration stated, "we, the
majority-ruled states of Southern Africa recognize our
responsibilities, both as separate nation-states and as

TABLE 7.1
SOUTHERN AFRICA - POPULATION AND
GROSS NATIONAL PRODUCT FOR 1980

Country	Population		GNP at Market Prices		
	Total mid-1980	Growth Rate % 1970- 1979	Total 1980 in US Million $	Per Capita $1980 $	Real GDP Growth Rate per capita 1970-1979
Angola	7,078,000	2.4	3.320	470	-9.6
Botswana	800,000	2.2	0.730	910	12.0
Lesotho	1,341,000	2.4	.520	390	9.5
Malawi	5,951,000	2.9	1.390	230	3.0
Mozam- bique	10,473,000	2.5	2.810	270	-5.3
Namibia	1,009,000	2.8	1.420	1,410	0.3
South Africa	27,735,000	2.7	66.960	2,290	0.6
Swaziland	557,000	2.6	0.380	680	4.0
Tanzania	19,000,000	2.8	3.850	580	-1.8
Zambia	5,766,000	3.1	3.220	560	-1.9
Zimbabwe	7,396,000	3.3	4.640	630	-1.7
Southern Africa	87,106,000	2.7	85.390	1,253	0.83

Source: Data from various sources

a group of neighbouring majority-ruled African countries to assist in achieving a successful culmination of our struggle".[8] In theory, this is a clear statement of purpose to mobilize and harmonize all men and material resources not only in the support of on-going liberation struggles in Namibia and South Africa, but also in reducing the susceptibility of the majority-ruled ones to external aggression; especially from South Africa.

The statement above should be evaluated in relation to the objectives as well as the potential capability of SADCC to contribute to the liberation of Namibia and South Africa. Without any doubt, the radical and militant states, particularly Angola, Mozambique and Zimbabwe have very strong Soviet, Cuban and Chinese support. This in itself, is the outcome of the ideological disposition of the leadership in those countries as well as of the protracted nature of their struggle for political independence. Following the attainment of political freedom, it was easy to eliminate or at least reduce their relationship with the Eastern bloc. Without neglecting the contribution of liberation armies and organizations, one can contend that to a large extent the struggle for liberation in those three countries mentioned above would have been delayed or failed entirely if not for the assistance rendered by the Soviet Union, Cuba, China and other Socialist countries. Contemporary security in these countries is mainly put in charge of foreign troops. For those SADCC countries which do not have foreign troops on their territories, they go round mostly to the Western capitals for their security.[9] For example, Mozambique has signed an agreement with Britain to train its army. This scenario introduces major and serious issues into the question of confronting the white racist apartheid regime in South Africa. Should there be a continued reliance on the Eastern bloc, Cuba and North Korea? Are the SADCC countries prepared to cooperate militarily to support the ANC in South Africa and SWAPO in Namibia? To what extent can they rely on the West for support in their quest for the political liberation of Southern Africa as a whole?

These are some of the crucial questions which are relevant to the political goals and future of SADCC. Reliance on external sources for military aid and the maintenance of security is not the way to build self-reliance, because this negates the <u>1980 Lagos Plan of Action</u> which has now become the corner stone of the African development and which SADCC subscribed to.[10] The Western world on which the majority of the SADCC states are dependent is also responsible to a very large extent for the survival of the minority white regime in South Africa. This was shown in Chapter Four under SADCC external linkages, especially its link with EEC countries. In fact, in places like Angola, Mozambique and Zimbabwe, the West is in total support of the opponents of the political parties in power today in the respective countries. The Western opposition and collaboration with the dissidents reactionary groups[11] were dealt with and elaborated on in Chapter Five of this book. It is the same group of countries on which SADCC states are economically dependent.

The internal basis of political and economic action in SADCC states also differ. For the Socialist economies, of Angola, Mozambique and Tanzania, their contemporary armies are mostly made up of guerrilla cadres (with only exception of Tanzania) and the states have been striving since their liberation to build what we can call "peoples' armies" or "popular armies".

These popular armies are mostly ideologically motivated, this means that, their conception and interpretation of war, liberation, power and society cannot be exactly similar to those of the armies in the so-called moderate and conservative countries like Botswana, Lesotho, Malawi, Swaziland and Zambia. This is a pointer to the fact that were there to be an agreement to pull their resources together, effectiveness and mobility could be major problems. The question, therefore, remains, what resources do the Southern Nine have to pull together to confront South Africa and perhaps the Western world who is aiding South Africa?

The Military Equation in Southern Africa

On a comparative basis all SADCC states are militarily inferior to South Africa, their economic situation is equally weak to that of South Africa. In spite of the 1984 moves to enter into peace agreements with some of the SADCC States, especially the non-aggression pacts signed with Angola on 16 February 1984 and Mozambique on 16 March 1984, South Africa still continues to destabilize the region.[12] All these are not enough to trust the white regime in South Africa, which has been very recalcitrant and aggressive for decades on issues of self-determination, majority right and rule in the Southern Africa sub-continent. South Africa has a very well equipped, well trained army, the best and largest armed forces in the whole of Africa, including nuclear weapons.[13] It is the strongest country in Africa militarily, with armed forces strength of 404,500 including reserves. This is more than the total armed forces of all SADCC member-states combined, and this is clearly shown from the figures of the indicators of the Southern African Military balance in

Table 7.2 (page 273). According to the 1982 report of the study Commission on U.S. policy toward Southern Africa, "the Republic of South Africa regularly accounted for some 50 percent of all sub-Saharan African arms imports".[14] The military spending per capita – shows that South Africa spends four to five times as much as any of its African neighbours. It has also been shown that in all of Africa only Libya spends more per person on defense than South Africa. And in local manufacture of equipment South Africa ranks with such countries as Brazil, Argentina, India, Israel and Taiwan as a significant arms producer.[15]

The partial exception is Zimbabwe which is the only SADCC member-state that is militarily strong with a 65,000-man armed force and 25,000 trained guerrillas on reserve. Most of the SADCC member-state's armies are poorly trained and equipped, except for Angola, Mozambique, Tanzania and Zimbabwe. And all depend on external sources for weapons and ammunitions. in fact, their dependence on the Western World which is also sustaining the South African army is a major impediment to any ability or effort to mobilize total armed strength in pursuit of overt political goals in order to further pursue economic liberation.

Table 7.2 (page 273) provides a quantitative sketch of the (force) military relationships between SADCC states and South Africa, plus Nigeria. The South African and Nigerian navies are the only ones possessing units heavier than patrol craft and neither has much capacity to inflict damage on the other in its own waters. The South African Air Force is the only one listed in the table with sufficient trained pilots, logistical support and numbers necessary to be considered an operational combat force. In fact, troop

TABLE 7.2
INDICATOR OF THE SOUTHERN AFRICAN MILITARY BALANCE IN 1980

Country	Total Armed Forces	Combat Aircraft	Helicopters	Naval Combatants[1]	Tanks	Other Armored Vehicles	Defense Budget Million $
Angola	40,000	31	51	13	285	350	362.8
Botswana	3,000**	–	–	–	–	–	29.3
Lesotho	1,000	–	–	–	–	–	–
Malawi	5,000	–	2	–	–	10	40.6
Mozambique	24,000	35	4	8	240	–	191.85
Swaziland	2,000	–	–	–	–	–	2.0*
Tanzania	50,000	20	6	33	40	–	180.0
Zimbabwe	60,000	–	–	–	–	–	555.0
Zambia	14,300	37	35	–	30	28	617.2
Subregional	199,300	123	98	54	595	388	1,978.4
Nigeria	173,000	21	30	12	50	118	1,750.0
Subregional and Nigeria	372,300	144	128	66	645	506	3,728.4
South Africa	81,400 (404,500 including reserves)	416***	170	23	270	3,160	2,760.0

Source: The Military Balance, 1979-80 and 1982/83 (London: ILSS).

[1]All armed naval units counted equally; only Nigeria and South Africa have armed units beyond patrol craft.
*Data for 1977 from World Military Expenditures and Arms Transfers, 1968-77 and 1972-82 (Washington, D.C.: ACDC, April 1984).
**Includes paramilitary forces.
***Does not include armed helicopters, transport and utility aircraft.

and equipment totals means little without an analysis of other, less quantifiable variables. For instance, the capacity of a nation's force to deploy, maneuver, and resupply units in combat is perhaps the most decisive factor. South Africa has the military capacity to strike hundreds of miles beyond its borders. None of the SADCC states or any other of the African states has at present the capacity to deploy more than a token force to a potential combat zone on South Africa's periphery without substantial outside logistical and other support. There are both political and logistical advantages accruing from South Africa's unitary command structure and internal lines of supply when contrasted with a possible wartime coalition of SADCC states or the African States as a whole. SADCC states are not only militarily weak and preoccupied with their own internal security, they are also autonomous political units with their own specific interests. A common military stance may perhaps not be easy or simple to maintain for SADCC, at least for sometime.

We are not contending that the size of an army per se determines its effectiveness in combat. But if we look at the economies of the SADCC states, their structural problems as well as dependence on South Africa and the Western World; the huge costs of reconstruction and rehabilitation in the newly liberated countries are enormous. Dependence of some Southern African states on foreign troops for survival and antecedents or inability to contain South African aggression there is little reason not to regard as rhetoric the SADCC objective of political liberation. Most SADCC states, in spite of their abhorrence of minority white rule and condemnation of South Africa's aggression, have either been compelled to sign peace agreements, are discussing the possibility of signing one or have declared, even without signing such an agreement that they would not provide training facilities for liberation movements or use their own forces against South Africa. For instance, immediately after Mozambican independence in 1975, its Foreign Minister, Joaquim Chissano declared that, "Mozambique would become a revolutionary base against imperialism and colonialism in Africa and at the same time it will co-exist with apartheid South Africa". He went further and said, "we do not pretend to be the saviours of the world, we will not be saviours or the reformers of South Africa themselves".[16] Similarly, Swaziland's Foreign Minister, Velaphi Dlamini declared in March 1980, that his country "would not support sanctions against South Africa".[17] This was only a restatement of a declaration made by King Sobhuza II of Swaziland in an address to the Swazi Parliament in 1980, in which King Sobhuza II categorically stated that his government "would not allow any organization to use Swaziland as a spring board for attacks against South Africa".[18] In any case, Swaziland has secretly signed a non-aggression agreement with South Africa in 1982. And in February 1985, South Africa opened a consulate office in Mbabane, Swaziland, as a result of the signing of an agreement on 28 December 1984 establishing official trade links between Swaziland and South Africa.[19] In the same vein, Botswana, Lesotho, Malawi and Zimbabwe have made such declarations after attaining their independence. To cap the whole issue Angola and Mozambique have signed a non-aggression agreement with South Africa early in 1984.[20] Despite these agreements, UNITA, and MNR with the covert support of South African troops, and overt support of

UNITA by the Reagan administration continued destabilizing the Southern African states.[21]

Though, the actions of Angola and Mozambique had the support of SADCC states (see Appendix 7, page 310) it shocked most observers who saw it as a sell out, a betrayal of Marxian principles of armed struggle to overthrow imperialism, a retreat from earlier positions and failure to follow a path which won them their own independence. However, it is essential not to be too emotional about the developments, even if we must admit that these kinds of agreements no doubt would make a serious dent in SADCC's political objectives, and a compromise of its liberation objectives. The SADCC member-states should realize, that the Boer ruling authority in South Africa cannot be trusted, and while the Angolan and Mozambican moves might be reflective of softening political positions and coalition with South Africa, it could also reflect a deepening crisis within apartheid system and the need to buy some breathing space. The move on the side of Angola and Mozambique must also be seen as reflective of the crisis that these countries have faced since achieving political independence in 1975. They have never really been allowed by South Africa to build their brands of socialism, meet the basic needs of their peoples, mobilize internal human and material resources, and supports for national security, and reconstruction facilities which were destroyed during the liberation struggles. In fact, it is only when they are secure and stable that they can mobilize and utilize, their human and material resources for the development of their countries. As shown in the foregoing chapters, especially in Chapter Five, South Africa's aggression against its neighbouring states has wasted lives and properties, schools, bridges, hospitals, roads, farmlands and so on - all these have been destroyed by the racist South African troops in pursuit of freedom fighters of the ANC and SWAPO.[22] But still, the 1983-1984 non-aggression agreements with South Africa have not allowed the SADCC states to reconsolidate, rehabilitate and put themselves on a stronger footing to contribute to the "anti-racial" and "anti-white minority dominance" principles of SADCC. In the short run, these agreements could be a cover up, to buy peace while continuing to support the liberation movements.

In any case, South African President P. W. Botha has suggested the formation of a Joint Regional Security Commission between South Africa, Botswana, Lesotho, Mozambique, Swaziland and Zimbabwe. This is a new and latest South African strategy of desperation to dominate its neighbours, since its so-called constellation of states of Southern Africa has failed. This strategy will also fail just like that of the constellation of states' strategy.[23]

Alternative Options for Southern Africa

For any meaningful development to take place in Southern Africa sub-region, the Southern Nine has to break its unequal relationship with the Western Capitalist world. The present arrangement whereby the organization is looking up mainly to the west for assistance amounts to putting all its eggs in one basket. We have been able to establish in this book, especially in Chapters Two, Three and Four that the West's activities in the Southern Africa sub-region is not borne out of economic altruism but for the satisfaction of their own ends.

As Judith Hart, a former British Minister for the Overseas Development Ministry, has frankly admitted that "much of what goes under the rubric of aid is highly questionable".[24] Evidence available in the case of Africa as a whole suggests that aid programmes and international capitalism, as currently administered, and in so far as they are concerned with economic development, frequently are counter-productive. And moreover, they have resulted in a growing debt burden of African countries, precipitating acute balance of payments problems, and severe restrictions upon the conduct of domestic policy. It is not being suggested, however, that economic development of Southern Africa will depend solely or exclusively on the flow of external resources. For it cannot be blindly assumed that there is a direct positive relationship between external assistance and economic development. The relationship may exist, but it has to be demonstrated. Moreover, much of the success of the development programmes will also depend on the extent of commitment of the Southern African governments themselves, that is, whether they are primarily "interested" in the development of their countries. However, this may depend upon what one means by "development".

The SADCC might do well to call for investments which will be of mutual benefit to both sides from the countries of Eastern Europe and the Nordic countries. The activities of the latter in Southern Africa show that of being committed to African economic development, at least more than the western powers.[25] As of now Scandinavian countries are already involved in projects being embarked upon by the SADCC. Sweden for example is involved in projects for technological development in eight of the nine Southern Africa countries.

It is not difficult to point out the incompatibility of interest between the West and the SADCC states. The former has an institutionalized machinery which serves the purpose of getting the world within its sphere of influence especially in the economic sense. The latter on the other hand will like to see the cycle of dependence broken and become less dependent on the West. The forces of history have therefore, made the West the controller of the economic fortunes of Southern Africa in particular and Africa in general. SADCC countries therefore, have a natural ally in the struggle for economic emancipation. The organization should regard the Soviets, the East Germans, and other Eastern powers as dependable partners in the struggle for economic emancipation.

It will be to the advantage of SADCC if it could embrace investors who are interested in ventures in Southern Africa. Instead of investing to make quick money, this group of investors is interested in projects that will eventually enhance the technological development of the region. They are also interested in going into joint ventures with either the SADCC or indegenous business concerns. To back SADCC projects, "India has agreed to more than $75 million in export credits for SADCC industrial projects, including several joint ventures".[26] Furthermore, the sum of India's joint venture programmes in Africa is the largest in the world when measured in terms of capital actually invested or committed.[27] For instance, Tanzania, a SADCC member state has entered into joint venture with India in the area of fertilizer production.[28] So also have some of the ECOWAS nations, Nigeria being a good example.

Another area in which India is a well-qualified partner for development is in food and industrial products, in which India is now one of the world's leading nations. Overall, the "green revolution" which is something of a non-event in most of Africa, but in India it has been a sensational success. Over the last ten years, food-grain output has risen by nearly 50 percent, and at least as significant - irrigation advances have evened out the troughs caused by savagely unreliable climate. In industry there is hardly any product that India does not produce, including sophisticated communications satellites and the vehicles to launch them. Her key resource is a huge and highly trained workforce. The extensively regulated economy uses these skills to make and export complex products including complete plants for the industrial development that so many African nations are seeking.[29] India is especially important because it has similar historical experience, and as a Third World nation like the SADCC. India was colonized by Britain which left an economic set up that was supposed to put India in the position of an exporter of primary products to the industries of Britain to the latter's advantage.

Given the Southern African experiences with the colonial imperialism and the white minority settler domination, it is high time that the SADCC states should stop believing that their salvation lies in the developed countries of the West coming to their rescue, and adopt politics of (collective) regional economic cooperation and national self-reliance. First, I here suggest that rather than continuing to associate with the Western European powers or organizations, such as the European Economic Community, the SADCC states should endeavour to harmonize their economic, industrial and agricultural policies within the framework of an African Common market which is the essence of the Lagos Plan of Action. To be sure, regional economic cooperation and national self-reliance is one of the major objectives of the Lagos Plan of Action. In many ways, the Lagos Plan of Action and the Final Act of Lagos constitute not only new ideas and concepts of development and growth but also new strategies of initiating and pursuing development and economic objectives. These strategies call not only for a radical restructuring of African economies; they also call for the mobilization of Africa's immense human and natural resources in the pursuit of sectoral integration and regional economic cooperation.

Secondly, SADCC is increasing its efforts and preparedness to draw lessons from the experiences of other Third World integration schemes. For instance, in 1983, a delegation of SADCC visited the Caribbean to study the Caribbean Community. SADCC must make efforts to understand the reasons for the demise of the East African Community, the problems of ECOWAS and of the Andean group, especially in the areas of their connections with MNCs, and the Western Capitalist Powers. If anything, the activities and interests of the Western capitalist powers, since the 1960s, have shown that they are not interested in supporting collective self-reliance in Africa not to mention an organization like SADCC which combines political and economic goals. In addition, the cautious and limited support from the socialist Eastern bloc appears to arise from the ideological goals which the USSR must have deduced from SADCC realities and ambitions, to the extent that a collection of dependent states and some "socialist economies", cannot hope to overthrow apartheid, dependence and poverty by relying on the imperialist Western Powers. SADCC must therefore, redefine its current approach towards collective self-reliance development and be prepared to instill discipline within its ranks.

Thirdly, SADCC needs to cooperate with the donor countries from a position of strength and not from a position of weakness. Most of the donors and investors, have important economic and strategic interests in the Boer dominated South Africa, on which SADCC aims to reduce economic dependence. Whether further non-aggression pacts are reached between South Africa and its neighbours or not, the liberation of the White racist dominated South Africa is one of the SADCC objectives. The Western collaborators of South Africa know this, and the Boer authority in South Africa is scared of it. Most of the Western countries helping SADCC have large investments in South Africa and are scared of any change in the status quo in South Africa.

Therefore, many of these Western countries would even have wished to see the SADCC states remaining disunited and weak in relation to South Africa, and continuing to depend on it. Besides, the Nordic countries, many of the Western countries continued to trade with the white racist regime in South Africa, but because they want to be on the winning side of history and naturally continue to serve their strategic and economic interests in the Southern Africa sub-region,[30] even after the apartheid might have been dismantled.

Fourthly, on the aid issue, I here suggest that, SADCC ought to act swiftly in addressing the question of aid and foreign investment, and draw up an investment code for the organization that would better provide for more, by the organization, of the growth and development that takes place through their cooperation. Proper management of development is not really possible without a firmer public ethic and better understanding of development requirements by political leaders, therefore, more attention must be paid to trade than aid. Inter-States trade should be encouraged by the SADCC member States.

Fifthly, because of international sanctions being imposed on South Africa, the Lusaka based Southern African Team for Employment (SATEP) should set up a study commission to find ways of creating job opportunities for migrant workers into the home economy before South Africa decided to repatriate all migrant workers to their respective countries.

Sixthly, in addition I suggest a formalized military agreement between the SADCC States to strengthening their regional cooperation. This move has been made by the Frontline States which constituted two-thirds of the SADCC States. With SADCC now becoming a reality, there is a need for a formalized military cooperation between the member states through a formalized defense treaty.

CONCLUSION

In making predictions about the future of SADCC and
Southern Africa we have to put many factors and forces
into consideration. The fact is that such predictions
can at best be tentative and highly subject to
change(s). Considering changing configurations, economic and political - within the Southern African
states, as well as within the international division of
labour, Southern Africa is integrated into the capitalist system, the nature and direction of the liberation
struggles in the sub-region, the deepening economic crisis of the SADCC states, the increasing political problems of the member states and continuous contradictions
arising from underdevelopment and dependence on the
great powers, are all bound to have an impact upon the
future of the SADCC cooperation scheme. SADCC's
achievements in view of the Southern Africa's development needs are indeed modest and encouraging. However,
they are only the first steps on a very long road ahead,
successful SADCC projects are clearly a threat to South
Africa apartheid regime, which has imposed economic
sanctions, and declared war on SADCC.

As examined in the foregoing chapters, SADCC having
concretely re-defined regionalism as self-reliance and
having made a fundamental linkage between the political
and the economic issue, faces internal and external obstacles; both are precipitates of the historical experiences of the Southern African states economies as well
as the manner in which they are structurally incorpo-
rated into the world system. The dependence of SADCC
states - socialist or capitalist - on foreign aid, technology, military and technical assistance, food aid and
many other supports and consequently, the dependence of

SADCC on foreign aid are equally bound to have some impact on the organizations's autonomy and thus circumscribe its ability to mobilize internal resources for self-reliance, growth and development. It must alsu be emphasized that all the same, conditions are not static.

The experience of Third World integration schemes, for instance, the Caribbean Economic Community (CARICOM), Andean Group and ECOWAS, so far show that the over politicization of integration institutions, policies and projects, the promulgation of nationalistic economic policies which conflict with regional programmes and the specific and broad interests of TNCs, would continue for a long time to come to influence even in some cases determine cooperation schemes. Collective self-reliance, especially when conceptualized as a move to reverse the conditions of underdevelopment and dependence, must take those problems into consideration. SADCC does not appear to be in a position for now to effectively deal with these problems. This is not because at the level of declarations SADCC was unaware of the problems of underdevelopment, foreign domination and mass poverty, and particularly how these deepen the crisis of national economies and consequently the regional economy. At the Lusaka summit, President Kaunda declared:

> Let us face the economic challenge. Let us form a powerful front against poverty and all of its offshoots of hunger, ignorance, disease, crime and exploitation of man by man. Let this summit be our workshop for sharpening our tools, forging new weapons, working out strategy and tactics for fighting poverty and improving the quality of life of our people.[31]

These are the problems which would continue to militate against the ability of the SADCC states to absorb the shocks of regional cooperation, confront their traditional struggle against underdevelopment in the interests of the majority. It is a contradiction for the SADCC states to continue to depend on the West and South Africa, and at the same time talk about self-reliance, without concrete efforts or preparedness on their part to make sacrifices and break age-old dependence on the West.

The intensification of liberation struggles in South Africa and Namibia and the deepening struggles between the governments and rebel forces within other SADCC states will have direct impacts on the stability and functioning of Southern Nine. Hopefully Namibia will achieve its independence very soon, and majority rule in South Africa will follow shortly. Radical, or maybe socialist governments will come to power in these states, should this happen the number of radical or socialist states within the Southern African states will increase. This will affect debates and the nature of projects sponsored by the SADCC. The possibilities of deepening the liberation goals of the SADCC can then be taken seriously. In the case of the Nkomati accord, it is a strategy to confer legitimacy on South Africa's policy of destabilizing its neighbours in order to prevent any useful discussion of Namibiam independence and the institutionalization of perpetual racism under the white regime in South Africa.

Compared with most other African regional cooperation schemes, the objectives of the SADCC are fairly realistic. Given the political will in the leadership of member-states, they are succeeding in establishing and running some common training and research facilities, in streamlining the regulations governing intragroup trade, transport and related matters and in creating a community spirit. In this respect, a good example which is already in operation is Mozambique-Tanzania Permanent Commission of Cooperation. This Commission is referred to as the model for agreement in many of the SADCC papers. However, all these depend on many factors, and the future development of Southern Africa will depend on many outside factors too. Most important among these would be the course of the international economic system. The prevailing view among economists appears to be that this gives ground for serious concern, notably on account of the energy position, the poor and underdeveloped countries' increasing inability to cope with population growth, food needs, drought and refugee problems, and external indebtedness.[32] The apparent secular slowing down of industrial expansion and population growth in the highly industrialized countries, and growing East-West tension, which in turn reinforces the conflicts between rich and poor countries. The effects of recession and high rates of inflation in the Western economies have already affected their willingness to assist African countries financially in recent years. All these have decreased purchases of non-essential commodities.

SADCC needs to move swiftly to demonstrate the concrete benefits that it is capable of providing if it is to retain the allegiance of member-states. In this regard, SADCC may have the easier task ahead. Not only has it fewer members to satisfy and a lengthy catalogue of short term projects ready to process, but its leaders appear more committed to its success, personally and politically than is the case with the defunct East African Community and the former Central African Federation.

Partly, no doubt, this is because SADCC is less demanding of its members; its acceptance of the sovereign authority of national governments is more unqualified. On
the other hand, an excessive emphasis on the exercise of
state autonomy could prove a serious weakness. Cooperation is of course a means, not an end. The salvation of
Southern Africa is economic cooperation and with this
free trade idea Southern African liberation will surely
be achieved.

The above predictions take note of many factors and
forces, firstly, the increasing crisis within the
metropolitan countries; secondly, the geo-strategic and
economic interests of the West and MNCs; thirdly, the
possibility of deepening crisis within the radical and
socialist states; fourthly, the 1984 non-aggression
agreements signed between Angola and South Africa, and
between Mozambique and South Africa.[33] Fifth, changes
in oil and gold prices in the international markets, especially the low price of gold has affected the South
African economy besides, recent intensifying of the liberation struggles by the ANC and SWAPO which is paralyz-
ing and demoralizing the morales of the white population
in South Africa and in Namibia. Sixth, the cost of ser-
vicing the mounting debts of African nations which is
estimated at about $170 billion by 1985 figures.[34] Sev-
enth, the nuclear proliferation which is increasing the
tensions between the East and West are complicating
north-south relationships, and the developing countries
could easily become theatres of conflicts that might result in war between the nuclear powers.[35] Lastly, the
worldwide recession. Essentially, these developments
would generate a need to resolve regional problems collectively in Southern Africa, thus promoting agreement
and cooperation among and between "radical socialist"

and "conservative" states, even if disagreements continue to emanate from specific aspects.

So the record of SADCC is spotty and successes few. The key is transportation and communications. In this area some advances have been made but more need to be done. Getting the railways and ports of the nine independent black ruled Southern African states to operate would in a sense promote all of the goals of SADCC, reduce dependence, and promote integration, spur development and encourage regional cooperation. There is a tendency to blame transportation problems on the destabilizing effects of South African policy. But SADCC states have yet to prove they can operate a railway efficiently; even in the 1982-84 drought years, the Southern Africa sub-region was almost totally dependent on South African ports for the importation of food.

Other development plans in SADCC have dismal prospects. Each year the trade among the Southern Nine declines even further. Still, SADCC has survived. The organization is not moribund. For an African regional organization that alone is an achievement. It has raised international finance in a shrinking market. It has completed a number of projects in the transportation and communications sectors. It has avoided flamboyant proclamations and suppressed interstate disputes. SADCC has helped to expose the racist regime in South Africa, and aroused its anger. It has provoked the forces of apartheid to strike out openly. Dependence upon South Africa has increased but cannot be blamed upon SADCC. The degree of success of SADCC may be difficult to gauge. One way to estimate it might be by assessing the degree of concern it raises in Pretoria. Finally, the Southern African states must be willing to promote liberation and self-reliance within their own national economies before extending them to the regional level. SADCC has a future as a functional regional cooperation, with the initial enthusiasm and willingness of its members, but a better promising future will not be secured for Southern Africa without serious struggles - individually, collectively and institutionally.

The assumption that (foreign) Western capitalism or direct foreign investment or transnational corporations are an "engine" of development, in that they contribute resources not otherwise available or only available in insufficient quantities has proved to be mistaken in the case of Southern Africa and the Africa as a whole. However, it is important to emphasize, that external resources without internal reform will naturally not be in the best interest of Southern Africa. And to think that the way for a spontaneous development of the economy is free when "external differences" are overcome is dangerous self-deception. There is therefore, the need for general commitment by the Southern African countries to introduce relevant, practical, and effective measures to accelerate the pace of growth and development. In this regard, the adoption of the self-reliant and self-sustaining strategy of development is a step in the right direction. After all development is "endogenous"; it springs from the heart of each society, which relies first on its own strength and resources and "defines in sovereignty the vision of its future", cooperating with societies, sharing its problems and aspirations. Thus, the economic prosperity of the Southern African countries in the 1980s and beyond would depend, to a considerable extent, on their ability to transform the concepts and the objectives of the SADCC from political slogans into a framework for policy and effective action.

NOTES

[1]"Angola and South Africa: War and Blackmail",
Africa (London), March 1984, pp. 37-39.

[2]For   details   on   the   Zimbabwe's   Independence
Struggle   see   Olayiwola   Abegunrin,   *Nigeria and the*
Struggle for the Liberation of Zimbabwe (forthcoming).

[3]See Seretse Khama's Keynote Address in Amon J.
Nsekela (ed.) *op. cit.*

[4]*Ibid*.

[5]*Ibid*.

[6]R.   H.   Green,   "Constellation,   Association,
Liberation: Economic Coordination and the Struggle for
Southern Africa" in *ACR 1979/80* (1980), p. A. 37.

[7]Kenneth W. Grundy, *Confrontation and Accommodation*
in   Southern   Africa: The   Limits   of   Independence
(Berkeley: University   of   California   Press,   1973),
pp. 29-32.

[8]See Amon J. Nsekela (ed.), *op. cit.*, p. 2.

[9]In   October   1983   President   Samora   Machel   of
Mozambique   for   the   first   time   in   the   history   of
Mozambique undertook a trip which, apart from Yugoslavia
one of his traditional socialist allies, took him mainly
to   Western   European   countries   –   Belgium,   the
Netherlands,   Portugal,   France   and   Britain.   See
Marcelino Komba "Mozambique: Pledges of Aid from the
West" *Africa* (November 1983), pp. 29-30.

[10]For details see Organization of African Unity,
Lagos Plan of Action for the Economic Development of
Africa, 1980-2000 (Geneva: International Institute for
Labour Studies, 1981).

[11]See report of the Committee of Foreign Relations,
U.S. House of Representatives, Subcommittee on Africa,
Hearing   before   the   Subcommittee   on   Africa   of   the
Committee on Foreign Affairs, House of Representatives,

97th Congress, 2nd Session 8 December 1982, <u>Regional Destabilization in Southern Africa</u> (Washington, D.C.: U.S. Government Printing Office, 1983) pp. 2-12. See also Glenn Frankel, "South African backed Rebels Weaken Mozambique", <u>The Washington Post</u> 8 October, 1984, pp. 1 & 36.

[12]See Chapter Five and Appendix 6 on Nkomati Accords. See also "Racist Troops Leave Angola" <u>Daily Sketch</u> (Ibadan) 16 February, 1984.

[13]On the South African Nuclear Weapons see Zdenek Cervenka, and Rogers, Barbara, <u>The Nuclear Axis: Secret Collaboration Between West Germany and South Africa</u> (London: Julian Friedmann, 1978).

[14]Report of the Study Commission on United States Policy Toward Southern Africa, <u>South Africa: Time Running Out</u> (Berkeley: University of California Press, 1981), p. 239.

[15]<u>Ibid</u>.

[16]Tony Hodges, "Mozambique: The Politics of Liberation", in G. M. Carter and Patrick O'Meara (eds.) <u>op. cit.</u>, pp. 79-80.

[17]"Swaziland" <u>ACR 1980/81</u> (1981), p. B. 889.

[18]<u>Ibid</u>.

[19]Banji Adeyanju, "Racists Subdue Frontline States", <u>Sunday Concord</u> 29 April, 1984, p. 13. See also Roger Murray, "SWAZILAND: South African trade pact highlights closer relations", <u>African Business</u>, Feb., 1985, p. 23.

[20]Joanmarie Kalter, "Mozambique's Peace with South Africa". Also see Jose Luis Cabaco, "The Nkomati Accords", <u>Africa Report</u> May-June 1984, pp. 19-27.

[21]Sheilah Ocampo, "Rebels Invade Maputo Streets Following Accord", <u>National Concord</u>, 6 July 1984, p. 13. See also Colin Legum, "Angola-South Africa: Lusaka Accord in Danger", <u>New Africa</u> September 1984, pp. 28-29.

[22]See The Zimbabwean Herald (Harare) 27 April, 1983. See also Walton R. Johnson, "Destabilization in Southern Africa" Trans-Africa Forum, Vol. 2, No. 2, (Fall 1984), pp. 65-76.

[23]P. W. Botha's speech delivered to the white South African Parliament on 31 January 1986, Radio RSA broadcast (Johannesburg: 31 January, 1986).

[24]See Judith Hart, Aid and Liberation (London, 1973).

[25]Jorge Tavares de Carvalho Simoes (ed.). Energy, Environment and Development in Africa 2, SADCC: Energy and Development to the Year 2000. SADCC Energy Sector in collaboration with The Beijer Institute and the Scandinavian Institute of African Studies (Uddevalla: Bohuslaningens AB, 1984).

[26]Joseph Hanlon, "The business of Liberation: the SADCC fights to keep the taint of apartheid out of its trade", South December 1984, p. 70.

[27]"Joint Ventures spearhead export drive", African Business, March 1985, p. 59.

[28]Ibid., p. 60.

[29]Ibid., p. 58.

[30]O. Abegunrin, "Western Options Vis-a-Vis South Africa" The Western Journal of Black Studies, Vol. 6, No. 4, Winter 1982, p. 239.

[31]Amon J. Nsekela (ed.) op. cit., p. IX.

[32]Emergency Committee for African Refugees "U.S. Policy and the Current Refugee Crisis in Africa", ISSUE Vol. XII, Nos. 1/2 (1982), pp. 10-13. See also, Roberts Browns and E. I. M. Mtei, "Africa and the IMF" in Africa Report, September-October, 1984, pp. 14-21. See also "Africa's Drought", Africa Report July-August 1984, pp. 11-27.

[33]See Chapter Five (page 166) and Appendix 6 (page 303) in this book, also Sean Moroney, "Sympathy Alone is not Enough" African Business, March 1983, pp. 15-16.

[34]For details see "African Debt" South July 1985, pp. 31-32.

[35]Layi Abegunrin, "Why the arms race must be halted" Daily Sketch (Ibadan), 19 August 1982, p. 5.

APPENDICES

APPENDIX 1

The Organizational Structure of SADCC

THE ANNUAL SUMMIT   A

·

THE MINISTERIAL COUNCIL   B

STANDING COMMITTEE   EXECUTIVE SECRETARY   SECTORAL
OF OFFICIALS   SECRETARIAT   COMMISSIONS C

297

APPENDIX 2

SADCC PROGRAMME OF ACTION
Allocation of Responsibilities for Regional Coordination
of Sectoral Activities

Coordinating Government	Sector	Projects (1982)	Administrative Structure
Angola	Energy Conservation and Security		Technical unit, Ministry of Energy
Botswana	Animal disease control	3	
	Crop research in the semi-arid tropics		
Lesotho	Soil conservation and land utilization		Technical unit, Ministry of Agriculture
Malawi	Fisheries, forestry and wildlife	9	
Mozambique	Transport and communications	106	Technical unit, Southern African Transport and Communications Commission (SATCC)
Swaziland	Manpower development	1	
Tanzania	Industrial develop.	10	Technical unit
Zambia	Southern African development fund		
	Mining		Working Group, Ministry of Mines
Zimbabwe	Food security plan	9	Administrative support Unit Ministry of Agriculture
	Security printing		Fidelity Printers

Source: An expanded version of Table 2, in Douglas G.
Anglin, "Economic Liberation and Regional Cooperation in
Southern Africa : SADCC and PTA" International
Organization, Vol. 37, No.4 (1983) p. 694.

APPENDIX 3

SADCC: COOPERATING GOVERNMENTS AND AGENCIES

	SADCC 1 ARUSHA July 1979	SADCC 2 MAPUTO Nov. 1980	SADCC 3 BLANTYRE Nov. 1980
OECD MEMBERS			
1. Australia	X	X	X
2. Austria		X	*
3. Belgium	X	X	X
4. Canada	X	X	X
5. Denmark	X	X	X
6. Finland		X	X
7. France		X	X
8. Germany	X	X	X
9. Ireland		X	X
10. Italy		X	X
11. Japan		X	X
12. Luxembeurg		X	
13. Netherlands	X	X	X
14. Norway	X	X	X
15. Portugal			X
16. Sweden	X	X	X
17. Switzerland		X	X
18. United Kingdom	X	X	X
19. United States	X	X	X
CMEA MEMBERS			
1. Bulgaria		X	*
2. Czechoslovakia		X	
3. E. Germany		X	X
4. Hungary		X	
5. Rumania		X	
NON-ALIGNED STATES			
1. Algeria		X	
2. Brazil		X	X
3. India		X	X
4. Iraq		X	
5. Venezuela		X	*
6. Yugoslavia		X	*
TOTAL	9	29	20

* Invited but did not attend.

APPENDIX 3

SADCC: COOPERATING GOVERNMENTS AND AGENCIES

	SADCC 1 ARUSHA July 1979	SADCC 2 MAPUTO Nov. 1980	SADCC 3 BLANTYRE Nov. 1980
UNITED NATIONS			
1. United Nations	X	X	
2. UNDP		X	X
3. UNCTAD		X	X
4. World Bank	X	X	X
5. FAO	X	X	X
6. IFAD		X	X
7. ILO			X
8. ITU		X	
9. UNFPA			X
EUROPEAN ORGANIZATIONS			
1. EEC	X	X	X
2. European Investment Bank		X	X
3. Nordic Investment Bank		X	*
ARAB FUNDS			
1. BADEA	X	X	X
2. Kuwait Fund		X	*
3. OPEC		X	*
AFRICAN ORGANIZATIONS			
1. African Development Bank	X	X	X
2. ECA	X	X	X
3. OAU		X	
OTHER ORGANIZATIONS			
1. Commonwealth	X	X	X
2. CMEA		X	
TOTAL	8	18	12

*Invited but did not attend

APPENDIX 4
<u>CHRONOLOGY OF SADCC MEETING 1979-1984</u>

Date	Annual SADCC Conferences	Summit Conferences	Council of Ministers
1970			
May	--	--	Gaborone (FLS)
July	Arusha (SADCC 1)	--	Arusha (FLS)
November	--	--	Dar-es-Salaam (FLS)
1980			
April	--	Lusaka	Lusaka
July	Maputo	--	Maputo
August	--	--	Ezulwini
September	--	--	Beira
September	--	--	Harare
November	Maputo (SADCC 2)	--	Maputo
1981			
January	--	--	Maputo
March	--	--	Dar-es-Salaam
May	--	--	Maputo
June	--	--	Mbabane
July	--	Harare	Harare
July	--	--	Luanda
August	--	--	Lusaka
November	Blantyre (SADCC 3)	--	Blantyre
1982			
March	--	--	Maputo
June	--	--	Luanda
July	--	--	Gaborone
October	--	SADCC Secretariat opens in Gaborone	--
December	--	--	Harare

Date	Annual SADCC Conferences	Summit Conferences	Council of Ministers
1983			
January	Maseru (SADCC 4)	--	Maseru
May	--	--	Dar-es-Salaam
July	--	Maputo	Maputo
October	--	--	Dar-es-Salaam
1984			
January	--	--	Harare
February	Lusaka (SADCC 5)	--	Lusaka

Source: Richard F. Weisfelder "The Southern African Development Coordination Conference: A new factor in the Liberation Process" in Thomas M. Callaghy (ed.), South Africa in Southern Africa (New York: Praeger Publishers, 1983). African Research Bulletin, March-April 1980, January-February 1981, July-August 1981, February-March 1982, July-August 1982, January-February 1983, April-May 1983, October-November 1983. See also Africa Economic Digest (London) January-February 1984.

BASIC INDICATORS FOR THE SADCC STATES

COUNTRY	Population millions mid-1979	Area thousands of square kilometers	GNP per capita Average annual growth rate % 1960-79	Life Expectancy at birth (years) 1979	Average Index of food production per capita (1969-71 = 100) 1977-79	Income Terms of trade* (1975=100) 1960, 1970, 1979			Percentage share in total exports of three principal exports 1976-78 Average^xx
Angola	6.9	1,247	-2.1	42	85	30	93	102	60.9
Botswana	0.8	600	9.1	49	89	NA	NA	NA	99.1
Lesotho	1.3	30	6.0	51	100	NA	NA	NA	100.0
Malawi	5.8	118	2.9	47	100	40	83	112	83.1
Mozambique	10.2	783	0.1	47	75	89	167	32	25.6
Swaziland	0.5	17	7.2	47	109	NA	NA	NA	58.9
Tanzania	18.0	945	2.3	52	94	118	152	104	55.4
Zambia	5.6	753	0.8	49	99	99	238	91	96.2
Zimbabwe	7.1	391	0.8	55	100	NA	NA	NA	21.9

* = Income terms of trade are an index of the value of commodity exports divided by import unit value.

xx = Commodity concentration is the current value of the three principal commodities in the exports of each of the SADCC Member-States as a percentage of the total current value of merchandise exports.

NA = Not available.

Source: The World Bank, Accelerated Development in Sub-Saharan Africa: An Agenda for Action (Washington, D.C.: The World Bank, 1981), pp. 143, 155 and 156.

APPENDIX 6

Text of the Nkomati Accords signed by the Government of the People's Republic of Mozambique and the Government of the Republic of South Africa on 16 March, 1984.

The government of the people's Republic of Mozambique and the government of the Republic of South Africa, hereinafter referred to as the High Contracting Parties, recognizing the principles of strict respect for sovereignty and territorial integrity, sovereign equality, political independence and the inviolability of the borders of all states, re-affirming the principle of non-interference in the internal affairs of other states, considering the internationally recognized principle of the right of peoples to self-determination and independence and the principle of equal rights of all peoples, considering the obligation of all states to refrain, in their international relations, from the threat or use of force against the territorial integrity or political independence of any state, considering the obligation of states to settle conflicts by peaceful means, and thus safeguard international peace and security and justice, recognizing the responsibility of states not to allow their territory to be used for acts of war, aggression or violence against other states, conscious of the need to promote relations of good neighbourliness based on the principles of equality of rights and mutual advantage, convinced that relations of good neighbourliness between the High Contracting Parties will contribute to peace, security, stability and progress in Southern Africa, the continent and the world, have solemnly agreed to the following:

Article One

The High Contracting Parties undertake to respect each other's sovereignty and independence and in fulfillment of this fundamental obligation, to refrain from interfering in the internal affairs of the other.

Article Two

1. The High Contracting Parties shall resolve differences and disputes that may arise between them and that may or are likely to, endanger mutual peace and security or peace and security in the region, by means of negotiation, enquiry, mediation, conciliation, arbitration or other peaceful means, and undertake not to resort, individually or collectively, to the threat or use of force against each other's sovereignty, territorial integrity or political independence.

2. For the purpose of this article, the use of force shall include inter alia:
   (a) Attacks by land, air or sea forces
   (b) Sabotage
   (c) Unwarranted concentration of such forces at or near the international boundaries of the High Contracting Parties.
   (d) Violation of the international land, air or sea boundaries of either of the High Contracting Parties.

3. The High Contracting Parties shall not in any way assist the armed forces of any state or group of states deployed against the territorial sovereignty or political independence of the other.

Article Three

1. The High Contracting Parties shall not allow their respective territories, territorial waters or air

space to be used as a base, thoroughfare, or in any other way by another state, government, foreign military forces, organizations or individuals which plan or prepare to commit acts of violence, terrorism or aggression against the territorial integrity or political independence of the other or may threaten the security of its inhabitants.

2. The High Contracting Parties, in order to prevent or eliminate the acts or the preparation of acts mentioned in paragraph 1 of this article, undertake in particular to:

(a) Forbid and prevent in their respective territories the organization of irregular forces or armed bands, including mercenaries, whose objective is to carry out the acts contemplated in paragraph 1 of this article.

(b) Eliminate from their respective territories bases, training centres, places of shelter, accommodation and transit for elements who intend to carry out the acts contemplated in paragraph 1 of this article.

(c) Eliminate from their respective territories centres or depots containing armaments of whatever nature, destined to be used by the elements contemplated in paragraph 1 of this article.

(d) Eliminate from their respective territories command posts or other places for the command, direction and coordination of the elements contemplated in paragraph 1 of this article.

(e) Eliminate from their respective territories communication facilities between the command and the elements contemplated in paragraph 1 of this article.

(f) Eliminate and prohibit the installation in their respective territories of radio broadcasting stations, including unofficial or clandestine broadcasts, for the elements that carry out the acts contemplated in paragraph 1 of this article.

(g) Exercise strict control, in their respective territories, over elements which intend to carry out or plan the acts contemplated in paragraph 1 of this article.

(h) Prevent the transit of elements who intend or plan to commit the acts contemplated in paragraph 1 of this article, from a place in the territory of either to a place in the territory of the other or to a place in the territory of any third state which has a common boundary with the High Contracting Party against which such elements intended or plan to commit the said acts.

(i) Take appropriate steps in their respective territories to prevent the recruitment of elements of whatever nationality for the purpose of carrying out the acts contemplated in paragraph 1 of this article.

(j) Prevent the elements contemplated in paragraph 1 of this article from carrying out from their respective territories by any means acts of abduction or other acts, aimed at taking citizens of any nationality hostage in the territory of the other High Contracting Party, and

(k) Prohibit the provision on their respective territories of any logistic facilities for carrying out the acts contemplated in paragraph 1 of this article.

3. The High Contracting Parties will not use the territory of third states to carry out or support the acts contemplated in paragraphs 1 and 2 of this article.

Article Four

The High Contracting Parties shall take steps, individually and collectively, to ensure that the international boundary between their respective territories is effectively patrolled and that the border posts are efficiently administered to prevent illegal crossings from the territory of a High Contracting Party to the territory of the other, and in particular, by elements contemplated in Article Three of this agreement.

Article Five

The High Contracting Parties shall prohibit within their territory acts of propaganda that incite a war of aggression against the other High Contracting Party and shall also prohibit acts of propaganda aimed at inciting acts of terrorism and civil war in the territory of the other High Contracting Party.

Article Six

The High Contracting Parties declare that there is no conflict between their commitments in treaties and international obligations and the commitments undertaken in this agreement.

Article Seven

The High Contracting Parties are committed to interpreting this agreement in good faith and will maintain periodic contact to ensure the effective application of what has been agreed.

Article Eight

Nothing in this agreement shall be construed as detracting from the High Contracting Parties' right of self-defense in the event of armed attacks, as provided for in the charter of the United Nations.

Article Nine

1. Each of the High Contracting Parties shall appoint high-ranking representatives to serve on a joint security commission with the aim of supervising and monitoring the application of this agreement.

2. The commission shall determine its own working procedure.

3. The commission shall meet on a regular basis and may be specially convened whenever circumstances so require.

4. The commission shall:

    (a) Consider all allegations of infringements of the provisions of this agreement.

    (b) Advise the High Contracting Parties of its conclusions, and

    (c) Make recommendations to the High Contracting Parties concerning measures for the effective application of this agreement and the settlement of disputes over infringements or alleged infringements.

5. The High Contracting Parties shall determine the mandate of their respective representatives in order to enable interim measures to be taken in cases of duly recognized emergency.

6. The High Contracting Parties shall make available all the facilities necessary for the effective

functioning of the commission and will jointly consider its conclusions and recommendations.

Article Ten
This agreement will also be known as `The Accord of Nkomati'.

Article Eleven
This agreement shall enter into force on the date of the signature thereof. The agreement agreed to by the High Contracting Parties shall be affected by the exchange of notes between them. In witness thereof, the signatories, in the name of their respective governments, have signed and sealed this agreement, in quadruplicate in the Portuguese and English languages, both texts being equally authentic. Thus done and signed at the common border on the banks of the Nkomati River on this the sixteenth day of March 1984. Samora Moises Machel, Marshall of the Republic. President of the People's Republic of Mozambique, President of the Council of Ministers. For the government of the People's Republic of Mozambique. Pieter Willem Botha, Prime Minister of the Republic of South Africa. For the government of the Republic of South Africa.

APPENDIX 7

Communique of the Arusha
Front Line States Meeting
Arusha, Tanzania 29 April 1984 Final Communique
The Front Line States' Summit Meeting was held in
Arusha, Tanzania on Sunday 29 April 1984 to consider the
recent developments in Southern Africa. The Heads of
State and Government present were: President Eduardo
dos Santos of the People's Republic of Angola; President
Quett Masire of the Republic of Botswana; President
Samora Machel of People's Republic of Mozambique;
President Julius K. Nyerere of the United Republic of
Tanzania; President Kenneth Kaunda of the Republic of
Zambia and Prime MInister Robert Mugabe of the Republic
of Zimbabwe. Also in attendance were Comrade Oliver
Tambo, President of the African National Congress;
Comrade San Nujoma, President of Swapo of Namibia.

The leaders stood for one minute of silence in
tribute to the late Edward Moringe Sekoine, whose very
valuable and practical contributions to the liberation
struggle of Southern Africa will be greatly missed by
the Front Line States and the Liberation Movements.

The Heads of State and Government and the leaders
of the Liberation Movements reaffirmed their total and
unqualified commitment to the liberation struggles of
the people of Namibia against colonialism and of the
people of South Africa against apartheid. They
reasserted their conviction and that of the Organization
of African Unity, that the total liberation of Africa
from colonialism and racism is essential for the
security of all the independent states of the continent
and in particular the Front Line States.

Further, they reiterated that the root cause of the problems in South Africa is apartheid itself; apartheid is the cause of Africa's hostility to the South African racist regime and of the existence of South African and Namibian refugees. None of these things is caused by the Front Line or other States neighbouring South Africa. Apartheid has been condemned in categorically terms by the United Nations, and by the leaders of Europe, America, Australia and Asia as well as by Africa. It cannot be made acceptable by the use of South Africa's military power and economic strength, nor by the use of mercenaries and traitors.

The Heads of State and Government and the leaders of the Liberation Movements discussed the understanding reached by the People's Republic of Angola and the Pretoria Regime, and they hoped that South Africa will honour its commitment to withdraw its troops from Angola. This withdrawal will constitute an opportunity for the immediate and unconditional implementation of Security Council Resolution 435 of 1978. They welcomed Angola's reaffirmation of its continued commitment to the struggle of the Namibian people under the leadership of Swapo. The Heads of State and Government expressed their support for the Angolan Actions against the externally supported armed bandits who are causing death and misery to the Angolan people and destruction of the economic infrastructure of the State.

The Heads of State and Government and the leaders of the Liberation Movements exchanged views on the Nkomati Accord between Mozambique and South African Government. They expressed the hope that the South African Government will live up to the commitment to cease its acts aimed at the destabilization of Mozambique through the use of armed bandits, and gave their support to the Mozambican actions aimed at the total elimination of these vicious bandits. They expressed appreciation of Mozambique's commitment to continued moral, political and diplomatic support for the ANC in the struggle against apartheid and for majority rule in South Africa.

The Heads of State and Government and the leaders of the Liberation Movements declared that the immediate objective for Namibia is and must be the rapid implementation of UN Security Council Resolution 435 of 1978, in order that Namibia may attain full and internationally recognized independence on the basis of self-determination by all people of that country. They reiterated the continuing role of the UN Security Council and Secretary General in the implementation of Resolution 435. The leaders of the Front Line States again reaffirmed their support for Swapo as the sole and authentic representative of the Namibian people.

For South Africa, the objective of the Front Line States and Liberation Movements is the abolition of apartheid by whatever means are necessary. The Leaders present again reiterated their strong preference for apartheid to be brought to an end by peaceful means. This can be achieved only through a process agreed upon in free discussions between the present South African regime and genuine representatives of the people of South Africa who are unrepresented in the present government structure of that country. A prerequisite for any such discussions would be the unconditional release from prison, detention, house arrest or 'banning' of Nelson Mandela and all other political leaders. Difficult as this step may be in the eyes of the present South African Government, there is no way to peace in Southern Africa except through discussions between the South African Government and the African people of South Africa.

To avoid any misunderstanding, they stressed that the phrase `African People' includes all those who have been classified as being citizens of the so-called independent homelands in South Africa; the denial of their South African citizenship is not recognized in international law, nor by any independent state apart from South Africa.

The alternative to free negotiations within South Africa aimed at the ending of apartheid will inevitably be continued struggle against that system by other means, including armed struggle. This struggle is being waged and will be conducted and led by the people of South Africa themselves, on their own initiative and within their own country. However, their struggle is, and is seen by Africa to be, a struggle for the freedom and security of all men and women regardless of colour. It therefore received, and will continue to receive, the full support of the peoples and the nations represented by the Heads of State and Government of the Front Line States.

Involved in this struggle for the total liberation of Africa from colonialism and racism is the consolidation of the freedom and the security of the states which have already achieved independence. To that end, and in the light of the difficult circumstances which do from time to time confront such states, the leaders of the Front Line States and the Liberation Movements reaffirmed their understanding of steps which are taken for this purpose by states which are fully committed to the liberation struggles. They also reaffirmed their commitment to the internationally recognized boundaries in Southern Africa as these were defined when the free states achieved their political independence.

The Heads of State and Government of the Front Line States and the leaders of the Liberation Movements condemned without reservation the open and the covert aggressive actions of South Africa directed at the destabilization of the African states, and those aimed against refugees from Namibia and apartheid South Africa. There is no excuse in international law or civilized practice for these actions. The Heads of State and Government and the leaders of the Liberation Movements also repeated their rejection of the attempt to link the freedom of Namibia with any Angolan Government decisions relating to its security requirements and its internal political structures.

The political and armed struggles being waged by the peoples of Namibia and South Africa led by Swapo and ANC respectively, are taking place inside those two countries. The struggle is between the people of Namibia and the occupying power, and between the people of South Africa and the apartheid regime. Therefore, the strategy of the Liberation Movements is that of internal struggle, firmly based on the people's will and determination.

As the denial of human rights, and the ruthlessness of the oppressor, has made it impossible for many active leaders of the Liberation Movements to live and work inside their own countries, it has been necessary for both Swapo and ANC to have an external wing. The international implications of the problems with which the Liberation Movements are contending also require international diplomatic and political activity, together with offices and representatives in other countries.

The Front Line States reaffirm their recognition of these external operations of the Movements, and reassert their intention to give shelter to them. The Front Line States also reaffirm their right and duty under international Conventions to accord hospitality to refugees from Namibia and apartheid South Africa. They appeal to the international community for diplomatic and economic support and protection as they carry out these international responsibilities.

The Heads of State and Government of the Front Line States and the leaders of the Liberation Movements represented at the Arusha Meeting, in reasserting their commitment to the struggle for freedom in Namibia and South Africa, also draw attention to the burden they are carrying on behalf of the world conscience and the international condemnation of colonialism and apartheid. They therefore appeal for active participation in the struggle by all other nations, other organizations and institutions, and all people who accept the principles of human dignity and equality.

In particular the leaders of the Front Line States and Liberation Movements appeal for political, moral, material and diplomatic support to be given to the Liberation Movements. They appeal also for concrete support to be given to the efforts of the Front Line States aimed at the consolidation of their independence and their fragile economies, as these are of direct relevance to their ability to play a constructive role in the search for peace and freedom in Southern Africa.

For the Heads of State and Government of the Front Line States and the leaders of the Liberation Movements repeat a truism. Peace is incompatible with racism and colonialism. Man is so constituted that men and women will die for freedom and human dignity if they are prevented from the peaceful pursuit of these basic human rights. Neither military might nor devious political machinations, whether directed against the peoples inside Namibia and South Africa or against the free States of Africa, can defeat the idea of freedom and racial equality.

The struggle will be long and hard.

It will be carried on until final victory.

A luta continua.

APPENDIX 8

NKOMATI ACCORD-ANC RESPONSE

The National Executive Committee of the African National Congress has met to consider the current situation in Southern Africa. The meeting resolved to issue the following statement. Over the last few weeks, the racist and colonial regime of South Africa has been involved in a frantic diplomatic, political and propaganda counter-offensive in Southern Africa. Some of the principal objectives of this offensive are:

1. To isolate the ANC throughout Southern Africa and to compel the independent countries of our region to act as Pretoria's agents in emasculating the ANC, the Vanguard Movement of the South Africa struggle for national emancipation.

2. To liquidate the armed struggle for the Liberation of South Africa.

3. To gain new bridgeheads for the Pretoria regime in its efforts to undermine the unity of the frontline States, destroy the SADCC and replace it with a so-called constellation of States and thus to transform the independent Countries of Southern Africa into its Client States.

4. To use the prestige of the frontline States in the campaign of the white minority regime to reduce the international isolation of apartheid South Africa and to lend legitimacy to itself and its colonial and fascist state. In pursuit of these aims, the Botha regime has sought to reduce the independent countries of our region to the level of its bantustan creations by forcing to join the Transkei, Bophuthatswana, Venda and Ciskei bantustans in entering into so-called non-

aggression pacts with Pretoria. Such accords, concluded as they are with a regime which has no moral or legal right to govern our country cannot but help to perpetuate the illegitimate rule of the South African white settler minority. It is exactly for this reason that this minority has over the years sought to bind independent Africa to such agreements. The African National Congress is profoundly conscious of the enormous political, economic and security problems that confront many of the peoples of our region. The blame for many of these problems must be laid squarely on the Pretoria regime which has sought to define the limit of independence of the countries of our region through a policy of aggression and destabilization. We are convinced that this regime, which is dripping from head to foot with the blood of thousands of people it has murdered throughout Southern Africa, cannot be an architect of justice and peace in our region. Neither can the ally of this regime, the Reagan administration of the United States, with its pro-apartheid policy of "Constructive engagement" be an architect of justice and peace in this region, while it is an angel of war, reaction and repression in other regions of the world, including the United States itself.

A just and lasting peace in our region is not possible while the fountainhead of war and instability in this area, the apartheid regime and the oppressive system it maintains in South Africa and Namibia, continue to exist. The Botha regime knows that no peace has broken out: rather, it has resorted to other means to continue its war for the domination of Southern Africa.

The situation in our region continues to point to the correctness of the decisions of the Maputo Frontline States Summit held in March 1982. That Summit observed that: "under the leadership of ANC, the people, through strikes and armed action, are vigorously rising against apartheid". It went on to commit the Frontline States "to intensify their material and diplomatic support for the liberation movements, SWAPO and ANC of South Africa, so that they can intensify the armed struggle for the attainment of the national independence of their people. That statement was made in full recognition of the fact that the destruction of the apartheid regime and the liberation of South Africa and Namibia constituted the fundamental pre-requisites for peace, stability and uninterrupted progress in our area.

That commonly agreed position reaffirmed the obligation of the people of South Africa, under the leadership of the ANC, to escalate their offensive, using all means, including armed action, for the overthrow of the criminal apartheid regime and the transfer of power to the masses. We remain and shall remain loyal to this perspective.

The Pretoria regime is acting in the manner that it is, to try to extricate itself out of the crisis that confronts its racist and colonial system of apartheid. It hopes that after it has "pacified" our neighbours and driven the ANC out of our region, it will then have a free hand to suppress the mass democratic movement of our country and thus create the conditions for it to spin out its intricate web of measures for the refinement and entrenchment of the apartheid system. Our principal task at this moment therefore is, and must be, to intensify our political and military offensive inside South Africa. This is the urgent call that we make to the masses of our people, to all democratic formations and to all members and units of the ANC and Umkhonto we Sizwe. Relying on our own strength, through action, we will frustrate the schemes of the enemy of the peoples of Africa and continue our forward march to the destruction of the system of white minority colonial domination in our country.

The central and immediate question of South African politics is the overthrow of the white minority regime, the seizure of power by the people and the uprooting by these victorious masses of the entire apartheid system of colonial and racist domination, fascist tyranny, the superexploitation of the black majority and imperialist aggression and expansionism. This question will be and is being settled, in struggle, within the borders of our country and nowhere else. We are entitled to expect that all those anywhere in the World, who count themselves among the anti-colonial and anti-racist forces, will join hands with us to bring about this noble outcome.

The peoples of Southern Africa know from their own experience that there can be no peaceful coexistence between freedom and independence on the one hand and colonialism on the other. We are confident that these masses, their Parties and governments which have over the years, demonstrated their commitment to the cause of the total liberation of Africa, will themselves remain loyal to this cause and firm in resolve to stand with our people, until victory is won.

We are equally certain that the people of South Africa and the World Progressive community will continue to deny the Botha regime the legitimacy it craves so desperately, adopt new measures to isolate it and increase their political, diplomatic moral and material support to the ANC.

The struggle for the liberation of South Africa, under the leadership of the ANC, will continue to grow in scope and effectiveness, until we have won our victory. Forward to a people's government!

Alfred Nzo,
Secretary General

For the National
Executive Committee
March 16, 1984

APPENDIX 9
SELECTED CURRENCY RATES[*]

Country	Name of Currency	Rate per Dollar
Angola	Kwanza	29.91
Botswana	Pula	2.15
Lesotho	Maluti	2.67
Malawi	Kwacha	1.68
Mozambique	Metical	41.55
Namibia	Rand	2.67
Nigeria	Naira	0.90
South Africa	Rand	2.67
Swaziland	Lilangani	2.67
Tanzania	Shilling	16.50
Zambia	Kwacha	5.65
Zimbabwe	Z $ (dollar)	1.67

[*]Source – Rates quoted as of 31 December 1985 from Financial Times of London. The Currency exchange rates fluctuate nearly everyday.

SELECTED BIBLIOGRAPHY

BOOKS

Abegunrin, Olayiwola, Nigeria and the Struggle for the Liberation of Zimbabwe (forthcoming).

Abegunrin, Olayiwola and Newsum, H. E., United States Foreign Policy Towards Southern Africa: Andrew Young and Beyond (London: Macmillan Press, 1987).

Ajala, Adekunle, Pan-Africanism: Evolution, Progress and Prospects (London: Andre Deutsch, 1973).

Arrighi, Giovanni and Saul, John S., Essays on Political Economic of Africa (New York: Monthly Review Press, 1973).

Astrow, Andre, Zimbabwe: A Revolution that Lost its Way? (London: Zed Press, 1983).

Balassa, Bela, Theory of Economic Integration (London: George Allen and Unwin, 1973).

Browne, Roberts, S. and Cummings, Robert Jr., The Lagos Plan of Action Vs. The Berg Report: Contemporary Issues in African Economic Development (Lawrenceville, Virginia: Brunswick Publishing Company, 1984).

Callaghy, Thomas C. (ed.), South Africa in Southern Africa (New York: Praeger Publishers, 1983).

Carter, Gwendolen, M. (ed.), African One-Party States (New York: Cornel University Press, 1962).

Carter, G. M. and O'Meara P. (eds.), Southern Africa: The Crisis Continued (Bloomington: Indiana University Press, 1977).

_____, Southern Africa: The Continuing Crisis (Bloomington: Indiana University Press, 1979).

324

_____, International Politics in Southern Africa (Bloomington: Indiana University Press, 1983).

Cervenk, Zdenek and Rogers, Barbara, The Nuclear Axis: Secret Collaboration Between West Germany and South Africa (London: Julian Friedmann, 1978).

Claude, Inis L. Jr., Swords into Plowshares (New York: Random House, 1971).

Danaher, Kevin, In Whose Interest?: A Guide to U.S. - South Africa Relations (Washington, D.C. Institute for Policy Studies, 1984).

El-Khawas, Mohamed and Cohen, Barry (eds.), The Kissinger Study of Southern Africa: National Security Study Memorandum 39 (Westport, CT: Lawrence Hill 1976).

Engels, Frederick, The Origin of the Family, Private Property and the State (New York: Path Finder Press, 1972).

Feit, Edward, Urban Revolt in South Africa 1960-1964 (Chicago: Northwestern University Press, 1971).

Gavin, R. J. and Betley, J. A., The Scramble for Africa (Ibadan: University Press, 1973).

Gibson, Richard, African Liberation Movements: Contemporary Struggles Against White Minority Rule (New York: Oxford University Press, 1972).

Grundy, Kenneth W., Confrontation and Accommodation in Southern Africa: The Limits of Independence (Berkeley: University of California Press, 1973).

Haas, Ernst B., The Unity of Europe: Political, Social and Economic Forces 1950-1957 (Stanford: Stanford University Press, 1968).

Harris, Richard (ed.), The Political Economy of Africa (New York: Schenkman Publishing Company, 1975).

Hazlewood, Arthur, Economic Integration: The East African Experience (Ibadan: Heinemann Educational Books, 1975).

Hyam, R., The Future of South African Expansion 1908-1948 (New York: A.P.C. Press, 1972).

July, Robert W., A History of the African People (New York: Charles Scribner's Sons, 1974).

Kapungu, Leonard T., RHODESIA: The Struggle for Freedom (New York: Orbis Books, 1974).

Katznelson, Ira et al. (eds.), The Politics and Society Reader (New York: David McKay Co. 1974).

Legum, Colin et al. (eds.), Africa in the 1980s: A Continent in Crisis (New York: McGraw-Hill Book, 1979).

Lenin, V. I., The State and Revolution (Moscow: Progress Publishers, 1981).

Mandela, Nelson, No Easy Walk to Freedom (London: Heinemann, 1965).

_____, The Struggle is My Life (London: International Defense and Aid Fund for Southern Africa, 1978).

Marcum, John, The Angolan Revolution Volume I: The Anatomy of an Explosion 1952-1962 (Cambridge, MA: MIT Press, 1969).

_____, The Angolan Revolution Volume II: Exile Politics and Guerrilla Warfare 1962-1976 (Cambridge, MA: MIT Press, 1978).

Martin, David and Johnson, Phyllis, The Struggle for Zimbabwe: The Chimurenga War (New York: Monthly Review Press, 1981).

Mazrui, Ali A., The African Condition: A Political Diagnosis (London: Cambridge University Press, 1980).

Mitrany, David, The Functional Theory of Politics (London: Martin Robertson and Company, 1975).

_____, A Working Peace System (Chicago: Quadrangle Books, 1966).

Mytelka, Lynn K., Regional Development in a Global Economy: Multinational Corporation, Technology and Andean Integration (New Haven: Yale University Press, 1979).

Nkrumah, Kwame, Neo-Colonialism: The Highest State of Imperialism (New York: International Publishers, 1965).

_____, Africa Must Unite (New York: International Publishers, 1963).

Nsekela, Amon J. (ed.), Southern Africa: Toward Economic Liberation (London: Rex Collings, 1981).

Nye, Joseph S. Jr., Pan-Africanism and East African Integration (Cambridge: Harvard University Press, 1967).

Nyerere, Julius K., Uhuru na Ujamaa: Freedom and Socialism (Dar-es-Salaam: Oxford University Press, 1968).

Onwuka, Ralph I., Development and Integration: The Case of the Economic Community of West African States (ECOWAS) (Ile-Ife: Obafemi Awolowo University Press, 1982).

Onwuka, Ralph I. and Sesay, A. (eds.), The Future of Regionalism in Africa (London: Macmillan Press, 1985).

Oyediran, Oyeleye (ed.), Nigerian Government and Politics Under Military Rule 1976-1979 (London: Macmillan Press, 1979).

Pratt, Granford, The Critical Phase in Tanzania 1945-
1968: Nyerere and the Emergence of a Socialist
Strategy (Cambridge: Cambridge University Press,
1976).

Ray, Ellen, Schaap, William et·al. (eds.) Dirty Work 2:
The CIA in Africa (Secaucus, NJ: Lyle Stuart,
1979).

Renninger, John P., Multinational Corporation for
Development in West Africa (Toronto: Pergamon
Press, 1979).

Robson, Peter, Economic Integration in Africa (Evanston:
Northwestern University Press, 1968).

Rodney, Walter, How Europe Underdeveloped Africa
(Washington, D.C.: Howard University Press, 1974).

Rosenau, James N. (ed.), The Scientific Study of Foreign
Policy (New York: The Free Press, 1971).

Sampson, Anthony, The Sovereign State of ITT (New York:
Stein and Day Publishers, 1973).

Seidman, Ann and Seidman, Neva, Outposts of monopoly
Capitalism: Southern Africa in the Changing Global
Economy (London: Zed Press, 1980).

_____, South Africa and U.S. Multinational
Corporations (Westport, CT: Lawrence Hill, 1978).

Serapiao, Luis B. and El-Khawas, Mohamed A., Mozambique
in the Twentieth Century: From Colonialism to
Independence (Washington, D.C.,: University Press
of American, 1979).

Simoes, Jorge Tavares de Carvalho (ed.), SADCC: Energy
and Development to the Year 2000 SADCC Energy
Sector in Collaboration with the Beijer Institute
and the Scandinavian Institute of African Studies
(Uddevalla: Bohuslaningens AB, 1984).

Soremekun, Fola, ANGOLA: The Road to Independence (Ile-
Ife: Obafemi Awolowo University Press, 1983).

328

Spero, Joan Edelman, The Politics of International Economic Relations (New York: St. Martin's Press, 1977).

Stockwell, John, In Search of Enemies: A C.I.A. Story (New York: Norton Press, 1978).

Swell, James P., Functionalism and World Politics (Princeton, NJ: Princeton University Press, 1966).

Thompson, Carol B., Challenge to Imperialism: The Frontline States in the Liberation of Zimbabwe (Harare: Zimbabwe Publishing House, 1985).

Zehender, Wolfgang, Cooperation Versus Integration: The Prospects of the Southern African Development Coordination Conference (1983).

329

ARTICLES

Abegunrin, Olayiwola, "The Southern Nine", Current Bibliography on African Affairs, Vol. 14, No. 4 (1981-82).

_____, "Western Options vis-a-vis South Africa" The Western Journal of Black Studies, Vol. 6, No. 4 (Winter 1982).

_____, "Soviet and Chinese Military Involvement in Southern Africa", Current Bibliography on African Affairs, Vol 16, No. 3 (1983-84_.

_____, "The Arabs and the Southern African Problem", International Affairs (London) Vol. 60, No. 1 (Winter 1983-84).

_____, "Liberation Struggle in South Africa" Renaissance Universal Journal, Vol. 4, No. 1 (1984).

_____, "Angola and the U.S. Since 1975", Lusophone Areas Studies Journal, No 4 (June 1985) pp. 51-82.

Adeyanju, Banji, "Racists Subdue Frontline States" Sunday Concord (Ikeja, Lagos) 29 April, 1984).

Anglin, Douglas D., "Economic Liberation and Regional Cooperation in Southern Africa: SADCC and PTA" International Organization Vol. 37, No. 4 (Autumn 1983).

Block, Jonathan and Weir, Andrew "Pretoria's dirty trick army" Africa Now, October, 1982.

Browne, Roberts S. and Mtei, E. I. M., "Africa and the IMF" Africa Report September-October, 1984.

Cabaco, Jose Luis, "The Nkomati Accords", Africa Report, Vol. 29, No. 3 (May-June, 1984).

Campbell, Horace, "Total War and Total Failure", Zimbabwean Herald (Harare), 9 December 1983).

330

Caporaso, James A., "Introduction: Dependence and Dependency in the Global System" International Organization, Vol, 32, No. 1, (Winter 1978).

Campbell, Horace Nkomati, before and after war, Reconstruction and dependence in Mozambique Journal of African Marxists Issue 6, October 1984).

Crocker, Chester, "South Africa: Strategy for Change", Foreign Affairs, Vol. 59, No 2 (Winter 1980/81).

Cronge, Suzanne, "U.S. Moves against Namibia" West Africa, 5 December 1983.

Dimsdale, John, "Tanzania-Mozambique: Two Roads to Socialism", Africa Report September-October 1982.

Doyle, Mark, "Mozambique: The Nkomati Process" West Africa 17 October, 1983.

_____, "Southern Africa: Boers on the Offensive" West Africa, 17 October, 1983.

_____, "Angola: The Cost of Defending Independence" West Africa , 7 January 1985.

Edlin, John, "SADCC: Key to Southern Africa's Economic Independence" Africa Report, May-June, 1983.

Frankel, Glenn, "South African-banned Rebels Weaken Mozambique" The Washington Post, 8 October 1984.

Fauvet, Paul, "Energy Meeting Generates heat and light" Africa Now, September 1983.

_____, "Mozambique: The MNR's lingering war" Africa Now, October, 1981.

Green, Reginald H., "Southern African Development Coordination: The Struggle Continues" Africa Contemporary Record (ACR) 1980-1981), pp. A24-34.

_____, "Southern African Development Cooperation: From Dependence and Poverty Towards Economic Liberation" ACR (1981-1982), pp. A. 97-113.

_____, "SADCC and South Africa in Confrontation: Liberation Vs. Destabilization" ACR (1982-1983) pp. A. 73-85.

_____, "Constellation, Association, Liberation: Economic Coordination and the Struggle for Southern Africa" ACR 1979-1980, p. A. 37.

Gregory, Martin, "Rhodesia: From Lusaka to Lancaster House" The World Today, Vol, 36, No. 1 (January 1980).

Haas, Ernst B., "International Integration: The European and the Universal Process", International Organization, Vol. 15, 1961.

Hanton, Joseph, "Hostage to apartheid: Frontline Angola: South June, 1983.

Hill, Christopher R., "Regional Cooperation in Southern Africa", African Affairs, Vol, 82, No. 327 (1983).

Ihonvbere, Julius, "Social Aspects of Integration: The Case of ECOWAS" Korean Journal of International Studies Vol. 14, No. 1 (1982/83).

Isaacman, Allen and Barbara, "Mozambique: South Africa's Hidden War", Africa Report, Vol. 27, No. 6, Nov.-Dec., 1982.

Jensen, Holter and Younghusband, Peter, "Southern Africa: The Zone of Instability", Newsweek International 6 September 1982.

Johnson, Walton R., "Destabilization in Southern Africa" Trans-Africa Forum, Vol. 2, No. 2 (Fall 1984).

Kalter, Joanmarie, "Mozambique's Peace with South Africa" Africa Report Vol. 29, No. 3 (May-June, 1984).

332

Katjavivi, Peter, "Namibia: 100 years of Occupation" West Africa 1 October, 1984.

Kisanga, E. J., "Regional Cooperation: A Challenge for the Continent" Africa Now (April 1984).

Komba, Marcelino, "Mozambique's return to Arms" Africa (June 1981).

Kornegay, Francis A. Jr. and Vockerodt, Victor A., "Lusaka and Regional Cooperation in Southern Africa, Part I: The Zimbabwe Connection", SADEX, Vol. 2, No. 3 (May-June 1980).

_____, "Lusaka and Regional Cooperation in Southern Africa, Part II: The South African Dilemma", SADEX, Vol. 2, No. 4 (July-August 1980).

Legum, Colin (ed.)., "Southern Africa: The Road to and from Lancaster House" ACR 1979-1980.

_____, "Angola-South Africa: Lusaka Accord in danger" New African (September 1984).

_____, "Cease firing, start talking: South Africa counts the cost", New African (March 1984).

Lines, Thomas, "Zimbabwe Plans to take over metal sales" Africa Now (March 1982).

Mawani, Mohamed Musa, "Nkomati's False Dawn" New African (October 1984).

Mawarire, Gilbert, "Angola Encourages Foreign Investment" New African (May 1984).

Mboukou, Alexandra, "An African Triangle" Africa Report, Vol 27, No. 5 (September-October, 1982).

McGowan, Patrick J. and Smith, Dale L., "Economic Dependency in Black Africa: An Analysis of competing theories", International Organization, Vol. 32, No. 2 (1978).

Mhango, Mkwapatira, "Zambia-Zaire: Border flare-up" New African (August, 1984).

Mitrany, David, "The United Nations After 25 Years, Regional and Functional Devolution" International Relations, Vol. III, No. 10 (November 1970).

Moroney, Sean, "SADCC: Fighting for Regional Development" African Business (January 1983).

_____, "Sympathy alone is not enough" African Business (March 1983).

Mukela, John, "Border Watch" Africa Now (June 1982).

Ncube, M. M., "The U.S., South Africa and Destabilization in Southern Africa" Journal of AFrican Marxists, Issue 6 (October 1984).

Norman, Denis R., "Africa's Drought: Food Security for Southern Africa" Africa Report, Vol. 29, No. 4 (July-August 1984).

Nyerere, Julius K., "America and Southern Africa", Foreign Affairs (July 1977).

Ocampo, Sheilah, "Rebels invade Maputo Streets following Accord" National Concord 6 July 1984.

Onwuka, Ralph I., "African Common Market in the Year 2000: Myths and Shibboleths" Viertel Jahres Berichte (September, 1983).

Pahad, Aziz, "Apartheid Terror: How Pretoria Wages War on Africa", Sechaba (March 1983).

Robson, Peter, "Economic Integration in Southern Africa", Journal of Modern African Studies, Vol. 5, No. 4 (December, 1967).

Simango, Uria, "Mozambique My Country" African Communist (Second Quarter, 1966).

334

Sparks, Allister, "South Africa Announces Truce by Mozambique and Rebels" The Washington Post (4 October 1984).

Turner, Janice, "Rising Tide of Vengeance" South (July 1983).

Turner, Sue, "SADCC: Food Security Emerges as the key Issue" Africa Economic Digest (AED) (27 January, 1984).

Udokang, Okon, "Economic Community of West African States: Theoretical and Practical Problems of Integration" Nigerian Journal of International Affairs (April 1979).

Ward, David, "Malawi: Sabotage by South Africa" Africa (November 1982).

Weisfelder, Richard F., "The Southern African Development Coordination Conference (SADCC)", South Africa International, Vol. 13, No. 2 (1982).

Winer, Stan, "Botswana Prepares on SADCC Role" Africa Now (March 1982).

Wolfers, Michael, "SADCC means Business" West Africa (29 August, 1983).

CHAPTERS IN EDITED WORKS

Abegunrin, Olayiwola, "Southern African Development Coordination Conference: Politics of Dependence" in Ralph Onwuka and Amadu Sesay (eds.) The Future of Regionalism in Africa (London: Macmillan Press, 1985).

Grundy, Kenneth W., "South Africa in the Political Economy of Southern Africa" in G. M. Carter and P. O'Meara (eds.) International Politics in Southern Africa (Bloomington: Indiana University Press, 1982).

Henderson, Robert, "South Africa Customs Union: Politics of Dependence" In Ralph I. Onwuka and Amadu Sesay (eds.) The Future of Regionalism in Africa (London: Macmillan Press, 1985).

Hodges, Tony, "Mozambique: The Politics of Liberation" in G. M. Carter and P. O'Meara (eds.) Southern Africa: The Continuing Crisis (Bloomington: Indiana University Press, 1979).

Johnson, Dale, "Dependence and the International System", in Cockcroft, et al. Dependence and Underdevelopment: Latin America's Political Economy (New York: Anchor Books, 1972).

Legum, Colin, "The International Moral Protest" in G. M. Carter and P. O'Meara (eds.) International Politics in Southern Africa (Bloomington: Indiana University Press, 1982).

Marcum, John, "Angola: Perilous Transition to Independence" in G. M. Carter and P. O'Meara (eds.) Southern Africa: The Continuing Crisis (Bloomington: Indiana University Press, ?? (Date)

Morgan, Philip E., "Botswana: Development, Democracy and Vulnerability" in G. M. Carter and P. O'Meara (eds.) Southern Africa: The Continuing Crisis (Bloomington: Indiana University Press, 1979).

O'Conner, James, "The Meaning of Economic Imperialism", in K. T. Fann and Donald C. Hodges (eds.) Reading in U.S. Imperialism (Boston: F. Porter Sargent, 1971).

Thisen, J. K., "ECA and Africa's Economic Development 1983-2000: A Preliminary Perspective Study" in R. I. Onwuka and O. Abegunrin (eds.), African Development: The OAU/ECA Lagos Plan of Action and Beyond (Lawrenceville, VA: Brunswick Publishing Company, 1985).

Weisfelder, Richard F., "The Southern African Development Coordination Conference: A New Factor in the Liberation Process" in Thomas M. Callaghy (ed.) South Africa in Southern Africa (New York: Praeger Publishers, 1983).

_____, "Lesotho: Changing Patterns of Dependence" in G. M. Carter and P. O'Meara (eds.), Southern Africa: The Continuing Crisis (Bloomington: Indiana University Press, 1979).

PUBLIC DOCUMENTS

African National Council Manifesto (Lusaka: 1972).

Africa Year Book and Who's Who 1977 (London: Africa Journal Limited, 1976).

Accelerated Development in Sub-Saharan Africa: An Agenda for Action (Washington, D.C.: The World Bank, 1981).

ANGOLA, People's Republic, White Paper on Acts of Aggression by the Racist South African Regime Against The People's Republic of Angola: 1975-1982 (Luanda: Ministry of External Relations, 1982).

Banque des donnes, Eurostat (Brussels: European Information Development, 1981).

North-South: A Program for Survival, The Report of the Independent Commission on International Development Issues Under the Chairmanship of Whilly Brandt (Cambridge, MA: The MIT Press, 1983).

Organization of African Unity, Lagos Plan of Action for the Economic Development of Africa 1980-2000 (Geneva: International Institute for Labour Studies, 1981).

Preferential Trade Area Draft Treaty (Addis Ababa: Economic Commission for Africa, June 1978).

Records of SADCC Summit Conferences 1979-1984 Issues (Gaborone).

President Robert Mugabe, The Construction of Socialism in Zimbabwe: Policy Statement No. 14 (Harare: Zimbabwe, Department of Information, 9 July, 1984).

SADEX Volume 1 - Volume 3 (Washington, D.C.: African
Bibliographic Center, various issues 1979-1981).

South Africa: Time Running Out, The Report of the Study
Commission on U.S. Policy Toward Southern Africa
(Berkeley: University of California Press, 1981).

The Military Balance 1982-1983 (London: The
International for Strategic Studies, 1982).

United Nations Statistical Yearbook: Thirty-First Issue
(New York: U.N. Department of International
Economic and Social Affairs, Statistical Office,
1981).

U.S. House of Representatives, The Report of Committee
on Foreign Relations, Subcommittee on Africa,
Hearings before the sub-committee on Africa of the
Committee on Foreign Affairs, U.S. House of
Representatives, 97th Congress, 2nd Session 8
December 1982 (Washington, D.C., U.S. Government
Printing Office, 1983).

World Military Expenditures and Arms Transfers 1972-1982
(Washington, D.C.: U.S. Arms Control and
Disarmament Agency, April 1984).

PERIODICALS

Africa (London) 1077-1985.

Africa Contemporary Record: Annual Survey and Documents
- (London) 1979-1983.

Africa Economic Digest (London) - 1982-1985.

Africa Report (New York) - 1980-1984.

Africa Research Bulletin (London) - 1977-1985.

Africa Now (London) - 1981-1985.

African Business (London) - 1981-1985.

AIM (Maputo) - 1983.

MOTO (Harare) - 1983.

New African (London) - 1980-1985.

Newsweek International (New York) - 1980-1985.

South (London) - 1981-1987.

The Economist (London) - 1983.

West Africa (London) - 1979-1986.

NEWSPAPERS

Botswana Daily News (Gaborone) - 1982.

Daily Sketch (Ibadan) - 1983-1985.

Daily Times (Lagos) - 1983.

Financial Times (London) - 1985.

Le Matin de Paris (Paris) - 1984.

National Concord (Ikeja) - 1983-1984.

New Nigerian (Kaduna) - 1981.

Rand Daily Mail (Johannesburg) - 1983.

Sunday Sketch (Ibadan) - 1983-1984.

Sunday Concord (Ikeja) - 1983-1984.

The Guardian (Lagos) - 1985.

The Guardian (London) - 1980-1984.

The New York Times (New York) - 1983-1984.

The Observer (London) - 1978-1984.

The Sowetan (Soweto) - 1980-1984.

The Star (Johannesburg) - 1980-1983.

The Times (London) - 1980-1984.

The Times of Zambia (Ndola) - 1982-1984.

The Washington Post (Washington, D.C.) - 1979-1985.

The Zimbabwean Herald (Harare) - 1981-1984.

INDEX

343

Zambia, xi, 2, 12, 21-5,
    34, 37, 82, 86, 96,
    116, 118, 122-3,
    126-9, 132, 140,
    142-6, 152-3,
    159-160, 162, 182,
    225-6, 268, 271,
    273, 297, 302, 310,
    322
Zimbabwe, xi, 2, 20,
    22-5, 34, 37, 82-3,
    86, 92-3, 118-124,
    126-9, 131-3, 137,
    140, 144-6, 158,
    160-1, 165-8, 172,
    174, 213, 225-6,
    239, 243, 248, 265,
    268-70, 272-3, 277,
    290, 297, 301, 310,
    322
Zimbabwe African National
    Union (ZANU), 25,
    92-3, 197
Zimbabwe African People's
    Union (ZAPU), 92-3
Zinc, 41, 124

STUDIES IN AFRICAN ECONOMIC AND SOCIAL DEVELOPMENT

1. Richard Vengroff and Alan Johnston, **Decentralization and the Implementation of Rural Development in Senegal**

2. Olayiwola Abegunrin, **Economic Dependence and Regional Cooperation in Southern Africa: SADCC and South Africa in Confrontation**

3. Charles O. Chikeka, **Britain, France, and the New African States: A Study of Post-Colonial Relationships**

4. Daniel Teferra, **The Making and Economy of Ethiopa**

5. Santosh Saha, **A History of Agriculture in Liberia, 1882-1970: Transference of American Values**

6. Santosh Saha, **A History of Agriculture in West Africa: A Guide to Information Sources**